Depression in the Elderly

Depression in the Elderly

A MULTIMEDIA SOURCEBOOK

John J. Miletich

Bibliographies and Indexes in Gerontology, Number 36
Erdman B. Palmore, Series Adviser

GREENWOOD PRESS
Westport, Connecticut • London

Library of Congress Cataloging-in-Publication Data

Miletich, John J.
    Depression in the elderly : a multimedia sourcebook / John J.
Miletich.
        p.   cm.—(Bibliographies and indexes in gerontology, ISSN
0743–7560 ; no. 36)
    Includes index.
    ISBN 0–313–30113–1 (alk. paper)
    1. Depression in old age—Bibliography.   I. Title.   II. Series.
Z6665.7.D46M56   1997
[RC537.5]
016.61897′68527—dc21   97–16238

British Library Cataloguing in Publication Data is available.

Library of Congress Catalog Card Number: 97–16238
ISBN: 0–313–30113–1
ISSN: 0743–7560

First published in 1997

Greenwood Press, 88 Post Road West, Westport, CT 06881
An imprint of Greenwood Publishing Group, Inc.

Printed in the United States of America

The paper used in this book complies with the
Permanent Paper Standard issued by the National
Information Standards Organization (Z39.48–1984).

10 9 8 7 6 5 4 3 2 1

To the Memory of Dane Miletich (1905-1996) and Eva Miletich (1909-1997)

Contents

Acronyms

AChE	Acetyl Cholinesterase
AD	Alzheimer's Disease
ADDS	Alcohol, Drug, and Depression Screening
AIM	Associates in Internal Medicine
ARSMA	Acculturation Rating Scale for Mexican-Americans
ATQ	Automatic Thoughts Questionnaire
BCDRS	Brief Carroll Depression Rating Scale
BDI	Beck Depression Inventory
BDI-SF	Beck Depression Inventory - Short Form
BODES	Behavioral Observation of Depression in the Elderly Scales
BP	Blood Pressure
BPRS-D	Brief Psychiatric Rating Scale - Depression Factor
BSI	Brief Symptom Inventory
CARE	Comprehensive Assessment and Referral Evaluation
CAT	Computerized Axial Tomography
CBC	Complete Blood Cell Count
CDI-LTC	Computerized Depression Inventory for Older Adults Living in Long-Term Care Facilities
CES-D	Center for Epidemiological Studies - Depression Scale
CFQ	Crying Frequency Questionnaire
CIBA	Chemical Industry in Basle
CIRS	Cumulative Illness Rating Scale
CNS	Central Nervous System
COPD	Chronic Obstructive Pulmonary Disease
CPEI	Chronic Pain Experience Instrument
CPN	Community Psychiatric Nurse
CPRS-D	Comprehensive Psychopathological Rating Scale - Depression
CRH	Corticotrophin-Releasing Hormone
CRS	Carroll Rating Scale
CSDD	Cornell Scale of Depression in Dementia
CSF	Cerebrospinal Fluid
CT	Computed Tomography
CTS	Cognitive Therapy Scale
DDESE	Duke Depression Evaluation Schedule for the Elderly
DIS	Diagnostic Interview Schedule

DMS	Delayed Memory for Story
DRLA	Developmental Resources of Later Adulthood
DS	Demoralization Scale
DSD	Dementia Syndrome of Depression
DST	Dexamethasone Suppression Test
EAChE	Erythrocyte Acetyl Cholinesterase
ECA	Epidemiological Catchment Area
ECG	Electrocardiogram
ECT	Electroconvulsive Therapy
	Electroconvulsive Treatment
ED	Emergency Department
EEG	Electroencephalogram
EMSQ	Extended Mental Status Questionnaire
EPESE	Established Populations for Epidemiological Studies of the Elderly
FTQ	Feeling Tone Questionnaire
GAS	Global Assessment Scale
	Goal Attainment Scaling
GDS	Geriatric Depression Scale
GDS-LF	Geriatric Depression Scale - Long Form
GDS-SF	Geriatric Depression Scale - Short Form
GHS	Geriatric Hopelessness Scale
GIDT	Guided Imagery Discharge Teaching
HADQ	Hospital Anxiety and Depression Questionnaire
HAMA	Hamilton Anxiety Scale
HBS	Health Behavior Scale
HDRS	Hamilton Depression Rating Scale
Hp	Haptoglobin
HU	Hounsfield Units
IADL	Independent Activities of Daily Living
ICD	International Classification of Diseases
ID	Index of Depression
IIADL	Index of Independence in Activities of Daily Living
ILTB	Intentional Life-Threatening Behavior
IPC	Interpersonal Counseling
IPT	Interpersonal Theory for Depression
IRT	Item Response Theory
LSNS	Lubben Social Network Scale
MADRS	Montgomery-Asberg Depression Rating Scale
MAO	Monoamine Oxidase
MAOI	Monoamine Oxidase Inhibitor
MCMI	Millon Clinical Multiaxial Inventory

MD	Major Depression
MDRS	Mattis Dementia Rating Scale
MDS	Minimum Data Set
MI	Myocardial Infarction
MID	Multi-Infarct Dementia
MMS	Mini-Mental State
MMSE	Mini-Mental State Exam
MP	Methylphenidate
MRI	Magnetic Resonance Imaging
MSQ	Mental Status Questionnaire
MSW	Master of Social Work
NCHS	National Center for Health Statistics
NIMH	National Institute of Mental Health
NPT	Nurse-Psychotherapist
NT	Nortriptyline
OBS	Organic Brain Syndrome
OPPES	Older Persons Pleasant Events Schedule
OPUPE	Older Persons Unpleasant Events
PD	Parkinson's Disease
PDI	Pain Disability Index
PEP	Peer Counseling for Elderly Persons
PES-AD	Pleasant Events Schedule - Alzheimer's Disease
PET	Positron Emission Tomography
PGCM	Philadelphia Geriatric Center Morale
POMS	Profile of Mood States
PQOL	Perceived Quality of Life
PTSD	Post-Traumatic Stress Disorder
RA	Rheumatoid Arthritis
RDC	Research Diagnostic Criteria
	Rey Dot Counting
RDI	Rorschach Depression Index
RDT	Routine Discharge Teaching
REM	Rapid Eye Movement
RLCQ	Recent Life Change Questionnaire
RMT	Rey Memory Test
ROC	Receiver Operating Characteristic Curve
SAS	Srole Anomie Scale
SBPST	Simultaneous Bilateral Physical Stimulation Test
SCL-90	Symptom Checklist - 90
SCL-90-R	Symptom Checklist - 90 - R
SDAT	Senile Dementia of the Alzheimer Type
SEI	Self-Esteem Inventory

SHOP	Social Health Outreach Program
SLI	Somatostatin-Like Immunoreactivity
SMI	Severely Mentally Ill
SPSS	Statistical Package for the Social Sciences
SRH	Self-Rated Health
SRRS	Social Readjustment Rating Scale
SSRI	Selective Serotonin Reuptake Inhibitor
TCA	Tricyclic Antidepressant
TDI	Trapp Depression Inventory
TICS	Telephone Interview for Cognitive Status
UCLA	University of California Los Angeles
VA	Veterans Administration
VASD	Visual Analogue Scale of Depression
WAIS	Wechsler Adult Intelligence Scale
WHYMPI	West Haven-Yale Multidimensional Pain Inventory
WMS	Wechsler Memory Scale

Preface

Depression, common in the elderly, is likely to become more prevalent, as the population ages and lives longer, especially as the baby boomer generation grows older. Depression is associated with loss, and the elderly - because they have outlived many other individuals - experience multiple losses, during their life cycle. Loss of family and friends through death, loss of health, loss of employment, and loss of social status are examples of losses experienced by these persons. The highest rates of major depression are found in the elderly who reside in institutions. These individuals have lost, among other things, home, autonomy, and privacy. Increasing numbers of the elderly will live in institutions in the twenty-first century.

Depression can be explained psychopharmacologically in terms of brain chemistry altered by negative emotions. Depression is attributed to decreased amounts of the neurotransmitters norepinephrine and serotonin in the brain. The tricyclic antidepressants, for example, increase the amounts of these substances and thus elevate mood.

There are specific risk factors for depression as the following risk factors indicate: negative health habits (excessive alcohol consumption), certain medical illnesses (hypothyroidism), prescription drugs (reserpine), and prior psychiatric illnesses (anxiety disorders). Both psychological and somatic symptoms are found in the depressed elderly. A sad mood, decreased motivation, hopelessness, and a desire to die are some of the psychological symptoms. Loss of energy, difficulty sleeping, and changes in appetite are a few of the somatic symptoms. Depression, if left untreated, can lead to suicide, more so in men than in women, and especially in men over the age of eighty-five. Firearms are the usual method of suicide for these men.

Clinical presentations of depression in the elderly range from minor depression, such as dysthymic disorder, to major depression which has four subtypes: melancholic, psychotic, atypical, and seasonal. Grief-related depression and mood disorders caused by physical illnesses, medications, or mood-altering substances are other clinical presentations of depression in the elderly. However, social support - from supportive family and friends - and religious faith can counteract the effects of depression. Psychotherapy, especially cognitive behavioral therapy, is effective in the treatment of depression. Drug treatment and psychotherapy are combined when psychotherapy alone is not effective. Tricyclic antidepressants such as imipramine and amitriptyline, developed in the 1950s, are used to treat depression. The monoamine oxidase inhibitors (MAOIs), also developed in the 1950s, can cause hypertensive crisis. The selective serotonin reuptake inhibitors (SSRIs), a relatively new class of drugs (e.g., paroxetine and sertraline) are safer in overdose than the tricyclics or MAOIs.

Electroconvulsive therapy (ECT) is a safe treatment option when medications are not effective or when an immediate improvement in a patient's depression is desired.

This book is a compilation of diverse information on depression in the elderly, covering the time period 1970-1996. The information is in many forms including: articles, audiocassettes, books, conference papers, dissertations, television programs, theses, and videocassettes. This information is organized into twelve chapters, three appendices, a list of acronyms, and separate author and subject indexes. The annotations are informational, but are not intended to be abstracts.

This book is intended for health care and related professionals including: gerontologists, nurses, paramedics, primary care physicians, psychiatrists, psychologists, social workers, sociologists, and suicidologists. Librarians can use this volume as a starting point for locating detailed information on depression in the elderly.

I am grateful to the following for their assistance: in Durham, North Carolina: Erdman B. Palmore, Duke University Medical Center; in Washington, DC: Gerontological Society of America; in Calgary, Alberta: Maureen Wedderburn, Education Resource Center for Continuing Care; University of Calgary Library; in Edmonton, Alberta: Alberta Alcohol and Drug Abuse Commission Library; Teresa Bendall, Alberta Family and Social Services Library; Alberta Health Community Health Section Library; Concordia College Library; Sue Gamble, Edmonton General Hospital Health Sciences Library and Resource Center; Peter Schoenberg, Glenrose Hospital Library; Sylvia Flood, Grant MacEwan Community College Library; Grey Nun's Hospital Library; Misercordia Hospital Library; Northern Alberta Institute of Technology Library; Robert A. Jago, Jago Publications; Royal Alexandra Hospital Library; University of Alberta Library; in Ottawa, Ontario: Canadian Association on Gerontology; and in Vancouver, British Columbia: Kevin Lindstrom, University of British Columbia.

A special thank you to Nita H. Romer, Acquisitions Editor, and Jane Lerner, Production Editor, Greenwood Publishing Group.

◆ Chapter 1 ◆

Etiology, Epidemiology, Diagnosis

1.001. Abler, R., T. Drinka, J. Mahoney, G. Gunter-Hunt, C. Matthews, S. Gravenstein and M. Carnes. "Depression in Patients of a Geriatric Medicine Clinic: Comparison of Two Screening Instruments." Abstract in **Gerontologist** 31, Special Issue 2 (October 1991): 325.

Forty older adults from a geriatric medical clinic were the subjects. They had a mean Mini-Mental State Exam (MMSE) score of 27. The sensitivity of the Geriatric Depression Scale (GDS) was 56%, its specificity 90%. The sensitivity of the Yale Depression Screening Question was 78%, its specificity 87%. The question asked was: "Do you often feel sad or depressed?"

1.002. Abrams, Robert C., Robert C. Young, George S. Alexopoulos and Jonathan H. Holt. "Neuroticism May Be Associated with a History of Depression in the Elderly." **International Journal of Geriatric Psychiatry** 6 (July 1991): 483-488.

1.003. Addington, Jean and P.S. Fry. "Directions for Clinical Psychosocial Assessment of Depression in the Elderly." **Clinical Gerontologist** 5 (June 1986): 97-117.

Three models - medical, psychodynamic, and cognitive-behavioral - account for depression in later life. Each model has a particular focus. The psychodynamic model, for example, emphasizes underlying conflict in the patient. The cognitive-behavioral model emphasizes activity schedules. However, a multidimensional assessment is necessary for multidisciplinary intervention in the effective treatment of depression in the elderly. Author biographical information. 38 references.

1.004. Aenchbacher, Louis Edgar, III. "The Relationship between Physical Activity and Self-Rated Depression in Free-Living Women Aged 60 Years and Older." **Dissertation Abstracts International** 51: 5242B. ED.D. University of Georgia, 1990. UMI Order No. AAD91-07169. DIALOG, Dissertation Abstracts Online.

1.005. Agrell, Berit and Ove Dehlin. "Comparison of Six Depression Rating Scales in Geriatric Stroke Patients." **Stroke** 20 (September 1989): 1190-1194.

Eighteen men and twenty-two women, ranging in age from sixty-one to ninety-three years, participated in this study. These participants had a stroke four months to 2.5 years prior to the study. Self-rating scales - the Geriatric Depression Scale (GDS), the Zung Scale, and the Center for Epidemiological Studies Depression Scale (CES-D) - were used to assess depression. Examiner-rating scales - the Hamilton Rating Scale (HRS), the Comprehensive Psychopathological Rating Scale - Depression (CPRS-D), and the Cornell Scale - were also used. Examples of findings: (1) positive predictive value was highest (93%) for the Zung Scale and (2) the CPRS-D was the best examiner-rating scale. Author biographical information. Abstract. 3 tables. 1 figure. 24 references.

1.006. Alexopoulos, George S. "Biological Abnormalities in Late-Life Depression." **Journal of Geriatric Psychiatry** 22, No. 1 (1989): 25-34.

1.007. Alexopoulos, George S., Kenneth W. Lieberman, Robert C. Young and Charles A. Shamoian. "Platelet MAO Activity and Age at Onset of Depression in Elderly Depressed Women." **American Journal of Psychiatry** 141 (October 1984): 1276-1278.

Two groups of individuals were studied to determine if, in these groups, platelet monoamine oxidase (MAO) activity differed. Although heredity partly determines platelet MAO activity, this activity also increases with age. One group consisted of thirty-eight elderly, depressed and hospitalized women. The other group was the control group and consisted of sixteen elderly women, residing in the community. Research Diagnostic Criteria (RDC), Hamilton Rating Scale for Depression, and Schedule for Affective Disorders and Schizophrenia (SADS) were used to assess the subjects. Nineteen women who became depressed at age fifty-five or earlier had significantly lower MAO activity than controls or nineteen women who became depressed at a later age. Author biographical information. Abstract. 1 table. 10 references.

1.008. Allers, Christopher T., JoAnna White and David Horn-buckle. "Early Recollections: Detecting Depression in the Elderly." **Individual Psychology** 46 (March 1990): 61-66.

1.009. Arean, Patricia A. "Screening for Depression in Low Income and Medically Ill Older Adults." Abstract in **Gerontologist** 34, Special Issue 1 (October 1994): 275.

The Beck Depression Inventory (BDI) and the Center for Epidemiological Scale-Depression (CES-D) were administered to 703 elderly, low income and minority medical patients. After Receiver Operating Characteristic Curves (ROCs) were calculated, it was determined that both scales should have higher cut-scores to be valid measures of major depression. Neither scale was useful in detecting minor depression.

1.010. Bagley, M. "Depression and the Older Woman: Exploration of a Learned Helplessness Model." Abstract in **Gerontologist** 18, Special Issue (1978): 46.

1.011. Baker, F.M., C. Wiley, S.A. Velli and J.T. Johnson. "Reliability of the Geriatric Depression Scale and the Center for Epidemiologic Studies of Depression Scale in the Elderly." Poster Paper No. NR513 presented at the **1994 Annual Meeting of the American Psychiatric Association, Philadelphia, Pennsylvania, May 21-26, 1994.** DIALOG, Conference Papers Index.

1.012. Baldwin, Bob. "Age of Onset of Depression in the Elderly." **British Journal of Psychiatry** 156 (March 1990): 445-446.

1.013. Baldwin, R.C. "Is There a Distinct Subtype of Major Depression in the Elderly?" **Journal of Psychopharmacology** 8, No. 3 (1994): 177-184.

1.014. Barsa, John, John Toner, Barry Gurland and Rafael Lantigua. "Ability of Internists to Recognize and Manage Depression in the Elderly." **International Journal of Geriatric Psychiatry** 1 (July-September 1986): 57-62.

Internists assessed seventy-seven elderly patients for depression. These patients were sixty-five years of age and over and 75% were women. The SHORT-CARE Instrument was administered to the patients. Internists made management recommendations. A review of charts a year and a half later revealed that although internists were skilled at formulating management plans regarding depression, they did not follow through with counseling or referral of patients. Author biographical information. Abstract. 1 figure. Acknowledgments. 24 references.

1.015. Baum, Steven K. and Russell L. Boxley. "Depression and Old Age Identification." **Journal of Clinical Psychology** 39 (July 1983): 584-590.

The subjects were 308 elderly persons in Los Angeles, California. Their mean age was 75.5 years. The Symptom Checklist-90, Cornell Medical Index, and Purpose-in-Life Test were some of the research instruments used. One finding: depressed persons feel older than they are. A second finding: meaningful existence counters depression. A third finding: increased mobility counters depression. Author biographical information. Abstract. 2 tables. 28 references.

1.016. Beckingham, Ann C. and Bernard Lubin. "Reliability and Validity of the Trait Form of Set 2 of the Depression Adjective Check Lists with Canadian Elderly." **Journal of Clinical Psychology** 47 (May 1991): 407-414.

1.017. Bell, I., F. Morrow, D. Marby, S. Mirages, C. Perrone, J. Edman and J. Cole. "B Vitamin Patterns of Geriatric Versus Young Adult Inpatients with Major Depression." Abstract in **Gerontologist** 29, Special Issue (October 1989): 223A.

1.018. Ben-Arie, O., L. Swartz and B.J. Dickman. "Depression in the Elderly Living in the Community: Its Presentation and Features." **British Journal of Psychiatry** 150 (February 1987): 169-174.

1.019. Berkman, Lisa F., Cathy S. Berkman, Stanislav Kasl, Daniel H. Freeman, Jr., Linda Leo, Adrian M. Ostfeld, Joan Cornoni-Huntley and Jacob A. Brody. "Depressive Symptoms in Relation to Physical Health and Functioning in the Elderly." **American Journal of Epidemiology** 124 (September 1986): 372-388.

1.020. Bird, Anne S., Alastair J. MacDonald, Anthony H. Mann and Michael P. Philpot. "Preliminary Experience with the SELF-CARE (D): A Self-Rating Depression Questionnaire for Use in Elderly, Non-Institutionalized Subjects." **International Journal of Geriatric Psychiatry** 2 (January-March 1987): 31-38.

1.021. Bischmann, Dori Ann. "Food Identification, Taste Complaints and Depression in the Elderly." **Dissertation Abstracts International** 52: 4488B. Ph.D. University of Arkansas, 1990. UMI Order No. AAD92-04682. DIALOG, Dissertation Abstracts Online.

There were in this study thirty elderly adults, ranging in age from sixty-six to ninety-one years, and thirty young adults, ranging in age from twenty-four to forty-six years. Each group was balanced for gender. All the subjects were, during this study, nonsmokers. The subjects, while blind-folded, smelled then tasted ten pureed food items. The subjects were then asked to identify the food item. The Beck Depression Inventory (BDI) was used to assess depression. The elderly were significantly poorer at identifying food items than were younger adults. Overall depression did not correlate with, for example, self-assessed taste acuity in either group.

1.022. Blancarte, Ana Lilia. "Validity of Short and Long Forms of the Geriatric Depression Scale (GDS) among Elderly Medical Outpatients." **Dissertation Abstracts International** 54: 87A. Ph.D. Texas A & M University, 1992. UMI Order No. AAD93-15034. DIALOG, Dissertation Abstracts Online.

One hundred thirty-eight medical outpatients, at least sixty-five years of age, were the subjects in this investigation. It concerned the validity of the Geriatric Depression Scale (GDS) and the Geriatric Depression Scale-Short Form (GDS-SF) in relation to the Brief Psychiatric Rating Scale-Depression Factor (BPRS-D). Concurrent validity of the BPRS-D with the GDS and the GDS-SF was supported.

1.023. Blazer, D. "The Epidemiology of Depression in Late Life." **Journal of Geriatric Psychiatry** 22, No. 1 (1989): 35-52.

1.024. Blazer, D., C. Service, B. Burchett and L.K. George. "The Association of Age and Depression: An Epidemiologic Exploration." Abstract in **Gerontologist** 29,

Special Issue (October 1989): 102A.

Approximately 4,000 persons, sixty-five years of age and older, associated with EPESE (Established Populations for Epidemiological Studies of the Elderly), were assessed for depression. Bivariate analyses revealed that depressive symptoms, in these community-residing research subjects, were associated with a number of variables, including increased age. Multiple regression analysis revealed that the association of age and depressive symptoms were reversed. In other words, age alone was not a risk factor for depression.

1.025. Blazer, D.G., L.K. George and Richard Landerman. "Are Depressive Symptoms Different in the Depressed Elderly?" Abstract in **Gerontologist** 24, Special Issue (October 1984): 133.

1.026. Blazer, Dan. "Depression in Late Life: An Update." Chapter in **Annual Review of Gerontology and Geriatrics** 9 (1989): 197-215.

1.027. Blazer, Dan, James R. Bachar and Dana C. Hughes. "Major Depression with Melancholia: A Comparison of Middle-Aged and Elderly Adults." **Journal of the American Geriatrics Society** 35 (October 1987): 927-932.

Eighteen middle-aged and nineteen elderly inpatients, at Duke University Medical Center, were suffering from major depressive episode with melancholia, according to DSM-III diagnosis. These inpatients were administered the Duke Depression Evaluation Schedule for the Elderly (DDESE). Both groups of inpatients were relatively homogenous, regarding cognitive capacity and severity of depressive symptoms. Older inpatients were less likely to report suicidal thoughts. Approximately 78% of the middle-aged and approximately 52% of the elderly inpatients reported crying spells. Author biographical information. Abstract. 3 tables. 28 references.

1.028. Blazer, Dan, Dana C. Hughes and Linda K. George. "The Epidemiology of Depression in an Elderly Community Population." **Gerontologist** 27 (June 1987): 281-287.

Five epidemiological research studies constitute the Epidemiological Catchment Area Program. Independent research teams and staff from the National Institute of Mental Health (NIMH) do the research studies. Dan Blazer and Linda K. George are the principal investigators for the Piedmont of North Carolina. Over 1,300 adults, sixty years of age and older, in the Piedmont Health Survey, were screened, in part, with the Diagnostic Interview Schedule (DIS). Twenty-seven percent of the subjects reported depressive symptoms: mild dysphoria (19%), symptomatic depression (4%), dysthymia (2%), mixed depressive and anxiety syndrome (1.2%), major depression (0.8%). Abstract. Author biographical information. 4 tables. 22 references.

1.029. Blazer, Dan and Candyce D. Williams. "Epidemiology of Dysphoria and Depression in an Elderly Population." **American Journal of Psychiatry** 137 (April 1980): 439-444.

1.030. Blazer, Dan G. "Affective Disorders in Late Life." Chapter in **Geriatric Psychiatry**, edited by Ewald W. Busse and Dan G. Blazer, 369-401. Washington, DC: American Psychiatric Press, 1989.

1.031. Blazer, Dan G. "Current Concepts: Depression in the Elderly." **New England Journal of Medicine** 320 (January 1989): 164-166.

1.032. Blazer, Dan G., Bruce Burchett, Connie Service and Linda K. George. "The Association of Age and Depression among the Elderly: An Epidemiologic Exploration." **Journals of Gerontology** 46 (November 1991): M210-M215.

1.033. Blazer, Dan G., II. **Depression in Late Life**. St. Louis, MO: C.V. Mosby, 1982.

Primary care physicians, psychiatrists, psychologists, and social workers are some of the professionals most likely to provide treatment for depressed elderly persons. The author, as a clinician at Duke University, learned about the widespread prevalence of depression, particularly in patients at Duke Hospital. His orientation is eclectic and he is aware of multiple factors in the etiology of and multiple targets in the intervention of depression in the elderly. Biological, social, epidemiological, and other data should be part of a comprehensive approach to treatment. Unipolar and bipolar affective disorders; late life bereavement and depressive neurosis; and depressive disorders associated with physical illness and alcohol use are the common depressive disorders of late life. Psychotherapy; family therapy; pharmacological treatment; and electroconvulsive, physical, and nutritional therapies are used in the treatment of late life depression.

1.034. Bonner, D. and R. Howard. "Clinical Characteristics of Resistant Depression in the Elderly." **International Journal of Geriatric Psychiatry** 10 (December 1995): 1023-1027.

1.035. Bonner, Dierdre and Robert Howard. "Treatment Resistant Depression in the Elderly." **International Journal of Geriatric Psychiatry** 10 (April 1995): 259-264.

1.036. Borson, Soo, Robert A. Barnes, Walter A. Kukull, Joseph T. Okimoto, Richard C. Veith, Thomas S. Inui, William Carter and Murray A. Raskind. "Symptomatic Depression in Elderly Medical Outpatients. I. Prevalence, Demography, and Health Service Utilization." **Journal of the American Geriatrics Society** 34 (May 1986): 341-347.

1.037. Brink, T.L., Jerome A. Yesavage, Owen Lum, Philip H. Heersema, Michael

Adey and Terrence L. Rose. "Screening Tests for Geriatric Depression." **Clinical Gerontologist** 1 (Fall 1982): 37-43.

1.038. Brumback, Roger A. "'Terminal Drop' as a Sign of Depression in Elderly Individuals: An Hypothesis." **Psychological Reports** 57 (August 1985): 84-86.

Low scores by geriatric patients on certain psychological tests, such as the Bender-Gestalt Test, and deterioration in cognitive functioning, also referred to as "terminal drop," have both been associated with impending death in elderly persons. The deterioration in test performance (tests of right-hemisphere function, in particular) may be a form of masked depression. Pharmacotherapy and electroconvulsive therapy (ECT) have both improved neuropsychological function in depressed persons. Improved test scores have been correlated with longer survival. Author biographical information. Abstract. 20 references.

1.039. Buckwalter, Kathleen C. "How to Unmask Depression." **Geriatric Nursing** 11 (July-August 1990): 179-181.

Memory, orientation, and speech are three of thirteen variables to consider when differentiating senile dementia, delirium, and depression from each other. Depression can be attributed to the destabilization of receptor sites in the brain to which chemical messengers - norepinephrine and serotonin - attach. The effectiveness of certain drugs, as well as electroconvulsive therapy (ECT), is due to these treatments "resetting" the receptors - restoring them to normal levels of activity. Author biographical information. 8 references.

1.040. Burch, Earl A. and Thomas J. Goldschmidt. "Depression in the Elderly: A Beta-Adrenergic Receptor Dysfunction?" **International Journal of Psychiatry in Medicine** 13, No. 3 (1983-1984): 207-213.

1.041. Burdman, Geri Marr. "Depression." in **Healthful Aging**, by Geri Marr Burdman, 71-75. Englewood Cliffs, NJ: Prentice-Hall, 1986.

The whole person must be considered in the diagnosis and treatment of depression. Physical disorders have to be taken into account when a person is depressed, but does not have a history of recent losses or psychological stress. The causes of depression in older individuals are many and varied. Stroke, pneumonia, failing sight, alcoholism, absence of meaningful life roles, and increasing social isolation are some of these causes.

1.042. Burnette, Denise and Ada C. Mui. "Determinants of Self-Reported Depressive Symptoms by Frail Elderly Persons Living Alone." **Journal of Gerontological Social Work** 22, No. 1-2 (1994): 3-19.

1.043. Burvill, P.W., W.D. Hall, H.G. Stampfer and J.P. Emmerson. "A Comparison of

Early-Onset and Late-Onset Depressive Illness in the Elderly." **British Journal of Psychiatry** 155 (November 1989): 673-679.

1.044. Burvill, Peter W., Hans G. Stampfer and Wayne D. Hall. "Issues in the Assessment of Outcome in Depressive Illness in the Elderly." **International Journal of Geriatric Psychiatry** 6 (May 1991): 269-277.

1.045. Busse, Ewald W. "Depression." in **Normal Aging**, Reports from the Duke Longitudinal Study, 1955-1969, edited by Erdman Palmore, 86-88. Durham, NC: Duke University Press, 1970.

The depressed elderly can, like younger individuals who experience a grief reaction, identify their loss. The loss of an adequate social role or financial insecurity in old age can precipitate depression in elderly persons. These persons lose their self-esteem. They feel discouraged, worried, troubled sometimes to the point of wishing for a painless death.

1.046. Butler, Robert N. and Myrna I. Lewis. "Late-Life Depression: When and How to Intervene." **Geriatrics** 50 (August 1995): 44-46, 49-50, 52 and 55.

Up to 20% of individuals age sixty-five and older may suffer from some form of depression. Neurotransmitter abnormalities pertaining to norepinephrine may be a physiological cause of depression. Hypertension, multiple sclerosis, lymphoma, and renal dialysis are examples of medical conditions associated with depression. The suicide rate for persons age sixty-five and older is 35 per 100,000. The selective SSRIs (selective serotonin reuptake inhibitors), paroxetine and sertraline, are useful for older patients because these drugs have short half-lives.

1.047. Callahan, C.M., J.G. Kesterson and W.M. Tierney. "The Use of Diagnostic Testing among Elderly Primary Care Patients with Depression." Abstract in **Gerontologist** 36, Special Issue 1 (October 1996): 206-207.

A study over two years of 3,767 elderly patients, who visited their primary care physician and were screened for depression, revealed that depressive symptoms were associated with increased use of diagnostic testing. Median/mean total test charges were higher for patients who were depressed than for patients who were not depressed.

1.048. Cappeliez, Philippe. "Some Thoughts on the Prevalence and Etiology of Depressive Conditions in the Elderly." **Canadian Journal on Aging** 7 (Winter 1988): 431-440.

1.049. Carpiniello, Bernardo, M.G. Carta and N. Rudas. "Depression among Elderly People: A Psychosocial Study of Urban and Rural Populations." **Acta Psychiatrica Scandinavica** 80 (November 1989): 445-450.

1.050. Chaisson-Stewart, G. Maureen. Editor. **Depression in the Elderly: An Interdisciplinary Approach**. New York, NY: Wiley, 1985. DIALOG, LCMARC-Books.

1.051. Charatan, Fred B. "Depression and the Elderly: Diagnosis and Treatment." **Psychiatric Annals** 15 (May 1985): 313-316.

1.052. Coffey, C. Edward, Gary S. Figiel, William T. Djang and Richard D. Weiner. "Subcortical Hyperintensity on Magnetic Resonance Imaging: A Comparison of Normal and Depressed Elderly Subjects." **American Journal of Psychiatry** 147 (February 1990): 187-189.

The subjects in this investigation were fifty-one inpatients sixty years of age or older. A DSM-III checklist was used to diagnose severe major depression. The patients, prior to receiving electroconvulsive therapy (ECT) for the depression, received brain MRI (magnetic resonance imaging). Sixteen patients also had mild dementia, stroke, Parkinson's Disease. There was no DSM-III indication of an organic affective disorder. Twenty-two elderly volunteers from the community, matched for age and sex, were the control group. There was no history in the control group of neurological or psychiatric illness. When the two groups were compared for subcortical hyperintensity, this condition was, in the elderly depressed patients, significantly more common and severe than in the control group. Author biographical information. Abstract. 1 table. 10 references.

1.053. Cole, Martin G. "Age, Age of Onset and Course of Primary Depressive Illness in the Elderly." **Canadian Journal of Psychiatry** 28 (March 1983): 102-104.

1.054. Cole, Martin G., Denise T. Rochan, Frank Engelsmann and Danka Ducic. "The Impact of Home Assessment on Depression in the Elderly: A Clinical Trial." **International Journal of Geriatric Psychiatry** 10 (January 1995): 19-23.

1.055. Cosgray, Robert E. and Vickie Hanna. "Physiological Causes of Depression in the Elderly." **Perspectives in Psychiatric Care** 29 (January-March 1993): 26-28.

1.056. Davidson, Harriet, Penny H. Feldman and Sybil Crawford. "Measuring Depressive Symptoms in the Frail Elderly." **Journals of Gerontology** 49 (July 1994): P159-P164.

1.057. Davies, Ann D. and K.J. Gledhill. "Engagement and Depressive Symptoms in a Community Sample of Elderly People." **British Journal of Clinical Psychology** 22 (June 1983): 95-105.

1.058. Davis-Berman, J.L. "Self-Efficacy and Depression in Older Adults: An Exploratory Study." Abstract in **Gerontologist** 25, Special Issue (October 1985): 165.

Members of the Golden Age Senior Center in Xenia, Ohio, were the subjects. They were interviewed by telephone and were administered a number of assessment instruments, including the Depression Adjective Checklist. Self-efficacy was the most important predictor of depression in these subjects.

1.059. DeForge, Bruce R. and Jeffery Sobal. "Self-Report Depression Scales in the Elderly: The Relationship between the CES-D and ZUNG." **International Journal of Psychiatry in Medicine** 18, No. 4 (1988): 325-338.

1.060. Depression and the Elderly. 25 minutes. 1990. Distributed/Produced by Terra Nova Films, Chicago, IL. Videocassette. DIALOG, A-V Online.

1.061. Dhondt, A.D.F. and C. Hooijer. "Iatrogenic Origins of Depression in the Elderly: Is Medication a Significant Aetiologic Factor in Geriatric Depression? Considerations and a Preliminary Approach." **International Journal of Geriatric Psychiatry** 10 (January 1995): 1-8.

1.062. Dovenmuehle, Robert H., John B. Reckless and Gustave Newman. "Depressive Reactions in the Elderly." in **Normal Aging**, Reports from the Duke Longitudinal Study, 1955-1969, edited by Erdman Palmore, 90-97. Durham, NC: Duke University Press, 1970.

In a comparison of normally functioning community volunteers and hospitalized subjects, depression in the volunteers was less severe with less guilt and no suicidal thoughts. Although there was in these volunteers occasional sleep disturbance, there was frequent anxiety and irritability. Symptomatology in the hospitalized subjects was more severe. 1 table. 6 references.

1.063. Downes, John J., Ann D. Davies and J.R. Copeland. "Organization of Depressive Symptoms in the Elderly Population: Hierarchical Patterns and Guttman Scales." **Psychology and Aging** 3 (December 1988): 367-374.

1.064. Dreyfus, Joan K. "Depression Assessment and Interventions in the Medically Ill Frail Elderly." **Journal of Gerontological Nursing** 14, No. 9 (1988): 27-36.

Change of appetite, criticism of others, and social withdrawal are examples of symptoms frequently found in the depressed elderly. Ibuprofen, clonidine, cycloserine, and digitalis are drugs with a potential side effect of depression. Gout, hyperthyroidism, pancreatitis, hepatitis, uremia, leukemia, multiple sclerosis, and psoriasis are medical conditions associated with depression. Fifteen things, including memory and hallucinations can be considered in differentiating dementia and depression in the elderly. Cognitive interventions can be used concerning loss of motivation. Author biographical information. 8 tables. 27 references.

1.065. Dunn, Victoria K. and William P. Sacco. "Psychometric Evaluation of the Geriatric

Depression Scale and the Zung Self-Rating Depression Scale Using an Elderly Community Sample." **Psychology and Aging** 4 (March 1989): 125-126.

1.066. Dush, David M. and R.R. Hutzell. "A Brief MMPI Depression Screening Scale for the Elderly." **Clinical Gerontologist** 5 (June 1986): 175-185.

1.067. Edlavitch, Stanley, Barry J. Gurland, Robert Golden, Merwyn Greenlick, H. Mitchell Perry and James Schoenberger. "Rates of Depression in Elderly Volunteers with Isolated Systolic Hypertension." **International Journal of Geriatric Psychiatry** 2 (January-March 1987): 111-117.

The SHORT-CARE is an assessment instrument which measures depression, cognitive impairment, and disability. This instrument was administered to 551 elderly persons with isolated systolic hypertension. The SHORT-CARE was administered at baseline interview and over a follow-up period of eighteen months. Rates and levels of depression in these subjects were remarkably low, when compared to community norms. Author biographical information. Abstract. 6 tables. 11 references.

1.068. Eisdorfer, C. "Depression in Aged: An Overview." Paper presented at the **6th World Congress of Psychiatry, Honolulu, Hawaii, August 28-September 3, 1977.** DIALOG, Conference Papers Index.

1.069. Encyclopedia of Aging, s.v. "Depression."

Depression, a self-limiting illness, is easily confused with various conditions, including dementia and hypochondriasis. For these reasons older adults, who are clinically depressed, are often not identified. The Dexamethasone Suppression Test (DST) is effective in the diagnosis of depression in the elderly. Rapid eye movement (REM) latency in these individuals is relatively short and, REM latency like the DST, is a way of identifying depression in this age group.

1.070. Encyclopedia of Gerontology, s.v. "Depression."

1.071. Etemad, B. "Sudden Losses and Depression in the Elderly." Paper presented at the **56th Annual Meeting of the American Orthopsychiatric Association, Washington, DC, March 31-April 4, 1979.** DIALOG, Conference Papers Index.

1.072. Evans, M.E. "Development and Validation of a Brief Screening Scale for Depression in the Elderly Physically Ill." **International Clinical Psychopharmacology** 8 (Winter 1993): 329-331.

1.073. Fassler, Louise B. and Moises Gaviria. "Depression in Old Age." **Journal of the American Geriatrics Society** 26 (October 1978): 471-475.

A sixty-five-year-old, married female; a seventy-year-old, twice-widowed female; and a sixty-eight-year-old married, male retiree illustrate depression in old age. Author biographical information. Abstract. 14 references.

1.074. Ferrario, Joyce Ann. "Coexistence of Hypochondriasis and Depression in the Elderly." **Dissertation Abstracts International** 43: 3535B. Ph.D. Case Western Reserve University, 1982. UMI Order No. AAD83-06537. DIALOG, Dissertation Abstracts Online.

Thirty-two men and eighty-seven women, with a mean age of seventy-three years, were the subjects. These noninstitutional subjects were administered the Whitely Index for Hypochondriasis, the Levine Pilowsky Depression Scale, and the Life Satisfaction Index-A. Four hypotheses were tested regarding three groups of individuals. Subjects with high hypochondriasis had a significantly lower mean depression score.

1.075. Ferrucci, L., J. Guralnik, N. Marchionni and A. Baroni. "Aging and Prevalence of Depression." Abstract in **Gerontologist** 30, Special Issue (October 1990): 314A.

In 1987 in Florence, Italy, 488 men and women, ranging in age from sixty-five to ninety-five years, were evaluated concerning health and social conditions. The Geriatric Depression Scale was administered to these subjects. Depression increased with advancing age and was more prevalent in women than in men. Cognitive impairment and incontinence were strongly associated with depression.

1.076. Fitzgerald, Joseph M. "Issues of Stability and Predictability of Depression across Adulthood." Abstract in **Gerontologist** 33, Special Issue 1 (October 1993): 285.

1.077. Flynn, Michael S. and Patrick Flynn. "How to Identify and Treat Depression in the Elderly." **Canadian Journal of Geriatrics** 7 (November-December 1991): 27-29, 32-34, 36-37 and 41.

A complete blood cell count (CBC), urinalysis, liver function tests, and thyroid function studies are examples of laboratory procedures recommended for elderly depressed persons. A computerized axial tomography (CAT) scan and magnetic resonance imaging (MRI) may help detect Alzheimer's Disease. Methyldopa, propranolol, vinblastine, and cimetidine are drugs which cause depression. Elderly persons who live alone, and those who abuse alcohol or drugs, are at considerable risk for suicide. Abstract. Author biographical information. 2 photographs. 2 tables. 19 references.

1.078. Foelker, G.A., Jr. and R.M. Shewchuk. "Is the CES-Depression Scale Biased by Somatic Symptomatology?" Abstract in **Gerontologist** 30, Special Issue (October

1990): 226A.

1.079. Foelker, George A., Richard M. Shewchuk and George Niederehe. "Confirmatory Factor Analysis of the Short Form Beck Depression Inventory in Elderly Community Samples." **Journal of Clinical Psychology** 43 (January 1987): 111-118.

1.080. Fogel, Barry S. and Marsha Fretwell. "Reclassification of Depression in the Medically Ill Elderly." **Journal of the American Geriatrics Society** 33 (June 1985): 446-448.

1.081. Fopma-Loy, Joan. "The Prevalence and Phenomenology of Depression in Elderly Women: A Review of the Literature." **Archives of Psychiatric Nursing** 2 (April 1988): 74-80.

1.082. Forbes, B., C. Burger and M. Lichtenstein. "The Interrelationship of Three Depressive Scales among an Older Female Population." Abstract in **Gerontologist** 28, Special Issue (October 1988): 237A.

1.083. Frances, Allen and Paul Teusink. "Elderly Patient's Confusion Confounds Diagnosis and Treatment of Depression." **Hospital and Community Psychiatry** 35 (November 1984): 1091-1093.

1.084. Freeman, Sue and Ada Roca. "Confronting Depression and Substance Abuse in Older Adults: Identification and Intervention." Abstract in **Gerontologist** 35, Special Issue 1 (October 1995): 459-460.

The Alcohol, Drug, and Depression Screening (ADDS) Program has identified older adults at risk for substance abuse, substance misuse, depression, and social deficits.

1.085. Fry, P.S. "Development of a Geriatric Scale of Hopelessness: Implications for Counseling and Intervention with the Depressed Elderly." **Journal of Counseling Psychology** 31 (July 1984): 322-331.

Hopelessness, depression, and self-esteem were evaluated in depressed elderly men and women, ranging in age from sixty-five to eighty years. After these sixty elderly subjects were interviewed, a factor analysis was done on the interview contents. The results were hopelessness about recovering: (1) lost physical and cognitive abilities; (2) lost personal and interpersonal worth and attractiveness; (3) spiritual faith and receiving spiritual grace; and (4) receiving nurture and recovering respect and remembrance in the present and after death. The factor analysis data was used to develop a Geriatric Hopelessness Scale (GHS). The scale was validated after it was administered to seventy-eight elderly men and women. Author biographical information. Abstract. 4 tables. 43 references.

1.086. Fry, Prem S. **Depression, Stress, and Adaptations in the Elderly: Psychological Assessment and Intervention**. Rockville, MD: Aspen Publishers, 1986: DIALOG, LCMARC-Books.

1.087. Futterman, A., S. Hanser, P. Hanley-Peterson, A. Zeiss, L.W. Thompson, D. Gallagher and G. Ironson. "Endogenous Depression and Anhedonia: Five Definitions of Endogenous Depression and Pleasant Events in Depressed Elderly." Abstract in **Gerontologist** 30, Special Issue (October 1990): 269A-270A.

Five definitions of endogenous depression were used to diagnose seventy-four older adults. These older adults were also administered the Older Persons Pleasant Event Schedule (OPPES). A comparison sample, seventy-three nondepressed older adults, were also administered the OPPES. Only the RDC and DSM III-R predicted OPPES scores. Endogenously depressed older adults reported fewer pleasant events.

1.088. Gallant, M.P. and C.M. Connell. "Relationship between Depression Scores and Daily Physical and Mental Health Self-Ratings: A Health Diary Approach." Abstract in **Gerontologist** 31 (October 1991): 64.

1.089. Ganguli, Mary, Joanne Gilby, Eric Seaburg and Steven Belle. "Depressive Symptoms and Associated Factors in a Rural Elderly Population: The MoVIES Project." **American Journal of Geriatric Psychiatry** 3 (Spring 1995): 144-160.

1.090. Gatz, Margaret and Margo-Lea Hurwicz. "Are Old People More Depressed?: Cross-Sectional Data on Center for Epidemiological Studies Depression Scale Factors." **Psychology and Aging** 5 (June 1990): 284-290.

Four age-cohort groups, ranging from twenty to ninety-eight years, were administered the Center for Epidemiological Studies Depression Scale (CES-D). The oldest group, which ranged in age from seventy to ninety-eight years, scored highest on lack of well-being. Individuals aged seventy and older were not likely to express a hopeful outlook. Young adults - those persons ranging in age from twenty to thirty-nine years - scored highest on depressed mood. Author biographical information. Abstract. 4 tables. 34 references.

1.091. Geiselmann, B. and B. Ahrens. "Physical Health Complaints and the Diagnosis of Mild Depression in the Old and Very Old." Abstract in **Gerontologist** 33, Special Issue 1 (October 1993): 312-313.

1.092. Geiselmann, B. and M. Borchelt. "The Relationship between Somatic Impairment and Depression in the Old and Very Old." Abstract in **Gerontologist** 31, Special Issue 2 (October 1991): 87-88.

One hundred fifty persons, ranging in age from seventy to 105 years, from the Berlin Aging Study, were the subjects. A semistructured diagnostic interview and a comprehensive examination battery were used to diagnose these subjects. The Prevalence of somatic multimorbidity was 90%; the prevalence of depression was 16%.

1.093. Gilleard, C.J., M. Willmott and K.S. Vaddadi. "Self-Report Measures of Mood and Morale in Elderly Depressives." **British Journal of Psychiatry** 138 (March 1981): 230-235.

1.094. Glasser, Michael and Peter Rabins. "Mania in the Elderly." **Age and Ageing** 13 (1984): 210-213.

DSM-III criteria were used to identify forty-two patients, sixty years old and older, who had mania. Eighteen of these individuals were male, twenty-four female. The mean age for the first episode of mania was 51.1 years. There is the possibility a structural brain lesion contributed to certain late-onset cases of mania in the elderly patients. Otherwise, these patients were similar to younger patients with mania. Author biographical information. Abstract. Acknowledgments. 6 references.

1.095. Glavin, Y.W., J. Mezzich, B. Zimmer and W. Flynn. "Clinical Manifestations and Correlates of Depressed Geriatric and Young Adults." Abstract in **Gerontologist** 25, Special Issue (October 1985): 190.

Between July 1983 and June 1984, at a university psychiatric center, 147 individuals, sixty years of age and older, and 689 individuals, ranging in age from twenty to fifty-nine years, were diagnosed with major depression. When these two groups of subjects were compared, it was learned the geriatric subjects exhibited more of the following: (1) decreased motor activity, (2) decreased appetite, and (3) jealousy. Furthermore, geriatric patients had more frequent diagnoses of these disorders: (1) gastrointestinal, (2) cardiovascular, and (3) neurological-muscular.

1.096. Godderis, Jan. "Assessing Depression in Elderly Patients." **Acta Psychiatrica Belgica** 87 (May-June 1987): 288-301.

1.097. Gonzalez, Elizabeth W. "The Relationship of Nurses' Critical Thinking Ability and Patients' Self-Disclosure to Accuracy in Assessment of Depression in Elderly Medical Patients." **Dissertation Abstracts International** 52: 1351B. Ph.D. New York University, 1990. UMI Order No. AAD91-13091. DIALOG, Dissertation Abstracts Online.

1.098. Good, W.R., I. Vlachonikolis, P. Griffiths and R.A. Griffiths. "The Structure of Depressive Symptoms in the Elderly." **British Journal of Psychiatry** 150 (April 1987): 463-470.

1.099. Grau, L., L. Mills and M. Granucci. "Nursing Assessment of Depression in a Home Care Population." Abstract in **Gerontologist** 36, Special Issue 1 (October 1996): 296.

Nineteen nurses, using assessment instruments including the Geriatric Depression Scale (GDS), assessed one hundred home care patients. A modified version of the Schedule of Affective Disorders and Schizophrenia (SADS) indicated that 11% of these patients had major depression. The SADS revealed that 8% of the patients, who had GDS scores of 9 or less, were dysphoric/dysthymic.

1.100. Grau, Lois and Deborah Padgett. "Somatic Depression among the Elderly: A Sociocultural Perspective." **International Journal of Geriatric Psychiatry** 3 (July-September 1988): 201-207.

1.101. Grayson, Paula, Bernard Lubin and Rodney Van Whitlock. "Comparison of Depression in the Community-Dwelling and Assisted-Living Elderly." **Journal of Clinical Psychology** 51 (January 1995): 18-21.

1.102. Grayson, Paula S., Bernard Lubin and Rodney Van Whitlock. "Reliability and Validity of Set 1 of the Depression Adjective Check Lists with the Elderly." **Assessment** 1 (March 1994): 17-22.

1.103. Green, Sandra F. "Depression in the Elderly: A Comparative Study of Assessment Measures." **Dissertation Abstracts International** 46: 2062B. Ph.D. University of Detroit, 1985. UMI Order No. AAD85-18691. DIALOG, Dissertation Abstracts Online.

The Geriatric Depression Scale (GDS), Beck Depression Inventory (BDI), and Rorschach Depression Index (RDI) were used to assess forty subjects age sixty and over. The GDS score was used to establish a nondepressed group and a depressed group. Eleven Rorschach variables discriminated with 92.5% accuracy nondepressed from depressed elderly. The suicide constellation was not recommended as an assessment instrument with the elderly. It was determined the BDI was a reliable assessment instrument.

1.104. Gregoire, J., N. de Leval, P. Mesters and M. Czarka. "Validation of the Quality of Life in Depression Scale in a Population of Adult Depressive Patients Aged 60 and Above." **Quality of Life Research** 3 (February 1994): 13-19.

1.105. Groulx, B. "How to Recognize Depression in the Elderly." Paper presented at the **64th Annual Meeting of the Royal College of Physicians and Surgeons of Canada, Montreal, Quebec, September 13-17, 1995**. DIALOG, Conference Papers Index.

1.106. Hale, W. Daniel. "Correlates of Depression in the Elderly: Sex Differences and Similarities." **Journal of Clinical Psychology** 38 (April 1982): 253-257.

White residents of a Florida retirement center were the subjects in this investigation. There were forty-seven white females and twenty-one white males. The subjects ranged in age from sixty-three to ninety-four years. All the subjects completed a life satisfaction survey. Some of the variables related to depression were: (1) poorer financial status, (2) poorer physical health, and (3) concerns about death. Author biographical information. Abstract. 1 table. 15 references.

1.107. Hale, W. Daniel, C.D. Cochran and Bruce E. Hedgepeth. "Norms for the Elderly on the Brief Symptom Inventory." **Journal of Consulting and Clinical Psychology** 52, No. 2 (1984): 321-322.

The Brief Symptom Inventory (BSI) is an abbreviated form of the Symptom Checklist-90 (SCL-90). The BSI, a fifty-three item self-report inventory, measures psychopathology along nine primary symptom dimensions, and takes approximately ten minutes to administer. Somatic items did not inflate scores on the depression scale. The BSI was administered to 364 females and 201 males age sixty and over. The elderly, when compared to younger adults, reported higher levels of distress on most symptom dimensions. Author biographical information. Abstract. 1 table. 1 reference.

1.108. Halpert, S. and N. Peters. "The Use of the BDI as a Geriatric Assessment Measure." Abstract in **Gerontologist** 36, Special Issue 1 (October 1996): 110-111.

When the Beck Depression Inventory (BDI) was used to assess 101 individuals over sixty-four years of age, and living in the community, 19.9% of these individuals were depressed. Mean BDI scores were 6.14. This assessment instrument had good internal reliability, with a Cronbach's alpha of .75. There was a significant correlation between BDI and CES-D scores.

1.109. Hanley-Peterson, P., A. Futterman, D. Gallagher and C. Cohan. "The Relationship between RDC Diagnoses of Endogenous Depression and Severity of Depression in an Elderly Sample." Abstract in **Gerontologist** 29, Special Issue (October 1989): 45A.

1.110. Harper, Robert G., Doreen Kotik-Harper and Henry Kirby. "Psychometric Assessment of Depression in an Elderly General Medical Population: Over-or Underassessment?" **Journal of Nervous and Mental Disease** 178 (February 1990): 113-119.

The MMPI, Brief Symptom Inventory, and Geriatric Depression Scale were administered to 247 geriatric medical patients. Research Diagnostic Criteria identified major depression in 59% of these patients, minor depression in 21%. There was cognitive impairment in 80% of the patients. There were false-negative rates of up to 53% for major depression and 100% for minor depression. Psychometric misrecognition of depression was positively associated with verbal intelligence level and patient age. Author biographical information. Abstract. 5 tables. 15 references.

1.111. Hastrup, Janice L., John G. Baker, Deborah L. Kraemer and Robert F. Bornstein. "Crying and Depression among Older Adults." **Gerontologist** 26 (February 1986): 91-96.

In order to study crying and depression, two groups of subjects were compared. Older adult men and women were in the first group. There were forty-four women, ages sixty-five to seventy-one, and twenty men, ages sixty-five to seventy. The second group, the younger adult sample, consisted of 145 mothers, ranging in age from twenty-eight to fifty-eight years, and seventy-seven fathers, ranging in age from thirty-three to sixty-four years. Both groups were nonclinical samples and both used two measures of depression: (1) the Philadelphia Geriatric Center Morale (PGCM) Scale, and (2) the Beck Depression Inventory (BDI), short form. The Crying Frequency Questionnaire (CFQ) was also used. This study did not offer any evidence for decreased or increased frequency of crying among the older adult men and women. However, there was a weak relationship between crying and depression in the older sample. Some individuals used crying to cope with stress. Crying did not necessarily indicate depression. Abstract. Author biographical information. 2 tables. 37 references.

1.112. Hawranik, Pamela and Beth Kondratuk. "Depression in the Elderly." **Canadian Nurse** 82 (October 1986): 25-29.

Hypothyroidism may be an organic cause of depression. Certain antihypertensive drugs cause depression. Some individuals may have a genetic predisposition to this illness. The elderly often become depressed when they lose family and friends. Decreased social ties are another cause of depression in the elderly. Furthermore, social values which place the elderly in a negative context contribute to this medical condition. Author biographical information. 2 photographs. French abstract. 15 references.

1.113. Hayes, Pamela M., Diana Lohse and Irving Bernstein. "The Development and Testing of the Hayes and Lohse Non-Verbal Depression Scale." **Clinical Gerontologist** 10, No. 3 (1991): 3-13.

Self-reported depression instruments cannot quantitatively test older nursing home residents for depression. Aphasia, deafness, restlessness, and other communication deficits prohibit the administration to these individuals of verbal pencil-and-paper tests. This is the reason the Hayes and Lohse Non-Verbal Depression Scale was developed. This scale, which has twenty items, has five answer options for each item, the answer options ranging from "always" to "almost never." Option four, for example, is "avoids eye contact." Option twenty is "cannot concentrate." The Hayes and Lohse Non-Verbal Depression Scale is statistically sound and can be administered by professionals such as registered nurses and social workers. Author biographical information. Abstract. 1 scale. 5 tables. 10 references.

1.114. Hendrie, Hugh C. and Judith H. Crossett. "An Overview of Depression in the Elderly." **Psychiatric Annals** 20 (February 1990): 64-69.

1.115. Herrmann, Nathan, Susan Lieff and Michael Silberfeld. "The Effect of Age of Onset on Depression in the Elderly." **Journal of Geriatric Psychiatry and Neurology** 2 (October-December 1989): 182-187.

1.116. Herron, Dorothy Gabell. "The Effect of Diet on Mood in the Elderly." **Dissertation Abstracts International** 56: 1936B. Ph.D. University of Maryland Baltimore Professional Schools, 1994. UMI Order No. AADAA-I9526599. DIALOG, Dissertation Abstracts Online.

Three well men and twenty-five well women, ranging in age from sixty-three to eighty-three years, were the subjects. These subjects ate, in random order, a high carbohydrate, a high protein, or a control snack. Two different instruments were used to measure mood before and one hour after the snacks were eaten. The carbohydrate snack significantly improved depression.

1.117. Hickie, Catherine and John Snowdon. "Depression Scales for the Elderly: GDS, Gilleard, Zung." **Clinical Gerontologist** 6 (Spring 1987): 51-53.

Three depression scales - Geriatric Depression Scale (GDS), Gilleard, Zung - were used to assess thirty-nine subjects. There were twenty-six female subjects and thirteen male subjects. Seventy-five years was the mean age. Twenty subjects had, according to DSM-III criteria, major depression. Nineteen subjects were not depressed. All three scales distinguished to a satisfactory degree between depressed subjects and a nondepressed group. The GDS was simpler than the Zung. Author biographical information. 1 table. 5 references.

1.118. Hunt, G., S. Gravenstein and M. Schmidt. "The CRS: More than Just a Depression Screen." Abstract in **Gerontologist** 29, Special Issue (October 1989): 286A-287A.

The Carroll Rating Scale (CRS), used to assess depression, consists of fifty-two items. The CRS is burdensome to administer and score. However, this instrument - in addition to providing information on depression - provides data on sleep disturbance and appetite changes.

1.119. Hybels, Derek Cushman. "Depression in the Elderly: An Application of the Reformulated Learned Helplessness Model." **Dissertation Abstracts International** 48: 1153B. Ph.D. Temple University, 1987. UMI Order No. AAD87-16375. DIALOG, Dissertation Abstracts Online.

1.120. Hyer, Lee and John Blount. "Concurrent and Discriminant Validities of the Geriatric Depression Scale with Older Psychiatric Inpatients." **Psychological Reports**

54 (April 1984): 611-616.

The Geriatric Depression Scale (GDS) is a thirty-item instrument, which assesses almost exclusively the psychological aspects of depression. The true/false answer format is relatively easy for older people to use. The subjects were sixty-one male inpatients at a Veterans Administration medical center, who were over fifty-five years of age. There was considerable overlap between the GDS and the Beck Depression Inventory (BDI), with which it was compared. The GDS was more precise in its diagnosis of depression than the BDI. Author biographical information. Abstract. 2 tables. 26 references.

1.121. Intrieri, R.C. and S.R. Rapp. "Confirmatory Factor Analysis of the Geriatric Depression Scale (GDS)." Abstract in **Gerontologist** 33, Special Issue 1 (October 1993): 251.

1.122. Jacoby, Robin J., Raymond J. Dolan, Raymond Levy and Robert Baldy. "Quantitative Computed Tomography in Elderly Depressed Patients." **British Journal of Psychiatry** 143 (August 1983): 124-127.

Elderly depressed patients, patients with senile dementia, and healthy controls were studied. Computed tomography (CT) scans - of twelve predefined brain areas - were used to obtain an index of brain tissue density in the depressed patients. These patients were compared, regarding Hounsfield Units (HU), to the other two groups of subjects. Controls had the highest HU values, dements the lowest. Ventricular dilatation, a predictor of increased mortality, was associated in the depressed patients with lower HU levels. Author biographical information. Abstract. 3 tables. Acknowledgments. 12 references.

1.123. Jimenez, Cristobal Jimenez, Trinidad Alcala Perez, Francisca Serrano Prieto and Pilar Martinez Navia-Osorio. "Behavioural Habits and Affective Disorders in Old People." **Journal of Advanced Nursing** 14 (May 1989): 356-364.

Two hundred seven men and women, over sixty-five years of age, and assessed with the Hospital Anxiety and Depression Questionnaire (HADQ), were the subjects studied. Selected findings: (1) three times as many women as men were depressed, (2) twice as many women as men experienced anxiety, (3) the subjects who frequently took walks were less depressed than those who rarely or never took walks, and (4) the subjects who slept less than seven hours tended to be more depressed and anxious than the subjects who slept more than seven hours. Author biographical information. Abstract. 4 tables. 2 figures. 33 references.

1.124. Jones, S.N. "Content Analysis of the Geriatric Depression Scale to Enhance Clinical Validity." Abstract in **Gerontologist** 32, Special Issue 2 (October 1992): 254.

1.125. Jorm, A.F. "The Epidemiology of Depressive States in the Elderly: Implications for Recognition, Intervention and Prevention." **Social Psychiatry and Psychiatric Epidemiology** 30 (March 1995): 53-59.

1.126. Kalayam B., G.G. Brown, R.C. Young, G.S. Alexopoulos and F.E. Musiek. "Neuropsychological Deficits and P300 Latency in Elderly Non-Demented Depressives." Paper presented at the **1995 Annual Meeting of the American Psychiatric Association, Miami, Florida, May 20-25, 1995**. DIALOG, Conference Papers Index.

1.127. Kane, Robert L., Joseph G. Ouslander and Itamar B. Abrass. "Diagnosis and Management of Depression." Chapter in **Essentials of Clinical Geriatrics**, Third Edition, by Robert L. Kane, Joseph G. Ouslander and Itamar B. Abrass, 115-143. New York, NY: McGraw-Hill, 1994.

Four factors can predispose the elderly to depression: (1) biological (genetic predisposition), (2) physical (loss of vision), (3) psychological (anger), and (4) social (loss of income). High risk factors associated with suicide in the elderly male: (1) Protestant, (2) white, (3) widowed or divorced, (4) blue-collar, low-paying job, (5) retired or unemployed, (6) living alone, (7) poor health, (8) loneliness, and (9) dependent personality. 16 tables. 22 references. 4 suggested readings.

1.128. Kanowski, S. "Age-Dependent Epidemiology of Depression." **Gerontology** 40, Supplement 1 (1994): 1-4.

1.129. Keane, Sarah M. and Sharon Sells. "Recognizing Depression in the Elderly." **Journal of Gerontological Nursing** 16, No. 1 (1990): 21-25.

1.130. Keckich, Walter A. and Mitchell Young. "Anaclitic Depression in the Elderly." Abstract in **Gerontologist** 22 (October 1982): 148.

Protest, despair, and detachment associated with depression in infants results from the denial of proper maternal care. The institutionalized elderly who experience multiple relationship losses, sensory deprivation, and physical deterioration undergo a process similar to the process experienced by these infants. The process is evident in infants and elderly who lack meaningful nurturing relationships.

1.131. Kemp, Bryan. "The Older Adult Health and Mood Index: A New Measure of Geriatric Depression." Abstract in **Gerontologist** 33, Special Issue 1 (October 1993): 308.

A new twenty-two item measure of geriatric depression was based on fifty-five questions. The test-retest reliability coefficient for this measure was 87. Seventy-five percent of depressed individuals were properly identified.

1.132. Kennedy, G.J., H.R. Kelman and C. Thomas. "The Effect of Depressive Symptoms on Mini-Mental State Exam Performance in 1855 Older Community Residents." Abstract in **Gerontologist** 33, Special Issue 1 (October 1993): 208.

1.133. Kennedy, Gary J., Howard R. Kelman and Cynthia Thomas. "The Emergence of Depressive Symptoms in Late Life: The Importance of Declining Health and Increasing Disability." **Journal of Community Health** 15 (April 1990): 93-104.

The sample for this investigation consisted of 1,457 Medicare recipients, residing in the community. The dependent study variable, depressive symptoms, was assessed at baseline and twenty-four months, with the Center for Epidemiological Studies Depression (CES-D) scale. The authors learned significant levels of depressive symptoms emerged, over a twenty-four-month interval, in 11% of the subjects. The prevalence of depression was more adequately explained by poor health and disability than by social support and life events. Deterioration in health over twenty-four months appeared to be more important than, for example, the number of medical conditions, in accounting for the emergence of depression. It appears acuity - not severity - of disability accounts for development of depressive symptoms. Author biographical information. Abstract. 3 tables. 1 figure. 29 references.

1.134. Kennedy, Gary J., Howard R. Kelman and Cynthia Thomas. "Persistence and Remission of Depressive Symptoms in Late Life." **American Journal of Psychiatry** 148 (February 1991): 174-178.

A total of 1,855 elderly individuals, who were sixty-five years of age or older, and who were Medicare recipients, were the randomly selected sample. These subjects were administered the Center for Epidemiological Studies Depression (CES-D) scale. Two years later 1,577 individuals were assessed for depressive symptoms. Death, dropping out, or incapacity accounted for 15% fewer subjects. Depressive symptoms persisted over two years for ninety-seven subjects; depressive symptoms remitted for 114 subjects. Differences in age and sleep disturbance were among the reasons for more than 30% variance between the two groups of depressed individuals. Advanced age was associated with persistent symptoms; improved health was associated with remission. Author biographical information. Abstract. 2 tables. 34 references.

1.135. Kennedy, Gary J., Howard R. Kelman, Cynthia Thomas, Wendy Wisniewski, Helen Metz and Polly E. Bijur. "Hierarchy of Characteristics Associated with Depressive Symptoms in an Urban Elderly Sample." **American Journal of Psychiatry** 146 (February 1989): 220-225.

A hierarchy of characteristics, associated with depressive symptoms, was found in an urban sample of 2,137 elderly persons. Illness, isolation, and poverty were some of the characteristics revealed by the Center for Epidemiological Studies Depression

(CES-D) scale. Author biographical information. Abstract. 2 tables. 25 references.

1.136. Kim, Kye Y., and Linda A. Hershey. "Diagnosis and Treatment of Depression in the Elderly." **International Journal of Psychiatry in Medicine** 18, No. 3 (1988): 211-221.

1.137. Kitchell, M., J. Okimoto, R. Barnes, R. Veith and M. Raskind. "Depression in the Geriatric Medical Inpatient." Abstract in **Gerontologist** 20, Special Issue (1980): 140.

In a study of patients age sixty and over, who were administered the Zung Self-Rating Depression Scale (SDS) and the Popoff Index of Depression (ID), sensitivity for the SDS was 65% and 92% for the ID. Specificity for the SDS was 87% and 43% for the ID. Forty-three percent of these individuals were depressed.

1.138. Kitchell, Margaret A., Robert F. Barnes, Richard C. Veith, Joseph T. Okimoto and Murray A. Raskind. "Screening for Depression in Hospitalized Geriatric Medical Patients." **Journal of the American Geriatrics Society** 30 (March 1982): 174-177.

1.139. Knauper, Barbel and Hans Ulrich Wittchen. "Diagnosing Major Depression in the Elderly: Evidence for Response Bias in Standardized Diagnostic Interviews?" **Journal of Psychiatric Research** 28 (March-April 1994): 147-164.

1.140. Koenig, H., P. Pappas, T. Holsinger and J. Bachar. "Assessing Strategies for Diagnosing Depression in Hospitalized Elderly Medical Patients: How Well Can Clinicians Determine the Etiology of Symptoms?" Abstract in **Gerontologist** 34, Special Issue 1 (October 1994): 237.

1.141. Koenig, Harold. "Depression and Dysphoria among the Elderly: Dispelling a Myth." **Journal of Family Practice** 23 (October 1986): 383-385.

1.142. Koenig, Harold G., Keith G. Meador, Harvey J. Cohen and Dan G. Blazer. "Detection and Treatment of Major Depression in Older Medically Ill Hospitalized Patients." **International Journal of Psychiatry in Medicine** 18, No. 1 (1988): 17-31.

1.143. Koenig, Harold G., Keith G. Meador, Harvey J. Cohen and Dan G. Blazer. "Screening for Depression in Hospitalized Elderly Medical Patients: Taking a Closer Look." **Journal of the American Geriatrics Society** 40 (October 1992): 1013-1017.

1.144. Koenig, Harold G., Keith G. Meador, Harvey J. Cohen and Dan G. Blazer. "Self-Rated Depression Scales and Screening for Major Depression in the Older Hospitalized Patient with Medical Illness." **Journal of the American Geriatrics**

Society 36 (August 1988): 699-706.

One hundred twenty-eight men, seventy years of age and over, who were patients at a Veterans Administration (VA) hospital, were the subjects. They underwent structured psychiatric interviews and were assessed with the Geriatric Depression Scale (GDS) and the Brief Carroll Depression Rating Scale (BCDRS). Eleven was the optimal cut-off score for the GDS, 6 for the BCDRS. The GDS had a sensitivity of 92% and a specificity of 89%. The BCDRS had a sensitivity of 100% and a specificity of 93%. Author biographical information. Abstract. 2 tables. 1 figure. Acknowledgment. 56 references.

1.145. Kongstvedt, Sheryl J. "Characteristic Symptoms of Elderly Depressives on Selected Measures of Depression." **Dissertation Abstracts International** 51: 5578B. Ph.D. University of Nebraska-Lincoln, 1990. UMI Order No. AAD91-08229. DIALOG, Dissertation Abstracts Online.

Younger adults, ranging in age from twenty to forty years, and geriatric individuals, sixty years and older, were studied. The Schedule for Affective Disorders and Schizophrenia (SADS); Beck Depression Inventory (BDI); Geriatric Depression Scale (GDS); and Symptom Checklist-90-R (SCL-90-R) were used to assess the subjects. The geriatric depressives endorsed fewer and milder depressive symptoms than the younger-adult depressives. Late-onset geriatric depression was distinguished from early-onset geriatric depression.

1.146. Krause, N.M. "Stress, Coping and Depressive Symptoms among the Elderly." Abstract in **Gerontologist** 25, Special Issue (October 1985): 66.

1.147. Krause, Neal. "Stress, Alcohol Use and Depressive Symptoms in Later Life." **Gerontologist** 35 (June 1995): 296-307.

1.148. Krause, Neal. "Stress and Sex Differences in Depressive Symptoms among Older Adults." **Journal of Gerontology** 41 (November 1986): 727-731.

1.149. Krishnan, K. Ranga. "Organic Bases of Depression in the Elderly." **Annual Review of Medicine** 42 (1991): 261-266.

1.150. Kronauer, Margaret. **Depression in the Elderly: A Selected Bibliography**. N.p., Free Press, 1981. DIALOG, Books in Print.

1.151. Kunsak, Nancy Elizabeth. "Factors of Depression in the Elderly: Assessment and Implications for Diagnosis." **Dissertation Abstracts International** 49: 1392B. Ph.D. dissertation. North Texas State University, 1987. UMI Order No. AAD88-04326. DIALOG, Dissertation Abstracts Online.

1.152. Kutcher, S.P. "Clinical Utility of Dexamethasone Suppression Testing in the

Elderly Depressive: A Case Report." **Canadian Journal of Psychiatry** 29 (October 1984): 505-507.

1.153. Kutner, N.G., K.B. Schechtman, M.G. Ory, D.I. Baker, R.B. Wallace and D.M. Buchner. "Self-Reported Depression and Poor Sleep: Gender Differences among Older Persons in the Community." Abstract in **Gerontologist** 33, Special, Issue 1 (October 1993): 308.

1.154. LaGory, Mark and Kevin Fitzpatrick. "The Effects of Environmental Context on Elderly Depression." **Journal of Aging and Health** 4 (November 1992): 459-479.

Seven hundred twenty-five persons, with a mean age of 69.1 years, and residing in Alabama, were studied regarding environmental context and depression. One finding: functionally impaired persons had a high level of distress. A second finding: limited social supports increased the likelihood of depressive symptoms. A third finding: depression was lower in functionally less healthy elders, who had greater environmental satisfaction. Author biographical information. Abstract. 2 tables. 6 notes. 38 references.

1.155. Lawlor, Brian A. "Barriers to the Diagnosis and Treatment of Depression in the Community Dwelling Elderly." **Irish Journal of Psychological Medicine** 12 (March 1995): 22-23.

1.156. Leary, M., A. Futterman, L.W. Thompson and D. Gallagher-Thompson. "Five Definitions of Endogenous Depression and Psychopathology in Older Adults." Abstract in **Gerontologist** 31, Special Issue 2 (October 1991): 61.

1.157. Lee, Alison J. "The Effects of Unipolar Major Depression and Age on Two Malingering Tests: Rey Memory Test and Rey Dot Counting Test." **Dissertation Abstracts International** 56: 2333B. Ph.D. California School of Professional Psychology, Los Angeles, 1994. UMI Order No. AADAA-I9526783. DIALOG, Dissertation Abstracts Online.

Sixty-five outpatients with unipolar major depression (thirty-five females, thirty males), and fifty-three normal control subjects (thirty-four females, nineteen males), forty-six to eighty-five years of age, were assessed with the Rey Memory Test (RMT) and the Rey Dot Counting Test (RDC). The Hamilton Depression Rating Scale was administered to the depressed subjects. Depression in middle-aged and older adults was associated with lowered performance on the RMT, these patients obtaining lower recall scores than younger patients. The RDC may be less sensitive than the RMT to the effects of depression.

1.158. Lee, D.M. "Mediators of the Stressor-Depression Relationship." Abstract in **Gerontologist** 23, Special Issue (October 1983): 94.

1.159. Lee, Heidi and Brian A. Lawlor. "State-Dependent Nature of the Clock Drawing Task in Geriatric Depression." **Journal of the American Geriatrics Society** 43 (July 1995): 796-798.

1.160. Lichtenberg, Peter A., T. Ann Gibbons, Michael Nanna and Frank Blumenthal. "Physician Detection of Depression in Medically Ill Elderly." **Clinical Gerontologist** 13, No. 1 (1993): 81-90.

The subjects were 150 elderly patients in a geriatric rehabilitation unit and a stroke rehabilitation unit, components of a medical center in a midwestern city. These patients were studied between approximately January and October 1991. Each patient was administered the Geriatric Depression Scale. This scale, used to assess affective functioning, consists of self-referent statements. Findings regarding depression: (1) age was highly related to it; (2) it was more prevalent in patients between sixty and seventy-four years of age than in patients seventy-five years of age and older; (3) rates did not vary significantly for men and women; and (4) physicians were more apt to detect it in women than in men. Author biographical information. Abstract. 4 tables. 19 references.

1.161. Lindstrom, Andrea. "Personal Control, Depressive Symptoms and Causal Attributions in the Elderly." Abstract in **Gerontologist** 20, Special Issue (1980): 149.

1.162. Linn, Margaret W., Kathleen Hunter and Rachel Harris. "Symptoms of Depression and Recent Life Events in the Community Elderly." **Journal of Clinical Psychology** 36 (July 1980): 675-682.

The death of a friend or relative, personal serious illness, illness of a relative or friend, and arguments with family or close friends were associated with depression in 188 individuals sixty-five years of age or older, residing independently in Miami, Florida. Author biographical information. Abstract. 2 tables. 34 references.

1.163. Liu, O., and D.R. Hoyt. "Depressive Symptoms among Three Groups of Elderly." Abstract in **Gerontologist** 35, Special Issue 1 (October 1995): 376.

1.164. Liu, Qiaoming. "Patterns and Predictors of Depressive Symptoms among the Elderly." **Dissertation Abstracts International** 56: 1930A. Ph.D. Iowa State University, 1995. UMI Order No. AADAA-I9531763. DIALOG, Dissertation Abstracts Online.

Approximately 1,000 elderly persons were interviewed by telephone. Data pertaining to these persons was categorized according to three age groups: (1) the preretired old (age fifty-five to sixty-four), (2) the young old (age sixty-five to seventy-four), and (3) the very old (age seventy-five or older). Examples of findings: (1) the very old had significantly higher levels of depressive symptoms than the preretired old, (2) health perception is significantly related to depressive symptoms for each of the groups, (3) the very old are, compared to the other two groups, more likely to report poorer health, and (4) having fewer psychological resources plays an important role in depressive symptoms of the very old.

1.165. Lubin, Bernard and Christine M. Rinck. "Assessment of Mood and Affect in the Elderly: The Depression Adjective Check List and the Multiple Affect Adjective Check List." **Clinical Gerontologist** 5 (June 1986): 187-191.

1.166. Magni, Guido, Fabrizio Schifano and Diego de Leo. "Assessment of Depression in an Elderly Medical Population." **Journal of Affective Disorders** 11 (September-October 1986): 121-124.

1.167. Maiden, Robert Joseph. "The Attribution of Learned Helplessness and Depression in the Elderly." **Dissertation Abstracts International** 42: 1181B. Ph.D. New School for Social Research, 1980. UMI Order No. AAD81-16926. DIALOG, Dissertation Abstracts Online.

1.168. Marin, R., R. Biedrzycki and S. Firinciogullari. "Apathy and Depression in Neuropsychiatry." Abstract in **Gerontologist** 31, Special Issue 2 (October 1991): 250.

A study of 123 patients, mean age seventy-two years, revealed that apathy and depression may produce loss of motivation. Apathy, however, is not associated with the vegetative symptoms of depression.

1.169. Markson, E.W., M. Kelly-Hayes, R. D'Agostino and A. Belanger. "Depressive Symptoms and Health among Elderly Women in the Framingham Cohort." Abstract in **Gerontologist** 34, Special Issue 1 (October 1994): 304.

Depressed Framingham Cohort females, between sixty-three and ninety-four years of age, were studied for four years. Age was not related to depressive symptoms. Furthermore, depressive symptoms did not predict excessive risk of mortality.

1.170. Markson, E.W., S.V. Wilking, M. Kelly-Hayes, A. Belanger and B. Carpenter. "Depression among the Framingham Cohort." Abstract in **Gerontologist** 31, Special Issue 2 (October 1991): 325-326.

1.171. Mastrogeorge, Barbara Lee. "The Effects of Locus-of-Control and Chronic Illness Status on Geriatric Depression Scale Scores in Communities of Elderly Women." **Dissertation Abstracts International** 51: 4240A. Ph.D. Fielding Institute, 1990. UMI Order No. AAD91-11530. DIALOG, Dissertation Abstracts Online.

Somatic symptoms rather than chronic illness predicted depressive symptoms in elderly women with a mean age of 74.4 years. Seventy-three percent of these women were widows and reported a mean of 2.4 chronic illnesses. The Geriatric Depression Scale (GDS) revealed that 5% of these women scored in the severe depressive range.

1.172. McCullough, Philip K. "Geriatric Depression: Atypical Presentations, Hidden Meanings." **Geriatrics** 46 (October 1991): 72-76.

The depressed elderly, unlike depressed younger adults, are likely to have cognitive deterioration obscuring their depression. Cognitive decline in the elderly may simulate dementia. However, depressed patients, relative to the genuinely demented, are generally better oriented. Pain due to degenerative conditions, such as arthritis, is very common in the depressed elderly. Narcotic analgesics can often compound the depression. Fatigue and gastrointestinal complaints are found in many elderly patients, who deny being depressed. Ataxia and macrocytosis may suggest alcohol abuse in these individuals. Author biographical information. Abstract. 4 tables. 21 references.

1.173. McElroy, M., D. Carmelli, G. Swan and A. LaRue. "Perceived Health and Onset of Depressive Symptoms in Aging Men." Abstract in **Gerontologist** 35, Special Issue 1 (October 1995): 225.

Scores from the Center for Epidemiological Studies Depression (CES-D) scale were used to assess older men for the time periods 1986-1988 (time 1) and 1992-1994 (time 2). Mean CES-D scores increased from 4.6 to 6.6 from time 1 to time 2. The level of depressive symptoms increased in 3.8% of the sample to a degree that might warrant clinical attention. Men who exercised were the least likely to have increased symptoms.

1.174. Meeks, S., M.L. Francis, E.S. Jackson and L.L. Gibson. "Prevalence and Treatment of Affective Symptoms among Older Severely Mentally Ill (SMI) Persons in the Community." Abstract in **Gerontologist** 32, Special Issue 2 (October 1992): 144.

Affective symptoms were quite prevalent in 102 community-residing, severely mentally ill (SMI) adults, in the second half of life, even in those SMI without affective diagnoses. Neither antidepressants nor lithium were administered to up to one-third of individuals with depressive or manic symptoms.

1.175. Mendes de Leon, Carlos F., Stephen S. Rapp and Stanislav V. Kasl. "Financial Strain and Symptoms of Depression in a Community Sample of Elderly Men and Women: A Longitudinal Study." **Journal of Aging and Health** 6 (November 1994): 448-468.

1.176. Meyers, B.S., S. Alpert and B. Kalayam. "State Specificity of DST Abnormalities in

Geriatric Depression." Abstract in **Gerontologist** 30, Special Issue (October 1990): 221A.

1.177. Meyers, Barnett S., and Robert Greenberg. "Late-Life Delusional Depression." **Journal of Affective Disorders** 11 (September-October 1986): 133-137.

1.178. Meyers, Barnett S., Balu Kalayam and Varda Mei-Tal. "Late-Onset Delusional Depression: A Distinct Clinical Entity?" **Journal of Clinical Psychiatry** 45 (August 1984): 347-349.

1.179. Milanesi, L., and B. Colby. "Assessing Depression among Older Women: A Cross-cultural Validation of the CES-D Instrument." Abstract in **Gerontologist** 31, Special Issue 2 (October 1991): 60-61.

The CES-D was used to assess 212 Japanese-American and Anglo-American women, who were over the age of sixty. This instrument demonstrated good internal consistency across both groups of women. There were no ethnic differences noted among the higher CES-D scores.

1.180. Mitchell, J. and H. Mathews. "A Theoretical Assessment of the Multidimensional Characteristics of the Geriatric Depression Scale among the Rural Elderly." Abstract in **Gerontologist** 31, Special Issue 2 (October 1991): 120-121.

1.181. Mitchell, Jim, Holly F. Mathews and Jerome A. Yesavage. "A Multidimensional Examination of Depression among the Elderly." **Research on Aging** 15 (June 1993): 198-219.

1.182. Molloy, D.W., K. LeClair and E.A. Braun. "Depression." Chapter in **Common Sense Geriatrics**, edited by D.W. Molloy, 132-147. Boston, MA: Blackwell Scientific Publications, 1991.

1.183. Monopoli, John Anthony. "Relationship of Depression and Hypochondriasis to 16PF Scores in the Elderly." **Dissertation Abstracts International** 51: 2629B. Ph.D. Hofstra University, 1990. UMI Order No. AAD90-24933. DIALOG, Dissertation Abstracts Online.

1.184. Morrill, B., R. Scott and W. Simmons. "Depression, Hopelessness and Dietary Intake in an Elderly Population." Abstract in **Gerontologist** 33, Special Issue 1 (October 1993): 288.

1.185. Mossey, J.M. "Subsyndromal Depression in the Hospitalized Elderly: A Typical Reaction to Being Sick and Hospitalized or a Manifestation of a Pre-existing Condition." Abstract in **Gerontologist** 34, Special Issue 1 (October 1994): 237-238.

Subsyndromal depression in hospital represents, in most cases, the continuation of a pre-existing condition not an expected reaction to being sick and hospitalized.

1.186. Motoike, P., J. Steuer, R. Gerner, R. Rosen and L. Jarvik. "Depression and Bodily Concerns in the Elderly." Abstract in **Gerontologist** 20, Special Issue (1980): 168.

Depressed elderly community residents, ranging in age from fifty-five to seventy-nine years, rated themselves regarding body worries and body discomforts. The severity of depression did not correlate significantly with body worries or body discomforts.

1,187. Muffled Pleas for Help: Diagnosing and Treating Depression in the Elderly. 23 minutes. 1994. Distributed/Produced by Back East Productions, Allentown, PA. Videocassette.

1.188. Mullen, J.A., T.L. Orbuch and D.L. Featherman. "Change and Stability in the CES-D Depression Score over Time in an Elderly Sample." Abstract in **Gerontologist** 28, Special Issue (October 1988): 156A.

1.189. Murphy, Elaine. Editor. **Affective Disorders in the Elderly**. Edinburgh, Scotland: Churchill Livingstone, 1986. DIALOG, LCMARC-Books.

1.190. Murphy, Elaine. "Social Origins of Depression in Old Age." **British Journal of Psychiatry** 141 (August 1982): 135-142.

1.191. Murphy, Jane M. "The Epidemiologic Face of Late-Life Depression." **Journal of Geriatric Psychiatry** 22, No. 1 (1989): 67-75.

The Stirling County Study, Epidemiological Catchment Area (ECA) Program, and Midtown Manhattan Study discuss epidemiological factors concerning late-life depression. Author biographical information. 1 table.

1.192. Murrell, Stanley A., Samuel Himmelfarb and Katherine Wright. "Prevalence of Depression and Its Correlates in Older Adults." **American Journal of Epidemiology** 117 (February 1983): 173-185.

Nine hundred sixty-two males and 1,555 females, fifty-five years of age and older, residing in Kentucky in 1981, were the subjects. The Center for Epidemiological Studies Depression Scale revealed that 13.7% of the males and 18.2% of the females were depressed. Self-reported physical health had the strongest relationship with depression. Over half the subjects took prescribed medication. Only 3.9% of the males required help for mental health problems. The figure for females was 3.2%. Author biographical information. Abstract. 6 tables. 36 references.

1.193. Murrell, Stanley A. and Suzanne Meeks. "Depressive Symptoms in Older Adults: Predispositions, Resources and Life Experiences." **Annual Review of Gerontology and Geriatrics** 11 (1991): 261-286.

At any given time, at least 10% of older adults experience depressive symptoms. More enduring life-event stress has an increased impact on depressive symptoms in older adults. Poor health and weak social support are examples of characteristics which place older adults at increased risk for depressive symptoms. 1 figure. 117 references.

1.194. Musetti, Laura, Guilio Perugi, Adalgisa Soriani, Vedia M. Rossi, Giovanni B. Cassano and Hagop S. Akiskal. "Depression Before and After Age 65: A Re-examination." **British Journal of Psychiatry** 155 (September 1989): 330-336.

1.195. Musil, C.M., M.R. Haug, C.D. Beckette, D.L. Morris, M.L. Wykle and M. Clapp. "Patterns of Depressive Symptomatology in Older Adults over the Course of 18 months." Abstract in **Gerontologist** 35, Special Issue 1 (October 1995): 375.

1.196. Nadzam, Deborah Morris. "Depression and Demoralization of the Aged." **Dissertation Abstracts International** 47: 2834B. Ph.D. Case Western Reserve University, 1986. UMI Order No. AAD86-22843. DIALOG, Dissertation Abstracts Online.

The Geriatric Depression Scale (GDS) and the Demoralization Scale (DS) were used to investigate 160 individuals over sixty-five years of age. These individuals were classified as: (1) demoralized only, (2) clinically depressed only, (3) clinically depressed and demoralized, and (4) neither clinically depressed nor demoralized, None of the individuals were clinically depressed only. Fifty-seven were demoralized only. Forty-six were clinically depressed and demoralized. Fifty-seven were neither clinically depressed nor demoralized. Four discriminant analyses correctly classified subjects over 88% of the time. Demoralized only subjects were more likely to live alone. Subjects who were neither depressed nor demoralized had less education and were more likely to live with their children.

1.197. Nelson, J. Craig, Yeates Conwell, Kathy Kim and Carolyn Mazure. "Age at Onset in Late-Life Delusional Depression." **American Journal of Psychiatry** 146 (June 1989): 785-786.

Patients with unipolar major depression were studied. These patients were over sixty years of age. Thirty-nine were delusional; seventy were nondelusional. There was no significant difference in onset age in either of the two types of patients. Abstract. Author biographical information. 10 references.

1.198. Newman, Margaret A. and Judith K. Gaudiano. "Depression as an Explanation for Decreased Subjective Time in the Elderly." **Nursing Research** 33

(May-June 1984): 137-139.

Volunteers from a meal program were the subjects. These subjects were sixty-eight women with a mean age of 70.44 years. The Beck Depression Inventory, a personal data questionnaire, and a test concerning subjective time were administered at the meal center. Each subject was required to estimate an interval lasting forty seconds. Depression was related to decreased subjective time. The greater the level of depression, the greater the underestimation of the length of a short interval. Author biographical information. Abstract. 1 table. 12 references.

1.199. Newmann, Joy P., Marjorie H. Klein, Julie E. Jensen and Marilyn J. Essex. "Depressive Symptom Experiences among Older Women: A Comparison of Alternative Measurement Approaches." Abstract in **Gerontologist** 35, Special Issue, 1 (October 1995): 75.

1.200. Newmann, Joy Perkins, Rafael J. Engel and Julie E. Jensen. "Age Differences in Depressive Symptom Experiences." **Journals of Gerontology** 46 (September 1991): P224-P235.

A total of 368 women between fifty-one and ninety-two years of age were studied, regarding age differences and depressive symptoms. These women were divided into two groups: (1) a younger age cohort, fifty-one to sixty-five years, and (2) an older age cohort, sixty-six to ninety-two years. There were among the older age cohort higher levels of, for example, loneliness and sleep disturbance. Author biographical information. Abstract. 5 tables. 3 figures. Acknowledgments. 41 references. Appendix.

1.201. Norris, Jack T., Dolores Gallagher, Anne Wilson and Carol Hunter Winograd. "Assessment of Depression in Geriatric Medical Outpatients: The Validity of Two Screening Measures." **Journal of the American Geriatrics Society** 35 (November 1987): 989-995.

Sixty-five men and three women, with a mean age of seventy-eight years, were assessed with the Beck Depression Inventory (BDI) and the Geriatric Depression Scale (GDS). These subjects were veterans from a Veterans Administration medical center. Both the BDI and GDS were shown to have reasonable agreement with RDC (Research Diagnostic Criteria) and DSM-III diagnoses in elderly medical patients. Up to 87% sensitivity rating for the BDI, and up to 84% sensitivity rating for the GDS, was obtained when 10, the lower cut-off score, was used for each of these two screening scales. There were few false negatives for either scale, when 17 was used as the cut-off score for the BDI and 14 for the GDS. Author biographical information. Abstract. 2 tables. 22 references.

1.202. Okimoto, Joseph T., Robert F. Barnes, Richard C. Veith, Murray A. Raskind, Thomas S. Inui and William B. Carter. "Screening for Depression in Geriatric Medical

Patients." **American Journal of Psychiatry** 139 (June 1982): 799-802.

When the Zung Self-Rating Depression Scale and the Popoff Index of Depression were used to assess fifty-five elderly patients, the Zung correctly classified 80% of the subjects and the Popoff correctly classified 69% of the subjects. Author biographical information. Abstract. 2 tables. 11 references. 1 appendix.

1.203. Oltman, Andrew M., Timothy J. Michaels and Robert A. Steer. "Structure of Depression in Older Men and Women." **Journal of Clinical Psychology** 36 (July 1980): 672-674.

1.204. O'Riordan, Thomas G., James P. Hayes, Rory Shelley, Desmond O'Neill, J. Bernard Walsh and Davis Coakley. "The Prevalence of Depression in an Acute Geriatric Medical Assessment Unit." **International Journal of Geriatric Psychiatry** 4 (January-February 1989): 17-21.

The subjects in this research were thirty-seven men and seventy-four women. The mean age of the subjects was eighty years. The subjects were administered - three to seven days after admission to hospital - the Geriatric Depression Scale (GDS). Depression was clinically significant in 23.4% of the patients screened. Specific antidepressant medication was required by 13.5% of the patients. Author biographical information. Abstract. 3 tables. 18 references.

1.205. Oxman, Thomas E., James E. Barrett, Jane Barrett and Paul Gerber. "Symptomatology of Late-Life Minor Depression among Primary Care Patients." **Psychosomatics** 31 (Spring 1990): 174-180.

1.206. Palinkas, Lawrence A., Deborah L. Wingard and Elizabeth Barrett-Connor. "Chronic Illness and Depressive Symptoms in the Elderly: A Population-Based Study." **Journal of Clinical Epidemiology** 43, No. 11 (1990): 1131-1141.

In a study of 1,617 men and women, sixty-five years of age and older, residing in California, depressed mood was prevalent in 5.2% of these individuals. Women had a prevalence rate nearly twice that of men. Age, amount of exercise, and number of medications were a few of the risk factors associated with depressive symptoms. Author biographical information. Abstract. 7 tables. Acknowledgment. 80 references.

1.207. Paris, A., C. Hankin and A. Spiro, III. "Depressive Symptoms Predict Medical Utilization: The VA Normative Aging Study." Abstract in **Gerontologist** 36, Special Issue 1 (October 1996): 252.

1.208. Peper, Martin Carl. Editor. **Depression in the Elderly: The Growing Challenge**, Proceedings of a Symposium, CIBA Pharmaceutical Company, Rancho Mirage, California, February 16-18, 1984, Summit, NJ: Ciba Pharmaceutical Company,

1984. DIALOG, LCMARC-Books.

1.209. Phifer, James F. and Stanley A. Murrell. "Etiologic Factors in the Onset of Depressive Symptoms in Older Adults." **Journal of Abnormal Psychology** 95 (August 1986): 282-291.

1.210. Powers, Sandra M. and Mark D. Corgiat. "Relationship between Depression and Somatic Complaints among the Elderly." Abstract in **Gerontologist** 28, Special Issue (October 1988): 267A.

After ninety-five elderly subjects were assessed with the Zung Self-Rating Depression Scale, and multiple regression analysis was performed, it was determined that somatic complaints did not contribute much to the symptoms endorsed by individuals who scored within the depressed range.

1.211. Pratt, Clara C., Willetta Wilson, Alida Benthin and Vicki Schmall. "Alcohol Problems and Depression in Later Life: Development of Two Knowledge Quizzes." **Gerontologist** 32 (April 1992): 175-183.

There are relatively few instruments with which to assess knowledge of later life mental health issues. One is The Facts on Aging and Mental Health Quiz developed by Erdman B. Palmore. This quiz consists of twenty-five true/false items. Another instrument is The Alzheimer's Disease Knowledge Test, consisting of twenty multiple-choice items. A third is the Penn State Mental Health Questionnaire. Two new assessment tools are the Quiz on Alcohol Problems in Later Life and Quiz on Depression in Later Life. These latter two quizzes consist of true/false items. Abstract. Author biographical information. 2 tables. 39 references. 2 appendices.

1.212. Qualls, S.H. and S. Heroux. "Depression in Very Old Community Residents: Correlates and Predictors." Abstract in **Gerontologist** 27, Special Issue (October 1987): 188A.

Fifty-five very old community residents were interviewed in their homes. CES-D scores indicated sixteen of these individuals were depressed. Depression correlated significantly with, for example, social network variables and frequency of loneliness. Health variables, however, were not significantly correlated with depression.

1.213. Rabins, P.V. and G.D. Pearlson. "CT Changes in Late-Life Depression." Abstract in **Gerontologist** 25, Special Issue (October 1985): 190.

Head CT scan attenuation numbers were studied in twenty elderly persons with major depression, ten persons with senile dementia (Alzheimer type), and seventeen normal persons matched for age and sex. Depressed persons had significantly lower CT attenuation numbers than normals. Elderly persons with major depression had structural brain abnormalities.

1.214. Rabins, P.V., G.D. Pearlson and E. Aylward. "Cortical MRI Abnormalities in Elderly Depressives." Abstract in **Gerontologist** 30, Special Issue October 1990): 221A.

There were two groups of subjects in this study: (1) twenty-one elderly subjects with major depression and (2) fifteen age-matched normals. MRI scans were done for each subject. Depressives had more cortical atrophy and a greater extent of subcortical lesions. There were no differences between subjects who were delusional and subjects who were not delusional, and no differences between subjects who received ECT and subjects who did not receive this treatment.

1.215. Rajkumar, S., N. Rangarajan, R. Padmavathi and R. Sathianathan. "Diagnosis and Management of Depression in the Elderly." **Indian Journal of Psychological Medicine** 11 (July 1988): 201-213.

1.216. Ranieri, P., G. Bellelli, M. Traversi, B. Bertozzi, R. Rozzini and M. Trabucchi. "Low Seruum Cholesterol and Depression In Elderly Patients." Abstract in **Gerontologist** 36, Special Issue 1 (October 1996): 277.

Four hundred seventy-six elderly patients with a mean age of 78.8 years were studied, regarding low serum cholesterol and depression. Cognitive status, depressive symptoms, functional disability, nutritional status, and somatic health were investigated. Stratification of these patients in three groups of decreasing serum cholesterol concentrations, and depression scores, revealed the risk for depression was greatest in the lowest serum cholesterol group.

1.217. Rapp, Stephen R. and Kenneth M. Davis. "Geriatric Depression: Physicians' Knowledge, Perceptions and Diagnostic Practices." **Gerontologist** 29 (April 1989): 252-257.

Medical residents can through graduate training increase substantially their knowledge, concerning detection and treatment of geriatric depression. An education program consisting of four seminars can help reach this goal. The first seminar deals with the identification of geriatric depression. The second seminar is a review of etiological factors. The third seminar focuses on treatment. The fourth seminar pertains to detection and referral. Didactic presentations, open discussion, handouts, and selected journal articles are part of the seminar sessions. Author biographical information. Abstract. 3 tables. 34 references.

1.218. Rapp, Stephen R., Sharon A. Parisi, David A. Walsh and Clinton E. Wallace. "Detecting Depression in Elderly Medical Inpatients." **Journal of Consulting and Clinical Psychology** 56 (August 1988): 509-513.

One hundred fifty men, with a mean age of 69.3 years, who were admitted to a Veterans Administration hospital, were studied, regarding the detection of depression. Seven measures used were: (1) Schedule for Affective Disorders and Schizophrenia (SADS), (2) Beck Depression Inventory (BDI), (3) Self-Report Depression Scale (SDS), (4) Geriatric Depression Scale (GDS), (5) Brief Symptom Inventory (BSI), (6) Global Assessment Scale (GAS), and (7) Mini-Mental State Exam (MMSE). Instruments such as the BDI and GDS were especially sensitive to detecting major depression. Furthermore, these instruments had better predictive power than procedures used by hospital staff. Author biographical information. Abstract. 2 tables. 21 references.

1.219. Rapp, Stephen R. and Scott Vrana. "Substituting Nonsomatic for Somatic Symptoms in the Diagnosis of Depression in Elderly Male Medical Patients." **American Journal of Psychiatry** 146 (September 1989): 1197-1200.

Research Diagnostic Criteria (RDC) for depression were modified, concerning the 1984 research by J. Endicott, who assessed depression in cancer patients. Endicott suggested substituting alternative nonsomatic symptoms for RDC somatic symptoms. One hundred fifty male medical inpatients, at least sixty-five years of age, were studied, and the modified RDC examined for sensitivity and specificity. The specificity of the modified criteria was 97%. Ninety-six percent of the patients were correctly classified. This research supports Endicott's suggestions. Author biographical information. Abstract. 2 tables. 13 references.

1.220. Ravindran, Arun V., K. Welburn and J.R.M. Copeland. "Semistructured Depression Scale Sensitive to Change with Treatment for Use in the Elderly." **British Journal of Psychiatry** 164 (April 1994): 522-527.

1.221. Raymond, P., M. Fretwell and S. McGarvey. "The Factor Structure of the Zung Depression Scale among Hospitalized Medically Ill Elderly." Abstract in **Gerontologist** 28, Special Issue (October 1988): 267A.

1.222. Raymond, P., M. Fretwell, S. McGarvey, M. Traines, N. Owens and R. Silliman. "Patterns of Change in Depressive Symptoms After Acute Hospitalization: The Senior Care Study." Abstract in **Gerontologist** 29, Special Issue (October 1989): 35A

Depression was not a transient state in 161 elderly patients, who received acute hospital care. These patients were assessed for depression at admission and at six weeks. Discharged patients should be targeted for follow-up assessment because improvements during hospitalization may not last long.

1.223. Reed, Pamela G. "Developmental Resources and Depression in the Elderly." **Nursing Research** 35 (November-December 1986): 368-374.

Twenty-eight clinically depressed individuals were matched on age, sex, and years of education with twenty-eight mentally healthy older adults. The Developmental Resources of Later Adulthood (DRLA) scale and the Center for Epidemiological Studies Depression (CES-D) scale were administered on three occasions to these subjects. The depressed individuals had, on all three occasions, significantly lower developmental scores. There was a causal tendency in the mentally healthy individuals to influence level of depression with developmental resources. Abstract. Author biographical information. 2 tables. 2 figures. 35 references.

1.224. Reynolds, Charles F., III. "Depression in the Elderly." **Geriatrics** 50, Supplement 1 (October 1995): S4-S5.

Depression is found in elderly patients at primary care clinics, in community residents over age sixty-five, and in elderly residents of long-term care facilities. Declining health, increasing disability, isolation, and spousal loss are at-risk factors for depression in this age group. Depression is also a risk factor for mortality. Unrecognized or undertreated depression can lead to suicide. Author biographical information. 1 table. 12 references.

1.225. Reynolds, Charles F., III. "Recognition and Differentiation of Elderly Depression in the Clinical Setting." **Geriatrics** 50, Supplement 1 (October 1995): S6-S15.

1.226. Reynolds, Charles F., III, Gary W. Small, Elliott M. Stein and Linda Teri. "When Depression Strikes the Elderly Patient." **Patient Care** 28 (February 28, 1994): 85-92, 95-98 and 101-102.

1.227. Ries, Richard K., Patricia N. Prinz, Dianne E. Williams and Michael V. Vitiello. "Sleep Deficits in Geriatric Onset Depression Are Minimal." Abstract in **Gerontologist** 28, Special Issue (October 1988): 73A.

Forty-three geriatric depressed patients were compared with eighty-five nondepressed controls matched for age and health. Sleep was monitored for three consecutive nights. Multiple measures of sleep were conducted. The depressed patients did not differ significantly on any measure from the controls.

1.228. Rogers, Kelly Forbes. "A Signal Detection Analysis of Beck's Cognitive Model of Depression in the Elderly." **Dissertation Abstracts International** 51: 5589B. Ph.D. Auburn University, 1989. UMI Order No. AAD91-09123. DIALOG, Dissertation Abstracts Online.

1.229. Rohrbaugh, Robert M., Alan P. Siegal and Earl L. Giller. "Irritability as a Symptom of Depression in the Elderly." **Journal of the American Geriatrics Society** 36 (August 1988): 736-738.

1.230. Rosin, L., J. Marmion, L. Root and R. Chacko. "Assessment of Depression across Settings and Diagnostic Groups." Abstract in **Gerontologist** 28, Special Issue (October 1988): 283A.

Two hundred elderly subjects were from three settings: (1) a geropsychiatric outpatient clinic, (2) an inpatient geropsychiatric unit, and (3) a senior citizens center. All subjects were assessed with the GDS and MMSE. The inpatient subjects had the highest GDS mean score. There were no significant differences among MMSE scores.

1.231. Rozzini, Renzo, Bruno Bertozzi, Piera Barbisoni and Marco Trabucchi. "Risk of Depression Is Higher in Elderly Patients with Lowest Serum Cholesterol Values." **British Medical Journal** 312 (May 18, 1996): 1298-1299.

The subjects were 476 men and women with a mean age of 78.8 years. These subjects, 70% of whom were women, were admitted over twelve months to a geriatric unit of a hospital in Italy. When these subjects were divided into three groups, in order of decreasing serum cholesterol concentrations, the risk of depression was greater in the group with the lowest serum cholesterol concentration. Author biographical information. 1 table. 3 references.

1.232. Rozzini, Renzo, Angelo Bianchetti, Corrado Carabellese, Mariarosa Inzoli and Marco Trabucchi. "Depression, Life Events and Somatic Symptoms." **Gerontologist** 28 (April 1988): 229-232.

Elderly men and women - 386 men, 815 women - living at home in Brescia, Italy were the subjects studied. These subjects were interviewed at home by general practitioners. The assessment instruments used were: (1) Self-Evaluation of Life Function scale; (2) Instrumental Activity of Daily Living scale; (3) Beck Depression Inventory; and (4) Anxiety Scale and Personal Well-Being Scale. The researchers learned that depression was the most important factor associated with the appearance of somatic complaints. Author biographical information. Abstract. 2 tables. 33 references.

1.233. Ruegg, Robert G., Sidney Zisook and Neal R. Swerdlow. "Depression in the Aged: An Overview." **Psychiatric Clinics of North America** 11 (March 1988): 83-99.

1.234. Sadavoy, J., Isaac Smith, David K. Conn and Brian Richards. "Depression in Geriatric Patients with Chronic Medical Illness." **International Journal of Geriatric Psychiatry** 5 (May-June 1990): 187-192.

Geriatric patients at the Baycrest Hospital in Toronto, Ontario, were administered the Folstein Mini-Mental State (MMS) Exam and the Montgomery-Asberg Depression Rating Scale (MADRS). Thirty-five percent of the patients who completed the MADRS had scores in the depressed range. Of the patients who completed the MMS, 15% had mild cognitive impairment, 10% demonstrated moderate impairment, and 47% had severe impairment. Author biographical information. Abstract. 4 tables. 19 references.

1.235. Sagar, R.S., D. Mohan, Vinod Kumar and S.K. Khandelwal. "Elderly Depressives: Use of Medicines with a Potential to Cause Depression." **Indian Journal of Psychiatry** 32 (January 1990): 64-68.

1.236. Salive, Marcel E. and Dan G. Blazer. "Depression and Smoking Cessation in Older Adults: A Longitudinal Study." **Journal of the American Geriatrics Society** 41 (December 1993): 1313-1316.

The National Institute on Aging funded this cohort study, whose setting was five counties in North Carolina. The study participants were men and women sixty-five years of age and older, with an oversampling of African-Americans. Current smokers, former smokers, and never smokers were the three participant classifications at baseline. A modified Center for Epidemiological Studies Depression (CES-D) scale was used to measure depressive symptoms. Examples of results: (1) the highest prevalence of clinically significant CES-D scores (11.2%) was among the current smokers and (2) 25% (128 of 511) of baseline current smokers had quit, after three years. Depressed smokers are not necessarily less likely to quit smoking than nondepressed smokers. Author biographical information. Abstract. 3 tables. Acknowledgments. 23 references.

1.237. Salzman, Carl and Richard I. Shader. "Depression in the Elderly: II. Possible Drug Etiologies: Differential Diagnostic Criteria." **Journal of the American Geriatrics Society** 26 (July 1978): 303-308.

1.238. Schein, Rebecca L., Patricia A. Arean and Michael G. Perri. "Congruence between the BDI Cognitive-Affective Subscale and Research Diagnostic Criteria in Older Adults." Abstract in **Gerontologist** 33, Special Issue 1 (October 1993): 289.

1.239. Schein, Rebecca L. and Harold G. Koenig. "CES-D Assessment of Geriatric Depression in Medically-Ill Inpatients." Abstract in **Gerontologist** 34, Special Issue 1 (October 1994): 237.

1.240. Schneider, L.S., M. Zemansky, V. Pollock, E.P. Ros and R.B. Sloane. "Personality Dysfunction in Recovered Depressed Elderly Subjects." Abstract in **Gerontologist** 27, Special Issue (October 1987): 181A.

A past history of major unipolar depression was identified with a structured clinical interview in thirteen elderly subjects. There were also in this study nineteen controls without a family psychiatric history. The personality and interpersonal relations of both groups of subjects were assessed. There were no differences in age, sex, or marital status in either group. There were in the subjects, who had a past history of major unipolar depression, nearly twice the number of dysfunctional personality traits as in the control group.

1.241. Schuler, P., T. Pujol, R. Westerfield and J. Mego. "Relationship between Depression and Lipid Levels in a Normo-cholesterimic Elderly Sample." Journal Poster Paper presented at the **75th Annual Meeting of the Federation of American Societies for Experimental Biology, Atlanta, Georgia, April 21-25, 1991.** DIALOG, Conference Papers Index.

1.242. Schwalm, Virginia Clare. "The Relationship of Gender and Marital Status to Depression and Personality and Demographic Variables among the Well Elderly." **Dissertation Abstracts International** 53: 2576B. Ph.D. University of North Dakota, 1991. UMI Order No. AAD92-20366. DIALOG, Dissertation Abstracts Online.

Two hundred fourteen females and 103 males, ranging in age from fifty-five to over eighty years, were assessed with the following: (1) Center for Epidemiological Studies-Depression scale, (2) UCLA Loneliness Scale, (3) Rosenberg Self-Esteem Scale, (4) Schedule of Recent Events, and (5) Multidimensional Scale of Perceived Social Support. Depression scale scores did not reveal a significant difference between men and women. Men were significantly lonelier than women.

1.243. Scogin, F., L. Butler, D. Hamblin and A. Corbishley. "Reliability of the Short Form Beck Depression Inventory with Older Adults." Abstract in **Gerontologist** 27, Special Issue (October 1987): 191A.

1.244. Sen, P., E. Arnold, B.M. Kaveman and D. McCrea. "Pilot Study to Evaluate a Simple Screening Test for Depression in Elderly." Paper No. NR136 presented at the **1996 Annual Meeting of the American Psychiatric Association, New York, New York, May 4-9, 1996.** DIALOG, Conference Papers Index.

1.245. Shamoian, Charles A. "Assessing Depression in Elderly Patients." **Hospital and Community Psychiatry** 36 (April 1985): 338-339 and 345.

Certain laboratory tests should be included in the assessment of depression in the elderly. A complete blood count, urinalysis, chest X-ray, fasting blood sugar, and a CAT scan are a few of these tests. Depression and dementia scales should also be administered. An elderly individual who has recently lost a spouse and who lives alone is at high risk for suicide. Passive suicide - not complying with treatment - can be as effective as active suicide. Approximately 80% of depressed elderly individuals can be successfully treated. Author biographical information. 9 references.

1.246. Skoglund, Pennelope A. "An Assessment of Life Satisfaction and Depression in Community Elderly and Their Relationship to Other Demographic and Social Variables." **Dissertation Abstracts International** 47: 2030A. Ph.D. University of Colorado at Boulder, 1986. UMI Order No. AAD86-18999. DIALOG, Dissertation Abstracts Online.

Personal interviews, utilizing a structured interview, were conducted with 140 senior citizens. Health, contact with friends, and employment were related to life satisfaction. Health, employment, and income were inversely related to depression.

1.247. Slater, Stanley L. and Ira R. Katz. "Prevalence of Depression in the Aged: Formal Calculations Versus Clinical Facts." **Journal of the American Geriatrics Society** 43 (January 1995): 78-79.

1.248. Smallegan, M.J. "Depression in Older Adults." Abstract in **Gerontologist** 27, Special Issue (October 1987): 226A.

One hundred eighty-two people, sixty-five years of age or older, were interviewed. There were in this nonrandom sample men and women, blacks and whites. These subjects represented various socioeconomic classes. The subjects were administered the Hopkins Symptom Checklist and the Geriatric Depression Scale. Approximately 20% of the subjects were depressed. Upper class blacks had a very low level of depression.

1.249. Snowdon, John. "The Prevalence of Depression in Old Age." **International Journal of Geriatric Psychiatry** 5 (May-June 1990): 141-144.

1.250. Spivey, Elizabeth Sumner. "The Measurement of Depression in the Elderly." **Dissertation Abstracts International** 47: 2187B. Ph.D. University of South Dakota, 1986. UMI Order No. AAD86-16582. DIALOG, Dissertation Abstracts Online.

One hundred subjects over the age of sixty were divided into four equal groups: (1) community residing males, (2) community residing females, (3) institutionalized males, and (4) institutionalized females. These subjects were assessed with: (1) the Beck Depression Inventory, (2) Zung Self-Report Depression Scale, (3) Geriatric Depression Scale, (4) Life Satisfaction Index-A, and (5) Social Readjustment Rating Scale. Examples of findings: (1) institutionalized groups had significantly higher scores than community members on the Zung and the Geriatric Depression Scale, (2) women tended toward lower life satisfaction scores than men on the Zung, Geriatric Depression Scale, and Life Satisfaction Index-A, and (3) all the assessment instruments, except the Social Readjustment Rating Scale, correlated very highly with each other.

1.251. Steiner, David and Bernice Marcopulos. "Depression in the Elderly: Characteristics and Clinical Management." **Nursing Clinics of North America** 26

(September 1991): 585-600.

Aging itself does not necessarily lead to depression, even though older individuals experience certain changes, including psychological and social changes, as they grow older. Elderly patients with Alzheimer's Disease, Parkinson's Disease, postmyocardial infarction, and stroke are often depressed. Hypochondriasis, irritability, hopelessness, and guilt may be symptoms of depression in the elderly. The Geriatric Depression Scale (GDS) is reliable and valid in assessing a variety of depressed elderly, including community elderly, institutionalized elderly, hospitalized elderly, and elderly stroke patients. Fluoxetine and bupropion have, for example, minimal cardiovascular side effects. These drugs may cause less morbidity than the monoamine oxidase (MAO) inhibitors. Author biographical information. 1 table. 133 references.

1.252. Steiner, Meir, Ellen Bouchard Ryan, Gail Huxley, Patricia Stephenson-Cino and Lester Krames. "Health Correlates of Depressive Symptoms in Community Elders." Abstract in **Gerontologist** 29, Special Issue (October 1989): 46A.

Twenty-five percent of the variance in depression scores for 1,062 elders was consistently accounted for by physical health.

1.253. Stukenberg, Karl W., Jason R. Dura and Janice K. Kiecolt-Glaser. "Depression Screening Scale Validation in an Elderly, Community-Dwelling Population." **Psychological Assessment** 2 (June 1990): 134-138.

1.254. Talbott, Maria M. "Age Bias in the Beck Depression Inventory: A Proposed Modification for Use with Older Women." **Clinical Gerontologist** 9, No. 2 (1989): 23-35.

Sixty-four widows with a median age of seventy-one years, and residing in Oregon and California, took part in this research. Death records and bereavement self-help groups were the sources of data regarding sample selection. Each widow was interviewed and administered the Beck Depression Inventory (shortened version). Age bias, pertaining to these subjects, was identified. A proposal was made for a new version of the body image change item. Author biographical information. Abstract. 3 tables. 19 references.

1.255. Thorpe, Lillian U. "Depressive Disorders in Old Age: An Overview." **Canadian Family Physician** 35 (March 1989): 657-661.

Masked depression is one presentation of depression in the elderly. In this type of depression, the elderly individual tends to dwell on somatic complaints. Another presentation of depression in the elderly is delusional depression. Paranoid and somatic delusions are commonly associated with this type of depression. A third presentation is pseudodementia, a syndrome of cognitive impairment. Author biographical information. English abstract. French abstract. 5 charts. 7 references.

1.256. Toner, John, Barry Gurland and Jeanne Teresi. "Comparison of Self-Administered and Rater-Administered Methods of Assessing Levels of Severity of Depression in Elderly Patients." **Journals of Gerontology** 43 (September 1988): P136-P140.

This research was done at Associates in Internal Medicine (AIM), a medical group at Columbia Presbyterian Medical Center in New York. Eighty patients with a mean age of seventy-five years were assessed for depression with two instruments: (1) the Zung Self-Rating Depression Scale and (2) the SHORT-CARE. The former is a self-administered questionnaire, the latter a rater-administered interview. One hundred percent was the response rate of completed interviews for the SHORT-CARE, 65% for the Zung. Visual problems and illiteracy were two reasons for not filling out the Zung. The Primary Care Physicians Questionnaire was compared to the SHORT-CARE and the Zung. This comparison revealed that the SHORT-CARE was a better assessment instrument for obtaining useful information regarding depression than the Zung. Author biographical information. Abstract. 3 tables. Acknowledgment. 19 references.

1.257. Tower, R.B. and S.V. Kasl. "Gender, Marital Closeness and Depressive Symptoms in Elderly Couples." **Journals of Gerontology** 51 (May 1996): P115-P129.

1.258. Tucker, M.A., S.J. Ogle, J.G. Davison and M.D. Eilenberg. "Development of a Brief Screening Test for Depression in the Elderly." **Journal of Clinical and Experimental Gerontology** 8 (September-December 1986): 173-190.

1.259. Tucker, M.A., S.J. Ogle, J.G. Davison and M.D. Eilenberg. "Validation of a Brief Screening Test for Depression in the Elderly." **Age and Ageing** 16 (May 1987): 139-144.

The Short Zung Interviewer-Assisted Depression Rating Scale was administered by a psychiatrist to 104 elderly community volunteers and thirty-three elderly depressed patients. Lack of self-esteem and hopelessness were two factors scored highest by the depressed patients. Diurnal mood variation and tiredness were two factors scored highest by the community volunteers. Cognitive function was impaired in the depressed patients relative to the community volunteers. Author biographical information. Abstract. 3 tables. Acknowledgments. 16 references.

1.260. Turner, M.J. "Gender Differences in Factors Related to Depression among Rural Elders." Abstract in **Gerontologist** 35, Special Issue 1 (October 1995): 180.

1.261. Turpie, Irene D. and Gisele M.M. Muir. "Determining the Cause of Depression in the Medically Ill Elderly." **Canadian Journal of Geriatrics** 5 (January-

February 1989): 37-42.

Neither insomnia nor fatigue are exclusively associated with depression. Insomnia may be caused by bladder dysfunction; fatigue may be caused by anemia. Weight loss associated with thyroid dysfunction may be mistaken for depression. Depression may precede carcinoma and it may be difficult to differentiate between dementia and depression. Certain drugs - propranolol and reserpine are examples - may increase or cause depression. Tranquilizers such as the benzodiazepines are depressive. Abstract. Author biographical information. 3 tables. 21 references.

1.262. Usui, W.M. and S.A. Murrell. "Self-Esteem and Depression: A Confirmatory Factor Analysis." Abstract in **Gerontologist** 33, Special Issue 1 (October 1993): 251.

1.263. Valente, Sharon M. "Recognizing Depression in Elderly Patients." **American Journal of Nursing** 94 (December 1994): 18-25.

1.264. Vaughn, G.L. and G.F. Meunier. "Construct Validity of a Short Form of the Geriatric Depression Scale." Abstract in **Gerontologist** 30, Special Issue (October 1990): 221A.

A fifteen-item variation of the Geriatric Depression Scale (GDS) was used to survey approximately 3,000 elderly subjects. Four results provided strong support for the validity of this scale. For example, GDS scores were higher for widows and widowers than for married elderly persons.

1.265. Walz, Patricia Jean. "The Effect of Including Health Items in a Self-Reporting Multidimensional Measure of Depression in the Elderly." **Dissertation Abstracts International** 52: 4484B. Ph.D. University of Arkansas, 1990. UMI Order No. AAD92-04758. DIALOG, Dissertation Abstracts Online.

The Trapp Depression Inventory (TDI) includes life satisfaction items, five subscales, and health items. The Geriatric Depression Scale (GDS) does not include health items. This research examined TDI health items as a separate subscale. Comparison of TDI and GDS scores established the external validity of the TDI. There was no significant difference in TDI scores when health items were included.

1.266. Watkins, A. and E. Kligman. "Psychometric Properties of the Beck Depression Inventories When Used with an Elderly Population." Abstract in **Gerontologist** 29, Special Issue (October 1989): 120A.

1.267. Waxman, Howard M., Gerald McCreary, Risa M. Weinrit and Erwin A. Carner. "A Comparison of Somatic Complaints among Depressed and Non-Depressed Older Persons." **Gerontologist** 25 (October 1985): 501-507.

This research took place in Philadelphia, Pennsylvania, where the subjects were 127 elderly men and women. The Geriatric Depression Scale and Cornell Medical Health Index were two instruments used to assess the subjects. The researchers learned somatic complaints were associated with depression. Depression score and chronic medical illnesses were strong predictors of somatic complaints. Neither demographic variables nor social supports were generally related to somatic complaints. Abstract. Author biographical information. 2 tables. 1 figure. 39 references.

1.268. Weinstein, Walter S. and Prabha Khanna. **Depression in the Elderly: Conceptual Issues and Psychotherapeutic Intervention.** New York, NY: Philosophical Library, 1986. DIALOG, LCMARC-Books.

1.269. Weissman, Jay Ira. "The Neuropsychology of Depression in the Elderly." **Dissertation Abstracts International** 54: 3161A. Ph.D. Fairleigh Dickinson University, 1993. UMI Order No. AAD94-03368. DIALOG, Dissertation Abstracts Online.

1.270. West, C.G., D.M. Reed, G.L. Gildengorin and E.L. Schneider. "Can Money Buy Happiness?: Depressive Symptoms in an Affluent Elderly Population." Abstract in **Gerontologist** 34, Special Issue 1 (October 1994): 304.

Mean CES-D scores were lower in 2,018 community-dwelling elders in an affluent California county than in other population-based samples. Decreasing CES-D scores were significantly associated with increasing income and education.

1.271. Williamson, G.M. and R. Schulz. "Pain and Depression among Community-Residing Elderly." Abstract in **Gerontologist** 31, Special Issue 2 (October 1991): 121.

CES-D scores were used to assess 228 community-residing elderly persons. These subjects were classified as nondepressed or at risk for becoming depressed. There was more pain and greater activity restriction in at-risk subjects. This group was also in poorer health. Health status predicted in the at-risk group pain and increased symptoms of depression. Alleviating pain may alleviate depressive symptoms in persons not at risk for becoming depressed.

1.272. Woehr, Michelle Denise. "Investigation of the Validity of Two Depression Measures in an Elderly Medical Population." **Dissertation Abstracts International** 55: 4618B. Ph.D. Texas A & M University, 1994. UMI Order No. AAD95-06737.

1.273. Yesavage, Jerome A. "Depression in the Elderly." **Postgraduate Medicine** 91 (January 1992): 255-258 and 261.

The aging process may predispose a person to depression. As a person ages, brain metabolic activity decreases. Furthermore, cerebral blood flow is markedly reduced in the depressed elderly. Another deficit is decreased brain concentrations of neurotransmitters, such as serotonin and norepinephrine. Many elderly patients may have masked depression. This type of depression is usually characterized by physical rather than psychological symptoms. There are a number of tests used to screen for depression and each one can be administered in less than fifteen minutes. These tests are: (1) the Mini-Mental State Examination, (2) Geriatric Depression Scale, (3) Hamilton Depression Scale, and (4) Beck Depression Inventory. Author Biographical Information. Abstract. 2 tables. 1 photograph. 13 references.

1.274. Yoder, C., G. Shute, G. Tryban, J. Boyd, M. Smith and K. Morris. "Older Adults' Recognition of Depressive Symptomatology in Vignettes." Abstract in **Gerontologist** 27, Special Issue (October 1987): 190A.

One hundred twenty adults, sixty years and older, were contacted by telephone and read two vignettes. One vignette described classic depression. Another vignette described masked depression. Subjects were asked to state potential reasons for, and potential solutions to, the difficulty in each vignette. The researchers learned many elderly persons - especially older males - do not recognize depression.

1.275. Young, R.C., G.S. Alexopoulos, M. Brown, C.A. Shamoian, R. Roe and M. Deck. "Brain CT and DST in Elderly Depressives." Paper presented at the **15th Annual Meeting of the Society for Neuroscience, Dallas, Texas, October 20-25, 1985.** DIALOG, Conference Papers Index.

1.276. Zgourides, George, Mark Spofford and Lee Doppelt. "The Geriatric Depression Scale: Discriminant Validity and Elderly Day-Treatment Clients." **Psychological Reports** 64 (June 1989): 1082.

1.277. Zimmer, B., Y.W. Glavin, J. Himmelhoch and W. Flynn. "Geriatric Depression: Its Presentation and Treatment." Abstract in **Gerontologist** 25, Special Issue (October 1985): 4-5.

A semistructured clinical interview and symptoms inventory were used to assess - between July 1983 and June 1984 - 689 individuals less than sixty years of age. All these individuals had major depression. They were compared with 147 individuals who also had major depression, but were sixty years of age and older. The geriatric depressive group experienced, for example, more self-neglect; more obsessions and compulsions; and more delusions.

1.278. Zimmer, Ben and Diane Snustad. "Comparison of the Center for Epidemiologic Studies Depression Scale (C.E.S.D.) and the Diagnostic Interview Schedule (D.I.S.) in a Geriatric Population." Abstract in **Gerontologist** 23, Special Issue (October 1983): 65.

1.279. Zung, William W. and Elizabeth M. Zung. "Use of the Zung Self-Rating Depression Scale in the Elderly." **Clinical Gerontologist** 5 (June 1986): 137-148.

1.280. Zung, William W.K. "Affective Disorders." Chapter in **Handbook of Geriatric Psychiatry**, edited by Ewald W. Busse and Dan G. Blazer, 338-367. New York, NY: Van Nostrand Reinhold, 1980.

1.281. Zweig, R.A. and G.A. Hinrichsen. "Age of Onset and Presentation/Outcome of Geriatric Depression: A Prospective Study." Abstract in **Gerontologist** 34, Special Issue 1 (October 1994): 237.

A study of 150 older adults, hospitalized for major depression, revealed that age of onset is not associated with patient symptoms or treatment outcome. Early and late onset depression may not be two distinct entities.

♦ Chapter 2 ♦

Memory, Cognition, Dementia

2.001. Alexopoulos, George S., Robert C. Young, Kenneth W. Lieberman and Charles A. Shamoian. "Platelet MAO Activity in Geriatric Patients with Depression and Dementia." **American Journal of Psychiatry** 144 (November 1987): 1480-1483.

The subjects were 115 hospitalized geriatric patients with a mean age of 74.1 years. The control group consisted of twenty individuals with a mean age of 73.6 years. The following were used for assessment purposes: (1) Research Diagnostic Criteria, (2) Schedule for Affective Disorders and Schizophrenia, (3) Hamilton Rating Scale for Depression, and (4) Cognitive Capacity Screening Examination. Platelet MAO activity was higher in demented patients with and without depression than in nondemented depressed patients. Platelet MAO activity was also higher in depressed patients with reversible dementia than in nondemented depressed patients. A dementia syndrome may develop in persons with abnormally high platelet MAO activity. Author biographical information. Abstract. 1 table. 27 references.

2.002. Allen, Daniel Noble. "The Relation between Self-Rated Memory Ability, Standard Memory Test Performance and Depressive Symptomatology/Negative Affective State in Community-Dwelling Elderly Individuals." **Dissertation Abstracts International** 55: 581B. Ph.D. University of South Dakota, 1993. UMI Order No. AAD94-16600. DIALOG, Dissertation Abstracts Online.

2.003. Archibald, Joan W. and Marcia A. Ullman. "Is It Really Senility or Just Depression?" **RN** 46 (November 1983): 49-51.

Clues to watch for regarding depression in the elderly: (1) dysphoria and mood alteration (patients seem sad, helpless, worried); (2) appetite changes (most patients experience a decrease in appetite); (3) sleep disturbances (some patients may sleep little, others excessively); (4) lack of energy (patients tire easily); (5) difficulty with concentration (agitated patients wring their hands); (6) guilt feelings (not suffered frequently); and (7) recurrent thoughts of death (expressed directly or indirectly). Author biographical information. 2 photographs. 5 references.

2.004. Benedict, Kenneth B. and Denise B. Nacoste. "Dementia and Depression in the Elderly: A Framework for Addressing Difficulties in Differential Diagnosis." **Clinical Psychology Review** 10, No. 5 (1990): 513-537.

2.005. Blau, Ellen M. "The Effect of Depression on Memory Performance and Memory Complaint in Older Adults." **Dissertation Abstracts International** 47: 4294B. Ph.D. California School of Professional Psychology, Berkeley, 1986. UMI Order No. AAD86-29761. DIALOG, Dissertation Abstracts Online.

The subjects were fifty mildly to moderately depressed individuals over age sixty. They were assessed with: (1) the Mini-Mental State Exam, (2) Beck Depression Inventory, (3) Geriatric Depression Scale, (4) Memory Functioning Questionnaire, and (5) California Verbal Learning Test. Examples of findings: (1) depressed subjects achieved, by the final learning trial, the same level of recall as normals; (2) depressed subjects obtained in memory strategies a slightly lower level of performance than normals; (3) depressed subjects reported more memory problems than normals; and (4) depressives were more attuned to their memory abilities than normals.

2.006. Bowes, J.M., W.N. Robiner and T.B. MacKenzie. "Issues in Diagnosing Depression in Dementia Patients." Abstract in **Gerontologist** 31, Special Issue 2 (October 1991): 60.

2.007. Breen, Alan Richard. "Intellectual and Memory Abilities of Elderly Psychiatric Outpatients with Coexisting Dementia and Depression." **Dissertation Abstracts International** 43: 724A. Ph.D. University of Washington, 1982. UMI Order No. AAD82-18206. DIALOG, Dissertation Abstracts Online.

Thirty-five psychiatric outpatients, ranging in age between fifty-seven and eighty-eight years, participated in this investigation. These outpatients had Primary Degenerative Dementia. Fourteen of these subjects also had major depression. Twenty-one subjects were not depressed. The Wechsler Memory Scale (WMS) and Mini-Mental State (MMS) Exam were administered. Depression did not contribute significant additional cognitive impairment to individuals who had a mild to moderately severe dementing illness.

2.008. Burchett, B., C. Pieper, C. Fillenbaum, G. Wall and D. Blazer. "Interrelationship of Depression and Cognitive Impairment in an Elderly Community Sample." Abstract in **Gerontologist** 33, Special Issue 1 (October 1993): 312.

2.009. Carnes, M. and G. Gunter-Hunt. "Screening for Dementia and Depression in Elderly Medical Patients." Abstract in **Gerontologist** 25, Special Issue (October 1985): 245.

A survey of U.S. internal medicine residency programs, with university affiliations, revealed that three of the programs routinely used questionnaires to screen for dementia, and two of the programs to routinely screen for depression, in individuals over age sixty-five.

2.010. Carnes, M., J. Smith, N. Kalin and S. Bauwens. "The Dexamethasone Suppression Test in Demented Outpatients with and without Depression." Abstract in **Gerontologist** 23, Special Issue (October 1983): 114.

2.011. Cash, J., J. Crow and B.J. Feir. "Study Investigating Video Games and Their Effects on Memory and Depression in the Elderly." Paper presented at the **30th Annual Convention of the Southwestern Psychological Association, New Orleans, Louisiana, April 19-21, 1984.** DIALOG, Conference Papers Index.

2.012. Cash, Maureen Marks. "Correlates of Dementia and Depression in the Able Elderly." **Dissertation Abstracts International** 54: 5381B. Ph.D. Michigan State University, 1993. UMI Order No. AAD94-06470. DIALOG, Dissertation Abstracts Online.

The Geriatric Depression Scale and Hamilton Rating Scale for Depression were two instruments used to assign 146 able elderly to one of three groups: (1) mildly demented, (2) mildly depressed, or (3) normal control. Scores from the Brief Symptom Inventory, Selective Reminding Test, and a memory complaints measure were used to compare the three groups. One finding: depressed participants had significantly more memory complaints than control group participants. A second finding: depressed group participants and demented group participants differed regarding depression, paranoid ideation, and psychoticism. A third finding: depressed and control group participants significantly differed regarding all symptom dimensions.

2.013. Clark, Barbara Jeanne. "Compliance, Memory Loss and Depression in the Elderly." **Masters Abstracts** 30: 373. M.A. Michigan State University, 1991. UMI Order No. AAD13-46257. DIALOG, Dissertation Abstracts Online.

Forty elderly individuals, residing independently in the community, were the subjects. These subjects provided demographic information, a medical history, and took their prescribed medication without assistance. Four assessment instruments were used, including the Senile Dementia of the Alzheimer Type (SDAT) battery. Pill counts were used to determine compliance percentage. There may be a relationship between depression and compliance.

2.014. Clark, Barbara Jeanne. "Group Interventions for Memory Complaints, Memory Impairment and Depression in the Able Elderly." **Dissertation Abstracts International** 56: 1694B. Ph.D. Michigan State University, 1994. UMI Order No. AADAA-I9524911. DIALOG, Dissertation Abstracts Online.

One hundred fifty community-dwelling older adults were assigned to one of three experimental treatment conditions: (1) a cognitive-behavioral workshop, (2) a meditation-relaxation workshop, or (3) a waiting list that served as a control. The Mini-Mental State Examination, Beck Depression Inventory, and Geriatric Depression Scale were some of the instruments used to pretest the subjects. Examples of results: (1) all three groups had decreased memory complaints in post-testing, (2) no statistically significant relationship between depression and memory loss, and (3) no significant improvement in cognitive function regardless of type of treatment.

2.015. Collins, Michael William. "Subjective Memory Complaints and Depression in the Able Elderly." **Masters Abstracts** 33: 1973. M.A. Michigan State University, 1995. UMI Order No. AADAA-I1374949. DIALOG, Dissertation Abstracts Online.

Ninety community-dwelling elderly, with a mean age of seventy years, were studied. The Beck Depression Inventory, Geriatric Depression Scale, and Memory Assessment Clinic Self-Report Scale were the assessment instruments used. Test scores were combined to formulate an affective and somatic factor of depression and a sum total of subjective memory complaint. There were significant relationships between total subjective memory complaint and the affective factor of depression and total subjective memory complaint and the somatic factor of depression.

2.016. Copeland, J.R.M., B.J. Gurland, M.E. Dewey, M.J. Kelleher, A.M.R. Smith and I.A. Davidson. "The Distribution of Dementia, Depression and Neurosis in Elderly Men and Women in an Urban Community: Assessed Using the GMS-AGECAT Package." **International Journal of Geriatric Psychiatry** 2 (January-March 1987): 177-184.

AGECAT, a computerized diagnosis, was used to analyze data, pertaining to elderly persons sixty-five years of age and over. These elderly persons resided in New York and London, England. The distribution of mental illness between males and females was examined. One finding: more depression in females. A second finding: the prevalence of depression in males appeared to increase significantly with age. Author biographical information. Abstract. 5 tables. 3 figures. Acknowledgments. 20 references.

2.017. Copeland, John R., Michael E. Dewey and Hazel M. Griffiths-Jones. "Dementia and Depression in Elderly Persons: AGECAT Compared with DSM-III and Pervasive Illness." **International Journal of Geriatric Psychiatry** 5 (January-February 1990): 47-51.

2.018. Eggert, Mary Ann. "A Study of Concurrent Validity of the Fuld Object-Memory Evaluation in a Veterans Administration Medical Center Setting." **Dissertation Abstracts International** 45: 1910B. Ph.D. Ohio State University, 1984.

UMI Order No. AAD84-18936. DIALOG, Dissertation Abstracts Online.

2.019. Emery, Olga B. and Lawrence Breslau. "Cognitive Deficits in SDAT Compared to Old Age Depression and the Relation to Normal Aging." Abstract in **Gerontologist** 27, Special Issue (October 1987): 5A.

2.020. Emery, V.O.B. and R. Arora. "Interaction of Language and Memory in Depressive Dementia: Comparisons with SDAT and Major Depression/Unipolar." Abstract in **Gerontologist** 31, Special Issue 2 (October 1991): 88.

2.021. Finnell, Kathryn Cole. "The Relationship of Cognitive Predispositions to Previous and Current Episodes of Depression in an Elderly Sample." **Dissertation Abstracts International** 41: 3176B. Ph.D. University of Oregon, 1980. UMI Order No. AAD81-02283. DIALOG, Dissertation Abstracts Online.

2.022. Fish, Michael and Bert Hayslip. "The Clinical Use of the Kendrick Battery in Differentiating Dementia and Depression in the Elderly." **Clinical Gerontologist** 3 (Summer 1985): 54-57.

2.023. Forsell, Yvonne, Anthony F. Jorm and Bengt Winblad. "Association of Age, Sex, Cognitive Dysfunction and Disability with Major Depressive Symptoms in an Elderly Sample." **American Journal of Psychiatry** 151 (November 1994): 1600-1604.

2.024. Fox, L.S., B.G. Knight and E.M. Zelinski. "A Meta-Analysis of Cognitive Deficit in Depression across the Lifespan." Abstract in **Gerontologist** 35, Special Issue 1 (October 1995): 185.

2.025. Frazer, D., A. Glicksman, L. Sands, D. Libon and S. Cooley. "Differential Effects of Depression and Dementia on Cognitive Functioning of Elderly Clients." Abstract in **Gerontologist** 28, Special Issue (October 1988): 266A.

Three hundred seventy-seven patients were administered a battery of cognitive tests then, based on depression and cognition, grouped into four categories. Depression did not appear to contribute to cognitive dysfunction in the elderly intact nor in the demented.

2.026. Frazer, D., A. Glicksman, W. Whelihan and A. Best. "The Relationship between Dementia and Depression across Age Groups and Settings." Abstract in **Gerontologist** 27, Special Issue (October 1987): 188A.

Thirteen hundred twenty subjects were assessed over a seven year period with: (1) the Extended Mental Status Questionnaire (EMSQ), (2) Delayed Memory for Story (DMS) measure, and (3) Geriatric Depression Scale (GDS). The purpose of this investigation was to study dementia and depression across age groups and settings.

The researchers learned a linear relationship occurred in younger and middle-old age groups, but not in the old-old (eighty-five plus) group.

2.027. Gannon, Timothy Leo. "The Impact of Depressive Symptoms on Explicit Memory Performance in the Elderly." **Masters Abstracts** 33: 256. M.A. Michigan State University, 1994. UMI Order No. AAD13-57895. DIALOG, Dissertation Abstracts Online.

Forty-five community-dwelling elderly, with a mean age of sixty-eight years, were the study participants. The Hamilton Depression Rating Scale, Beck Depression Inventory, Geriatric Depression Scale, Selective Reminding Test, and Logical Memory Test were used to assess the participants. A depression and memory factor was developed with the test score, revealing a relationship between symptoms and memory performance.

2.028. Gibson, Andrew J. "A Further Analysis of Memory Loss in Dementia and Depression in the Elderly." **British Journal of Clinical Psychology** 20 (September 1981): 179-185.

2.029. Gray, Jeffrey W., Arlene I. Rattan and Raymond S. Dean. "Differential Diagnosis of Dementia and Depression in the Elderly Using Neuropsychological Methods." **Archives of Clinical Neuropsychology** 1, No. 4 (1986): 341-349.

2.030. Grut, Michaela, Anthony F. Jorm, Laura Fratiglioni, Yvonne Forsell, Matti Viitanen and Bengt Winblad. "Memory Complaints of Elderly People in a Population Survey: Variation According to Dementia Stage and Depression." **Journal of the American Geriatrics Society** 41 (December 1993): 1295-1300.

2.031. Gurland, Barry J., Robert R. Golden, Jeanne A. Teresi and Judith Challop. "The SHORT-CARE: An Efficient Instrument for the Assessment of Depression, Dementia and Disability." **Journal of Gerontology** 39 (March 1984): 166-169.

2.032. Haggerty, John J., Jr., Dwight L. Evans, Robert N. Golden and David S. Janowsky. "Differential Diagnosis of Pseudodementia in the Elderly." **Geriatrics** 43 (March 1988): 61-69 and 72-74.

A comparison of eight features of pseudodementia and dementia. Pseudodementia: (1) onset is relatively rapid; (2) duration, usually short; (3) mood, depressed; (4) behavior, unresponsive; (5) somatic symptoms, fatigue/appetite disturbance; (6) cognitive impairment pattern, worse on effortful tasks; (7) response to error, highlights; and (8) CAT, normal. Dementia: (1) onset is insidious; (2) duration, indeterminate; (3) mood, blunted or irritated; (4) behavior, distracted; (5) somatic symptoms, sleep disturbance; (6) cognitive impairment pattern, multiple impairments; (7) response to error, minimizes; and (8) CAT, possible cortical atrophy. Author biographical information. Abstract. 3 tables. 21 references.

2.033. Harrison, Robert, Navin Savla and Kalman Kafetz. "Dementia, Depression and Physical Disability in a London Borough: A Survey of Elderly People in and Out of Residential Care and Implications for Future Developments." **Age and Ageing** 19 (March 1990): 97-103.

Dementia, depression, and physical disability in dependent elderly people in Waltham Forest, a borough of London, England, were studied. Thirteen hundred three persons were studied. The Brief Assessment Schedule and the Barthel Index were used for assessment purposes. Although there was little disability outside private and voluntary residential accommodation, there was a high prevalence of depression in the study population as a whole. Author biographical information. Abstract. 5 tables. Acknowledgments. 27 references.

2.034. Hayslip, Bert, Jr., Kevin J. Kennelly and Robyn M. Maloy. "Fatigue, Depression and Cognitive Performance among Aged Persons." **Experimental Aging Research** 16 (Autumn 1990): 111-115.

Seventy-two elderly individuals, with a mean age of 71.58 years, volunteered for this study. These subjects, consisting of twenty males and fifty-two females, were assessed with the Beck Depression Inventory (BDI). They were then assigned to one of three conditions, each condition varying in effort and fatigue-inducing nature. Depressed subjects were more prone to fatigue. Depression impacted on performance concerning short-term memory. Author biographical information. Abstract. 3 tables. 24 references.

2.035. Henderson, A.S. and K. Hasegawa. "The Epidemiology of Dementia and Depression in Later Life." Chapter in **Aging and Mental Disorders: International Perspectives**, edited by Manfred Bergener, Kazuo Hasegawa, Sanford I. Finkel and Tsuyoshi Nishimura, 65-79. New York, NY: Springer, 1992.

2.036. Hoch, C., C. Reynolds, D. Buysse and D. Kupfer. "Two-Year Outcomes of Demented, Depressed and Mixed-Symptom Elderly." Abstract in **Gerontologist** 32, Special Issue 2 (October 1992): 159.

There were four groups of subjects: (1) fifty-one depressed, (2) thirty-four demented, (3) fifty-eight mixed-symptom, and (4) fifty-one control. These subjects were assessed for depression and dementia every six months for two years. Depressed improved, demented declined, mixed subjects depression improved, while cognitive impairment declined, and ratings remained stable for controls.

2.037. Hoch, C.C., C.F. Reynolds, P.A. Houck, D.J. Buysse and D.J. Kupfer. "Sleep Predictors of Two-Year Mortality in Mixed Depressed-Demented Patients." Abstract in **Gerontologist** 29, Special Issue (October 1989): 34A-35A.

2.038. Jones, James Denison. "Memory Complaints, Depression and Memory Functions in the Able Elderly." **Masters Abstracts** 33: 1974. M.A. Michigan State University, 1995. UMI Order No. AADAA-I1374978. DIALOG, Dissertation Abstracts Online.

The Geriatric Depression Scale, Rivermead Behavioral Memory Test, Logical Memory I, and Memory Assessment Clinics Self-Rating Scale were administered to 121 community-dwelling older adults. Depression scores accounted for the most variance in memory complaint scores.

2.039. Kahn, Robert L., Steven H. Zarit, Nancy M. Hilbert and George Niederehe. "Memory Complaint and Impairment in the Aged: The Effect of Depression and Altered Brain Function." **Archives of General Psychiatry** 32 (December 1975): 1569-1573.

2.040. Katz, I., M. Aronson and R. Lipkowitz. "Depression: Symptomatic Expression in the Normal and Demented Elderly." Abstract in **Gerontologist** 22 (October 1982): 240.

2.041. Keller, William Jefferson. "Forty Hertz EEG Activity in the Elderly: Dementia, Depression and Normal Aging." **Dissertation Abstracts International** 46: 2492B. Ph.D. University of Houston, 1985. UMI Order No. AAD85-20477. DIALOG, Dissertation Abstracts Online.

2.042. Kennedy, G.J., H.R. Kelman and C. Thomas. "The Longitudinal Interactions of Depression and Cognitive Impairment in Older Community Residents." Abstract in **Gerontologist** 31, Special Issue 2 (October 1991): 217.

2.043. Kennelly, Kevin J., Bert Hayslip and Sandra K. Richardson. "Depression and Helplessness-Induced Cognitive Deficits in the Aged." **Experimental Aging Research** 11 (Fall-Winter 1985): 169-173.

2.044. Kral, V.A. "The Relationship between Senile Dementia (Alzheimer Type) and Depression." **Canadian Journal of Psychiatry** 28 (June 1983): 304-306.

2.045. Kral, Vojtech A. and Olga B. Emery. "Long-Term Follow-Up of Depressive Pseudodementia of the Aged." **Canadian Journal of Psychiatry** 34 (June 1989): 445-446.

Forty-four patients with a mean age of 76.5 years, and afflicted with depressive pseudodementia, were treated for the depression. Cognitive function then reverted to premorbid level. These patients were interviewed and retested regularly at six-month intervals for an average of eight years. Depression recurred in some patients during the follow-up period. At the end of this period, 89% of the patients had developed a dementia of the Alzheimer type. Author biographical information. English abstract. French abstract. 9 references.

2.046. Kramer-Ginsberg, E. and B.S. Greenwald. "Predictors of Cognitive Impairment at Long-Term Follow-Up amongst Elderly Depressives." Abstract in **Gerontologist** 33, Special Issue 1 (October 1993): 307.

Elderly depressives participated in a seven-year follow up of cognitive assessment. They were administered the Telephone Interview for Cognitive Status (TICS). There was in 52% of these depressives significant cognitive impairment. At initial assessment, neuroradiological reports of brain abnormalities indicated cognitive impairment at follow-up.

2.047. Lamberty, Greg J. and Linas A. Bieliauskas. "Distinguishing between Depression and Dementia in the Elderly: A Review of Neuropyschological Findings." **Archives of Clinical Neuropsychology** 8 (March-April 1993): 149-170.

2.048. La Rue, A. and S. Goodman. "Clinical Correlates of Impaired Memory in Geriatric Depression." Abstract in **Gerontologist** 29, Special Issue (October 1989): 102A.

2.049. La Rue, A., G. Swan and D. Carmelli. "Depressive Symptoms and Cognitive Performance in Normally Aging Men." Abstract in **Gerontologist** 33, Special Issue 1 (October 1993): 20.

2.050. La Rue, Asenath. "Patterns of Performance on the Fuld Object Memory Evaluation in Elderly Inpatients with Depression or Dementia." **Journal of Clinical and Experimental Neuropsychology** 11 (August 1989): 409-422.

2.051. Levy, R.O. "Psychological and Physiological Changes in Elderly Depressive Dements and Controls." Paper presented at the **6th World Congress of Psychiatry, Honolulu, Hawaii, August 28-September 3, 1977**. DIALOG, Conference Papers Index.

2.052. Lichtenberg, P., B. Marcopulos, D. Steiner and J. Tabscott. "Comparison of Ham-D and GDS' Ability to Detect Depression in Dementia Patients." Abstract in **Gerontologist** 30, Special Issue (October 1990): 302A.

2.053. Lichtenberg, P. and M. Nanna. "Does Depression Predict Cognition in Geriatric Medical Patients?" Abstract in **Gerontologist** 33, Special Issue 1 (October 1993): 45-46.

Two hundred nineteen geriatric medical inpatients, with an average age of seventy-seven years, were the subjects. Twenty-nine percent of these subjects were depressed. Approximately 33% exhibited cognitive dysfunction. There was a modest but significant relationship between depression and cognition.

2.054. Lichtenberg, P. and M. Nanna. "The Role of Cognition and Depression in

Recovery During Geriatric Rehabilitation." Abstract in **Gerontologist** 34, Special Issue 1 (October 1994): 323.

2.055. Lindesay, James, Kate Briggs and Elaine Murphy. "The Guy's/Age Concern Survey: Prevalence Rates of Cognitive Impairment, Depression and Anxiety in an Urban Elderly Community." **British Journal of Psychiatry** 155 (September 1989): 317-329.

2.056. Lyness, Scott A., Elaine M. Eaton and Lon S. Schneider. "Cognitive Performance in Older and Middle-Aged Depressed Outpatients and Controls." **Journals of Gerontology** 49 (May 1994): P129-P136.

This research into cognitive performance had three groups of subjects: (1) older (sixty to seventy-five years) unmedicated outpatients, (2) middle-aged (forty to fifty-nine years) unmedicated outpatients, and (3) healthy controls. All the outpatients had major depression. Verbal, visual-spatial, and visuo-motor scanning tasks were used to assess cognitive performance. One finding: controls performed better on visuo-motor scanning tasks than depressed subjects. A second finding: older outpatients were slower on visuo-motor scanning tasks than middle-aged outpatients. A third finding: older depressed subjects performed worse than middle-aged depressed subjects because age and depression, together, were a negative additive factor. Author biographical information. Abstract. 4 tables. Acknowledgments. 45 references.

2.057. Marrocco, Geraldine Fahy. "Dementia and Depression: A Study of Prevalence in an Elderly Residential Setting." **Dissertation Abstracts International** 57: 595A. ED.D. Columbia University Teachers College, 1996. UMI Order No. AADAA-I9620160. DIALOG, Dissertation Abstracts Online.

In a study of 111 persons seventy-five years of age and older, residing in Connecticut, it was demonstrated cognitive functioning, age, and the diagnosis of cancer were some of the variables significantly correlated with depressive symptoms. Marital status and alcohol use, for example, were not significantly correlated with depression.

2.058. Matsuyama, S.S. and J. Joseph. "Haptoglobin Types in Depression and Dementia." Abstract in **Gerontologist** 22 (October 1982): 231.

Haptoglobin (Hp) typing was performed on seventy elderly, depressed individuals. Forty-three individuals with no mental disorders were also studied. There was in the depressed subjects, when compared to the nondepressed subjects, no significant difference in the distribution of Hp genotypes. Alzheimer patients were being studied to determine if these patients had significantly increased Hp gene frequency.

2.059. McCue, Michael, Gerald Goldstein and Carolyn Shelly. "The Application of a Short Form of the Luria-Nebraska Neuropsychological Battery to Discrimination between Dementia and Depression in the Elderly." **International Journal of Clinical Neuropsychology** 11, No. 1 (1989): 21-29.

2.060. McDougall, G.J. "Metamemory and Depression in Cognitively Impaired Older Adults." Abstract in **Gerontologist** 34, Special Issue 1 (October 1994): 238.

2.061. McNeil, J.K. "Neuropsychological Characteristics of the Dementia Syndrome of Depression (DSD): Onset, Resolution and Three-Year Follow-Up." Abstract in **Gerontologist** 36, Special Issue 1 (October 1996): 251.

2.062. McWilliam, C., N. Wood, J.R.M. Copeland and W.H. Taylor. "Erythrocyte Acetyl Cholinesterase in Elderly Patients with Dementia and Depression Compared with Normal Controls." **Age and Ageing** 19 (March 1990): 104-106.

Levels of acetyl cholinesterase (AChE) decrease as the brain ages. These levels decrease further in senile dementia of the Alzheimer type (SDAT). There are also in SDAT and endogenous depression decreased levels of erythrocyte acetyl cholinesterase (EAChE). After forty-six mentally well normal controls, ten subjects with SDAT, and twenty-seven subjects with depression were studied, it was learned there were in these groups no significant differences from normal in dementia or depression. In other words, changes in EAChE, according to this research, do not account for the presence of depression or dementia in persons with these afflictions. Abstract. 1 table. Acknowledgment. 12 references. Author biographical information.

2.063. Melton, Mary Elizabeth. "The Role of Anxiety and Depressive Symptoms in the Cognitive Functioning of Old and Young Women." **Dissertation Abstracts International** 53: 589B. Ph.D. University of North Carolina at Greensboro, 1991. UMI Order No. AAD92-08307. DIALOG, Dissertation Abstracts Online.

2.064. Miller, Edgar and Peter Lewis. "Recognition Memory in Elderly Patients with Depression and Dementia: A Signal Detection Analysis." **Journal of Abnormal Psychology** 86 (February 1977): 84-86.

Depressive, demented, and normal individuals were the subjects in this research. Twenty individuals comprised each of three groups. The subjects had a mean age as follows: depressive (77.4 years), demented (77.5 years), and normal (77.8 years). A modification of the Continuous Recognition Procedure, in which 160 cards were used to test recognition memory, was applied to each group. This study revealed depressives, unlike dements, did not have, regarding poor performance on memory tasks, a true memory deficit. Author biographical information. Abstract. 1 table. 1 reference note. 10 references.

2.065. Nelson, D.V., R.G. Harper, D. Kotik-Harper and H.B. Kirby. "Brief Neuropsychologic Differentiation of Depression Versus Dementia in Elderly Inpatients."

Abstract in **Gerontologist** 27, Special Issue (October 1987): 188A-189A.

2.066. Newton, N., A Schneider, L. Lazarus, L. Groves and K. Dellefield. "Relation between Psychiatric Treatment and Cognitive Functioning in Elderly Depressed Patients." Abstract in **Gerontologist** 22 (October 1982): 241.

Twenty elderly depressed persons, ranging in age from sixty-three to eighty-nine years, were the subjects. These subjects were assessed after admission to and prior to discharge from a psychiatric facility. The Sandoz Clinical Assessment Geriatric Scale and the Hamilton Depression Scale were two assessment instruments used. Concentration, memory, and verbal fluency were studied. One finding: depressed patients with moderate dementia were less responsive to psychiatric treatment. Another finding: psychopharmacological agents did not impair cognitive functioning.

2.067. Niederehe, G., R.E. Reichlin and B. Burns. "Ego Development, Locus of Control and Memory Function in Young and Old Depressed Women." Abstract in **Gerontologist** 28, Special Issue (October 1988): 151A.

2.068. Niederehe, G., C.W. Scott, D. Thomas, K. Nielsen-Collins and D. Volpendesta. "Depression and Age Effects on Reconstructive Memory Processes." Abstract in **Gerontologist** 23, Special Issue (October 1983): 239.

2.069. Nussbaum, Paul David. "Depression and Cognitive Deterioration in the Elderly: A Follow-Up Study." **Dissertation Abstracts International** 52: 5544B. Ph.D. University of Arizona, 1991. UMI Order No. AAD92-08027. DIALOG, Dissertation Abstracts Online.

2.070. Nussbaum, Paul David and Lori Sauer. "Self-Report of Depression in Elderly with and without Progressive Cognitive Deterioration." **Clinical Gerontologist** 13, No. 1 (1993): 69-80.

The fifty-four subjects in this research consisted of three groups of elderly individuals: (1) depressed with no cognitive deterioration, (2) depressed with cognitive deterioration, and (3) probable Alzheimer's Disease (AD) patients. The subjects were administered the Geriatric Depression Scale (GDS) and the Mini-Mental State Examination (MMSE); the GDS was also administered two years later. There were no differences, for either test period, on the GDS total score among the three groups. Author biographical information. Abstract. 3 tables. 1 figure. 25 references.

2.071. O'Connor, D.W. and M. Roth. "Coexisting Depression and Dementia in a Community Survey of the Elderly." **International Psychogeriatrics** 2 (Spring 1990): 45-53.

2.072. O'Flaithbheartaigh, S.F., P. Powchik, P.D. Harvey, M. Parella, L. White, M. Davidson and K.L. Davis. "Cognitive Deficits and Psychopathology in Elderly Schizophrenic and Affective Disorder Patients." Paper presented at the **1995 Annual Meeting of the American Psychiatric Association, Miami, Florida, May 20-25, 1995.** DIALOG, Conference Papers Index.

2.073. Owens, D.R. and P.A. Webber. "Dementia and Depression: Patient and Staff Concordance Rates." Abstract in **Gerontologist** 35, Special Issue 1 (October 1995): 88.

2.074. Pivarnik, Neil Charles. "A Comparison of Health Care Aide's and Self-Perceptions of Physical Functioning in Elderly Patients with Depression and Dementia." **Dissertation Abstracts International** 51: 960A. ED.D. Columbia University Teachers College, 1989. UMI Order No. AAD9013571. DIALOG, Dissertation Abstracts Online.

Ninety-four elderly individuals with depression, dementia, both or neither were the subjects. They were assessed with: (1) the Mental Status Questionnaire (MSQ), (2) Simultaneous Bilateral Physical Stimulation Test (SBPST), (3) Geriatric Depression Scale (GDS), and (4) Index of Independence in Activities of Daily Living (IIADL). There was in the depressed subjects no significant difference in health care aides and self-perceptions of physical functioning. The group with dementia perceived themselves significantly more independent than the depression group perceived themselves.

2.075. Poon, Leonard W. "Toward an Understanding of Cognitive Functioning in Geriatric Depression." **International Psychogeriatrics**, Supplement 2 (1992): 241-266.

2.076. Popkin, Samuel J., Dolores Gallagher, Larry W. Thompson and Martha Moore. "Memory Complaint and Performance in Normal and Depressed Older Adults." **Experimental Aging Research** 8 (Fall-Winter 1982): 141-145.

2.077. Portalska, Renata Z. and Marion Bernstein. "The Differentiation of Depression from Senile Dementia in the Elderly." **International Journal of Geriatric Psychiatry** 3 (April-June 1988): 137-144.

2.078. Price, S., S. Birge, K. Riggs and M. Michael. "Implications of Formal Assessment of Cognition and Depression." Abstract in **Gerontologist** 30, Special Issue (October 1990): 225A.

2.079. Prinz, P., M. Vitiello, D. Williams, L. Poon and F. Wilkie. "Cognitive Deficits in Geriatric Onset Depression Are Minimal." Abstract in **Gerontologist** 28, Special Issue (October 1988): 284A.

2.080. Rabins, Peter V. "Coexisting Depression and Dementia." **Journal of Geriatric Psychiatry** 22, No. 1 (1989): 17-24.

Dementia caused by depression is treatable, the onset of this disorder often being less than three months. The person with this condition usually has a past history of affective disorder. Guilt, appetite disturbance, and ideas of self-blame usually characterize this condition. Although depression may be treatable in a person who has depression secondary to irreversible dementia, cognition does not return to baseline. Author biographical information. 28 references.

2.081. Reedy, J., L. Roth and J. Burns. "Memory and Depression in Elderly Psychiatric Patients: Diagnosis Versus Self-Report." Poster Paper No. M-4 presented at the **102nd Annual Convention of the American Psychological Association, Los Angeles, California, August 12-16, 1994**. DIALOG, Conference Papers Index.

2.082. Reifler, Burton V. "Dementia Versus Depression in the Elderly." Chapter in **Aging and Mental Disorders: International Perspectives**, edited by Manfred Bergener, Kazuo Hasegawa, Sanford I. Finkel and Tsuyoshi Nishimura, 83-89. New York, NY: Springer, 1992.

2.083. Reifler, Burton V. "Depression with and without Dementia." **Hospital Practice** 25 (April 30, 1990): 47-51, 54, 59, 62-63 and 66.

2.084. Reifler, Burton V., Eric Larson and Ray Hanley. "Coexistence of Cognitive Impairment and Depression in Geriatric Outpatients." **American Journal of Psychiatry** 139 (May 1982): 623-626.

Fifty-eight elderly outpatients at the University of Washington, Seattle, Washington, were the subjects. The Kahn-Goldfarb Scale and Research Diagnostic Criteria were used to assess these subjects. All the subjects were cognitively impaired. Of these subjects, 23% were diagnosed with depression. Although 20% had depression only, 85% had depression superimposed on dementia. The more severe the cognitive impairment, the lower the rate of coexisting depression. Cognitively impaired women appeared to be more likely to be depressed than cognitively impaired men. Author biographical information. Abstract. 1 table. 16 references.

2.085. Richardson, E.D., R.L. Miller, M.A. Whisman and C. Mazure. "Screening for Depression in Cognitively-Impaired Geriatric Patients." Abstract in **Gerontologist** 35, Special Issue 1 (October 1995): 258.

2.086. Richardson, Sandra Kay. "Depression and Helplessness-Induced Cognitive Deficits among the Aged." **Masters Abstracts** 23: 219. M.S. North Texas State University, 1984. UMI Order No. AAD13-22946. DIALOG, Dissertation Abstracts Online.

2.087. Riley, K.P. and E. Redinbaugh. "Screening for Depression and Dementia in High Risk Elderly." Abstract in **Gerontologist** 30, Special Issue (October 1990): 270A.

One hundred forty-eight inner-city persons, over the age of seventy-five, were the subjects. The average age of these subjects, who lived alone in government-subsidized housing, was 82.9 years. Sixty-seven percent of these subjects were black, 89% female. A battery of tests revealed 38% of these subjects were possibly depressed or cognitively impaired.

2.088. Rohling, Martin L. and Forrest Scogin. "Automatic and Effortful Memory Processes in Depressed Persons." **Journals of Gerontology** 48 (March 1993): P87-P95.

The subjects consisted of thirty depressed patients, twenty psychiatric controls, and thirty normal controls, the subjects ranging in age from sixteen to seventy-five years. The Inventory to Diagnose Depression and the Hamilton Rating Scale for Depression were two assessment instruments used. Free recall and paired associates were tasks designed to be effortful. Memory for frequency and location were tasks designed to be automatic. Depression was not related to memory deficits. Psychiatric hospitalization, more so than depression, had a greater negative effect on memory. Author biographical information. Abstract. 5 tables. Acknowledgments. 36 references.

2.089. Sahakian, Barbara J. "Depressive Pseudodementia in the Elderly." **International Journal of Geriatric Psychiatry** 6 (June 1991): 453-458.

2.090. Scheier, L.M., M.H. Kleban and P.A. Parmelee. "Depression as a Predictor of Cognitive Functioning: Dynamic Versus Static Models." Abstract in **Gerontologist** 32, Special Issue 2 (October 1992): 142.

2.091. Scogin, Forrest, David Hamblin and Larry Beutler. "Validity of the Cognitive Error Questionnaire with Depressed and Non-Depressed Older Adults." **Psychological Reports** 59 (August 1986): 267-272.

The depressed participants were forty-three older adults, consisting of twenty men and twenty-three women, ranging in age from sixty-four to eighty-four years. The control group consisted of fifty-three older adults twenty men and thirty-three women, ranging in age from sixty to eighty-eight years. Both groups were administered the Cognitive Error Questionnaire and the Beck Depression Inventory Short Form. Questionnaire scores were factor analyzed, these analyses indicating one factor responsible for most of the variance. This suggested the questionnaire measured general dysfunctional thinking in older adults. The questionnaire evidenced high internal reliability, after collapsed scores reliably separated the depressed from the nondepressed elders. Scores were not significantly correlated with

Beck Depression Inventory scores. Author biographical information. Abstract. 2 tables. 9 references.

2.092. Scogin, Forrest Ray, Jr. "Memory Skills Training for the Elderly: The Efficacy of Self-Instructional Training on Memory Performance, Memory Evaluation and Depression." **Dissertation Abstracts International** 44: 3542B. Ph.D. Washington University, 1983. UMI Order No. AAD84-02213. DIALOG, Dissertation Abstracts Online.

Sixty elderly persons over age sixty took part, approximately one hour per day, in self-paced study for sixteen days, regarding four mnemonic techniques. After these persons were assigned to either an immediate-training condition or a control group, they were assessed concerning memory performance, memory evaluation, and affective status measures: (1) prior to training, (2) immediately following training, and (3) at one-month follow-up. Persons in the immediate training condition improved their performance on some memory performance measures. There were no corresponding significant changes in affective status at immediate post training. Improvements in memory performance were maintained at one-month follow-up.

2.093. Siegel, Barry, David Gurevich and Gregory F. Oxenkrug. "Cognitive Impairment and Cortisol Resistance to Dexamethasone Suppression in Elderly." **Biological Psychiatry** 25 (January 1989): 229-234.

2.094. Smith, J. and T. Drinka. "The Coexistence of Dementia and Depression in Geriatric Clinic Outpatients." Abstract in **Gerontologist** 23, Special Issue (October 1983): 102-103.

One hundred thirty male outpatients, ranging in age from sixty to ninety-two years, were diagnosed, with the Jacobs Cognitive Screening Capacity Exam, as having dementia. Berger's Severity Rating Scale was used to determine the severity of dementia. Ninety of the 130 subjects were depressed. The greater the severity of dementia, the lower the rate of coexisting depression.

2.095. Snowdon, John and Fred Lane. "The Botany Survey: A Longitudinal Study of Depression and Cognitive Impairment in an Elderly Population." **International Journal of Geriatric Psychiatry** 10 (May 1995): 349-358.

2.096. Snow-Turek, A.L. and M.P. Norris. "Self-Reported Depression in Demented Elderly." Abstract in **Gerontologist** 36, Special Issue 1 (October 1996): 253.

2.097. Steeman, E., I.L. Abraham and J. Godderis. "Risk Profiles for Institutionalization in a Cohort of Elderly People with Dementia or Depression." Abstract in **Gerontologist** 36, Special Issue 1 (October 1996): 46.

Seventy-five elderly individuals with dementia or depression were studied in order to develop risk profiles for institutionalization. Age, marital status, communication skills, cognition, and social support were some of the variables analyzed. Three profiles high, moderate, low were generated, each profile statistically different from each other.

2.098. Steingart, A. and N. Herrmann. "Major Depressive Disorder in the Elderly: The Relationship between Age of Onset and Cognitive Impairment." **International Journal of Geriatric Psychiatry** 6 (August 1991): 593-598.

2.099. Steuer, Joanne. "Cognition and Depression in Geriatric Patients." Abstract in **Gerontologist** 20, Special Issue (1980): 207.

In a study of sixty elderly community residents, ranging in age from sixty to ninety years, clinical depression in geriatric outpatients was not related to cognitive functioning.

2.100. Thuras, P.D., I.R. Katz and D.W. Frazer. "Dementia and the Validity of Depressive Symptom Checklists." Abstract in **Gerontologist** 31, Special Issue 2 (October 1991): 46.

Structured interview symptom checklists, using DSM-III-R criteria, were valid in the detection of depression, even when administered to individuals who had moderate cognitive impairment.

2.101. Toner, J., B. Gurland, J. Teresi and F. Tirumalasetti. "Detecting Depressive Symptoms in Dementia: The Feeling Tone Questionnaire (FTQ)." Abstract in **Gerontologist** 35, Special Issue 1 (October 1995): 24-25.

2.102. Truax P. and L. Teri. "Are Caregiver Depression Ratings of Demented Patients Biased by Their Own Mood?" Abstract in **Gerontologist** 30, Special Issue (October 1990): 236A.

2.103. Tucker, A.R., C.A. Langston, P. Parmelee and I.R. Katz. "Structure and Utility of the Cornell Scale of Depression in Dementia (CSDD)." Abstract in **Gerontologist** 36, Special Issue 1 (October 1996): 113.

2.104. Vitiello, M.V., P.N. Prinz, L.W. Poon and D.E. Williams. "Memory Impairment in the Elderly Is Associated with Validated Memory Complaint, But Not with Major Depressive Disorder." Abstract in **Gerontologist** 30, Special Issue (October 1990): 157A.

Objective assessments of cognition, and self-reports, should be considered by practitioners, in order to accurately judge the validity of patient complaints, regarding memory impairment. Depression alone is not necessarily associated with memory impairment.

2.105. Weinberger, David M. "Looking Beyond the Illness: Depression and Dementia in the Elderly." **Psychotherapy in Private Practice** 11, No. 4 (1992): 93-116.

2.106. Weinstein, Walter Samuel. "Mood Induction and Cognitive Self-Schemas in the Elderly Depressive: The Role of Cognition Versus Affect." **Dissertation Abstracts International** 47: 2638B. Ph.D. Memphis State University, 1986. UMI Order No. AAD86-19466. DIALOG, Dissertation Abstracts Online.

2.107. White, Nancy and Walter R. Cunningham. "The Relationships among Memory Complaint, Memory Performance and Depression in Young and Elderly Adults." Abstract in **Gerontologist** 24, Special Issue (October 1984): 205.

A memory questionnaire was administered to two groups of individuals. There were 141 young individuals and 142 elderly adults. The two groups of subjects were also given memory and reaction-time tasks. The groups were also assessed with a depression scale. Depression was related to memory performance and memory complaints in the elderly adults, but not in the young subjects.

2.108. Winegardner, Jill. "A Comparison of Cognitive, Affective and Life Experience Correlates of Depression in Young Adults and the Aged." **Dissertation Abstracts International** 42: 2556B. Ph.D. University of Montana, 1980. UMI Order No. AAD81-25540. DIALOG, Dissertation Abstracts Online.

2.109. Yoash-Gantz, R., B. Marcopolus and L. Thompson. "'Older Adults' Memory Self-Assessment and Performance Before and After Treatment for Depression." Abstract in **Gerontologist** 30, Special Issue (October 1990): 51A.

The Schedule for Affective Disorders and Schizophrenia was used to diagnose depression in fifty-two elderly subjects, who were subsequently treated for depression. These subjects were administered, before and after treatment, the Memory Functioning Questionnaire and several memory tests. Memory complaints and level of depression were both significantly reduced after treatment, but there was little significant change in actual memory functioning.

2.110. Young, R.C., R. Abrams, G.S. Alexopoulos and G.P. Smith. "Investigatory Behavior in Geriatric Affective Disorder and Dementia." Abstract in **Gerontologist** 26, Special Issue (October 1986): 112A.

Ten elderly persons with major depression, two elderly persons with bipolar disorder, and six elderly persons with primary degenerative dementia were studied, regarding investigatory behavior. A concealed observer monitored the extent of this behavior in these subjects, as they sat at a table for fifteen minutes and touched/manipulated novel objects. One finding: more persons with primary degenerative dementia than with major depression engaged in investigatory behavior. A second finding: investigatory behavior was more sustained in persons with bipolar disorder than in persons with primary degenerative dementia.

2.111. Zung, W.W. "Depression and Dementia in Aged: Emotional Status and Cognitive Findings." Paper presented at the **24th Annual Meeting of the Academy of Psychosomatic Medicine, Costa Mesa, California, November 13-16, 1977.** DIALOG, Conference Papers Index.

Chapter 3

Physical Illnesses, Disability, Sensory Impairment

3.001. Altergott, K. "The Social Context of Serious Illness and Depression: A Canadian-U.S. Comparison." Abstract in **Gerontologist** 32, Special Issue 2 (October 1992): 225-226.

The first group of subjects were forty-nine cancer patients in Indiana, ranging in age from sixty to seventy-five years. The second group of subjects were fifty-three cancer patients in Manitoba, ranging in age from sixty to seventy-nine years. Both groups were assessed for depression. Although 33% of the Indiana sample were depressed, only 18% of the Manitoba sample were depressed. Financial considerations were a risk factor for depression in Indiana, but not in Manitoba.

3.002. Andelin, Lisa C., Cathy A. Alessi and Harriet U. Aronow. "Reliability of Screening for Sensory Impairment in Depressed Versus Non-Depressed Older Adults." **Journal of the American Geriatrics Society** 43 (June 1995): 684-687.

3.003. Andersson, Gerhard, Lennart Melin, Per Lindberg and Berit Scott. "Dispositional Optimism, Dysphoria, Health and Coping with Hearing Impairment in Elderly Adults." **Audiology** 34 (March-April 1995): 76-84.

3.004. Bartmann, Judith Ann. "Middle-Aged and Older Women with Mastectomies: Coping Strategies and Depression." **Dissertation Abstracts International** 55: 2950A. Ph.D. University of Northern Colorado, 1994. UMI Order No. AAD9503705. DIALOG, Dissertation Abstracts Online.

One hundred women, ranging in age from forty-five to ninety-one years, were the subjects. These women, all of whom had had mastectomies, were divided into two groups: (1) middle-aged and (2) older. Examples of coping strategies and depression in these groups: (1) there were for both groups no significant differences between the use of active cognitive and active behavioral-type coping strategies, (2) approximately four times as many older women as middle-aged women used the avoidant-type coping strategy, and (3) women with higher education reported lower levels of depression.

3.005. Barton, Sandra L. "Conductive Hearing Loss: Life Satisfaction and Depression in the Aged Adult." **Masters Abstracts** 26: 101. M.S. Texas Woman's University, 1985. UMI Order No. AAD13-30795. DIALOG, Dissertation Abstracts Online.

A Beltone audiometer was used to test hearing in thirty-eight aged females. They were administered the Life Satisfaction Index-A (LSI-A) and the Self-Rating Depression Scale (SDS). Ceruen was removed from the ears of these subjects to increase conductive hearing. There were significant post-treatment differences in LSI-A scores, but not in SDS scores.

3.006. Bianchetti, A., G.B. Frisoni, D. de Leo, O. Zanetti and M. Trabucchi. "Prevalence of Depression in Alzheimer's Disease." Abstract in **Gerontologist** 33, Special Issue 1 (October 1993): 48.

Five depression scales were used to assess twenty-eight Alzheimer's Disease patients. Twenty-nine percent of these patients had major depression. The Geriatric Depression Scale and Zung scale correlated best with the other scales. The Hamilton scale provided the worst correlations and should not be used to assess this population.

3.007. Billig, N. and S.W. Ahmed. "An Assessment of Depression and Dementia Associated with Hip Fracture." Abstract in **Gerontologist** 25, Special Issue (October 1985): 60.

Thirty-three male and female patients, with an average age of 78.5 years, and afflicted with hip fracture, were evaluated at the time of their hospitalization. The General Health Questionnaire and the Zung Depression Scale were two instruments used. Eighteen percent of these patients were depressed when they sustained their hip fracture. Thirty-six percent were cognitively impaired. Approximately 88% did not have a prior psychiatric history.

3.008. Billig, Nathan and Susan Ahmed. "Hip Fractures, Depression and Dementia: A Follow-Up Study." Abstract in **Gerontologist** 26, Special Issue (October 1986): 187A.

3.009. Blankenship, Lana, A. Lynn Snow-Turek and Margaret P. Norris. Physical "Functional Impairment and Depression as Predictors of Verbal Fluency in the Elderly." Abstract in **Gerontologist** 33, Special Issue 1 (October 1993): 285.

3.010. Blixen, C., C. Kippes and S. Bowlin. "Osteoarthritis, Depression and Quality of Life in Older Adults: A Pilot Study." Abstract in **Gerontologist** 36, Special Issue 1 (October 1996): 274.

Fifty community-residing men and women, with a mean age of 70.5 years, and afflicted with moderate to severe pain due to osteoarthritis, were the subjects. They required assistance with activities such as laundry and meal preparation, relying on family and friends. These subjects were extremely satisfied with informal support. They had a relatively low level of depression.

3.011. Breen, Alan, Mark Davis, Carl Eisdorfer and Donna Cohen. "Anxiety and Depression in the Aged with Insomnia." Abstract in **Gerontologist** 20, Special Issue (1980): 70.

3.012. Buckwalter, K., D. Cusack, E. Sidles, D. Wheeler, L. Sayres and G. Blair. "Increasing Communication Ability in Elderly Stroke Patients: A Serendipitous Finding Related to Depression." Abstract in **Gerontologist** 25, Special Issue (October 1985): 5.

Nursing staff used, three times daily, individual therapy programs to increase communication in elderly stroke patients. Improvements in communication and unexpected and dramatic affective changes were observed in these patients. The use with thirty subjects of Goal Attainment Scaling (GAS) confirmed affective and behavioral improvement. Improvement was attributed to increased staff attention and not a specific nursing intervention.

3.013. Burns, R.A., N. Satish and M.T. Abou-Saleh. "Study of Corticotropin and Cortisol Response to CRH Following Dexamethasone in the Elderly with Alzheimer's Disease, Depressive Illness and Normal Subjects." Paper presented at the **1991 Annual Meeting of the Royal College of Psychiatrists, Brighton, United Kingdom, July 2-6, 1991.** DIALOG, Conference Papers Index.

3.014. Carpenter, Brian D., Milton E. Strauss and John S. Kennedy. "Personal History of Depression and Its Appearance in Alzheimer's Disease." **International Journal of Geriatric Psychiatry** 10 (August 1995): 669-678.

The medical charts of two groups of depressed geriatric inpatients were studied. One group had Alzheimer's Disease (AD) and major depression. The other group had major depression without dementia. Most depressed AD patients, unlike depressed patients without dementia, experienced their first episode of depression. Patients with AD may be at risk for the first lifetime occurrence of depression. These patients more frequently demonstrated tearfulness or had a sad face. Patients without AD more frequently expressed thoughts of death or a feeling of worthlessness. Author biographical information. Abstract. 1 figure. 2 tables. Acknowledgments. 55 references.

3.015. Chadwick, Terri Skinner. "The Effect of Stroke on Selected Characteristics of Depression in Elderly Nursing Home Residents." **Dissertation Abstracts International** 53: 4206A. Ph.D. Texas A & M University, 1992. UMI Order No. AAD93-00409. DIALOG, Dissertation Abstracts Online.

Forty-four nursing home residents (twenty-three stroke and twenty-one nonstroke) were interviewed. These persons were designated as: (1) depressed stroke, (2) depressed nonstroke, (3) nondepressed stroke, and (4) nondepressed nonstroke. Examples of findings: (1) 54% of the depressed stroke group reported loss of energy, (2) nondepressed nonstroke subjects tended not to express anxiety, and (3) depressed subjects were more cognitively impaired than nondepressed subjects.

3.016. "Chronic Illness in the Elderly: Doesn't Have to Lead to Depression." **Canadian Doctor** 55 (November-December 1989): 18.

According to a University of Southern California study, limited social support, or stressful situations, are more significantly associated with depression than physical disability. Seventy-three patients, with an average age of seventy-two years, were assessed physically and psychologically. These patients had chronic illnesses such as arthritis and diabetes. Twenty-three (31.5%) of these patients were depressed. These patients, unlike patients who were not depressed, experienced financial difficulties, death of a loved one, being a victim of crime, and other stressful life events.

3.017. Churchill, C.M., J.C.S. Breitner, C.E. Coffey, R. Krishnan, C.B. Nemeroff and C.V. Priolo. "Occult White Matter Disease in Elderly Depressives." Paper presented at the **World Psychiatric Association Regional Symposium, Washington, DC, October 13-16, 1988.** DIALOG, Conference Papers Index.

3.018. Conn, Vicki S., Susan G. Taylor and Phyllis Wiman. "Anxiety, Depression, Quality of Life and Self-Care among Survivors of Myocardial Infarction." **Issues in Mental Health Nursing** 12 (October-December 1991): 321-331.

Forty-seven women and forty-seven men, with a mean age of 73.44 years, were the sample. These men and women had had, one to two years prior to this study, a myocardial infarction (MI). The Profile of Mood States (POMS), Health Behavior Scale (HBS), and Perceived Quality of Life (PQOL) scale were used to assess the sample. Depression significantly predicted quality of life, depression accounting for 49% of the variance in quality of life. Exercise accounted for 21% of the variance in mood variables. Anxiety scores did not predict any self-care behavior score. Author biographical information. Abstract. 1 table. 40 references.

3.019. Decker, Susan D. and Richard Schulz. "Correlates of Life Satisfaction and Depression in Middle-Aged and Elderly Spinal Cord-Injured Persons." **American Journal of Occupational Therapy** 39 (November 1985): 740-745.

One hundred persons, 90% of them male, and with a mean age of fifty-six years, participated in this research. The Social Support Scale, Perceived Control Scale, Life Satisfaction Index-A, and Center for Epidemiological Studies Depression scale were used for assessment purposes. The Statistical Package for the Social Sciences and update were used to analyze data. The degree of well-being of these subjects was slightly lower than that of persons who were not disabled. The subjects who experienced high levels of well-being believed they had high levels of control and higher levels of social support. One tendency: persons with greater disability reported lower levels of well-being. Author biographical information. Abstract. 1 table. Acknowledgments. 22 references.

3.020. desRosiers, Gabriel, John R. Hodges and German Berrios. "The Neuropsychological Differentiation of Patients with Very Mild Alzheimer's Disease and/or Major Depression." **Journal of the American Geriatrics Society** 43 (November 1995): 1256-1263.

3.021. Downer, Patricia. "Characteristics of Depression in Neurologically Impaired and Normal Elderly." **Dissertation Abstracts International** 50: 4215B. Ph.D. University of Arizona, 1989. UMI Order No. AAD90-04968. DIALOG, Dissertation Abstracts Online.

Four groups of elderly individuals were studied: (1) patients with major depression, (2) patients with presumed dementia, Alzheimer's type, (3) patients with Parkinson's Disease, and (4) normal controls. The Hamilton Rating Scale for Depression and Beck Depression Inventory were used to assess these subjects. One finding: the Parkinson's Disease individuals had a significantly higher Hamilton Rating Scale for Depression vegetative factor mean than the individuals with presumed dementia, Alzheimer's type. A second finding: for Parkinson's Disease patients, Parkinson's Disease symptom severity ratings did not correlate more highly with clinician ratings than with self-report ratings of depression. A third finding: patients with presumed dementia, Alzheimer's type, did not, due to loss of insight, report less depression.

3.022. Dunkle, Ruth E. and Celia R. Hooper. "Using Language to Help Depressed Elderly Aphasic Persons." **Social Casework** 64 (November 1983): 539-545.

A speech-language pathologist and a social worker helped a sixty-three-year-old, retired male aphasic who was depressed. Reflective listening, correction of incorrect referents, and reinforcement of the aphasic's progress in language therapy were among the treatment techniques used. Author biographical information. 25 footnotes.

3.023. Emery, Olga B. and Lawrence D. Breslau. "Loss of Memory in Depression and Senile Dementia Alzheimer's Type." Abstract in **Gerontologist** 28, Special Issue (October 1988): 69A.

3.024. Essex, Marilyn J. and Marjorie H. Klein. "The Importance of the Self-Concept and Coping Responses in Explaining Physical Health Status and Depression among Older Women." **Journal of Aging and Health** 1 (August 1989): 327-348.

3.025. Everard, K.M., K.E. Freedland and E.B. Fisher, Jr. "Depression and Social Support Received, Provided and Desired by Older Adults with Congestive Heart Failure." Abstract in **Gerontologist** 36, Special Issue 1 (October 1996): 383.

3.026. Fagerstrom, Ritva. "Correlation between Depression and Vision in Aged Patients Before and After Cataract Operations." **Psychological Reports** 75 (August 1994): 115-125.

3.027. Fernandez, M.E., E. Mutran, D. Reitzes and J. Mossey. "The Role of Social Support and Depression in Recovery from Hip Fracture." Abstract in **Gerontologist** 33, Special Issue 1 (October 1993): 112.

3.028. Fitz, Allan G. and Linda Teri. "Depression, Cognition and Functional Ability in Patients with Alzheimer's Disease." **Journal of the American Geriatrics Society** 42 (February 1994): 186-191.

This study, which compared Alzheimer's Disease (AD) patients with and without depression, took place at the University of Washington, Seattle, Washington. The participants were forty-six AD patients with major depression and forty-five without. The Mattis Dementia Rating Scale (MDRS), Hamilton Depression Rating Scale (HDRS), and Independent Activities of Daily Living (IADL) were used for assessment purposes. The presence and severity of depression significantly predicted functional status, but the degree of association varied, according to the level of cognitive severity. Author biographical information. Abstract. 2 tables. 2 figures. Acknowledgments. 29 references.

3.029. Gierz, Monika and Dilip V. Jeste. "Physical Comorbidity in Elderly Veterans Affairs Patients with Schizophrenia and Depression." **American Journal of Geriatric Psychiatry** 1 (Spring 1993): 165-170.

3.030. Gruetzner, Howard. "Depression and Alzheimer's." Chapter in **Alzheimer's: A Caregiver's Guide and Sourcebook**, Updated and Revised, by Howard Gruetzner, 37-44. New York, NY: John Wiley and Sons, 1992.

3.031. Guerrero, Jose and Marc-Antoine Crocq. "Sleep Disorders in the Elderly: Depression and Post-Traumatic Stress Disorder." **Journal of Psychosomatic Research**, Supplement 1 (1994): 141-150.

3.032. Gugel, Rita Nacken. "The Effects of Group Psychotherapy on Orientation, Memory, Reasoning Ability, Social Involvement and Depression of Brain Damaged and Non-Brain-Damaged Aged Patients Exhibiting Senile Behavior." **Dissertation Abstracts International** 40: 2365B. Ph.D. New York University, 1979. UMI Order No. AAD79-25268. DIALOG, Dissertation Abstracts Online.

3.033. Harkins, S.W., F.M. Bush and D.M. Laskin. "Diagnosis, Symptoms, Depression,

Personality and Age in Chronic Orofacial Pain Patients." Abstract in **Gerontologist** 32, Special Issue 2 (October 1992): 277.

When forty-three young and forty-one old pain patients were studied, the researchers learned there are greater similarities than differences regarding age and this type of patient. Young and old patients had the same frequency of pain in the jaw and head. Furthermore, both groups had the same depression level.

3.034. Harris, M. Jackuelyn, Monika Gierz and James B. Lohr. "Recognition and Treatment of Depression in Alzheimer's Disease." **Geriatrics** 44 (December 1989): 26-30.

The depressed Alzheimer patient may not be able to adequately verbalize the depressed mood. This patient may have masked depression. There will be symptoms of depression, but the patient will not complain about feeling sad. It is important to interview caregivers about patient symptoms. A ninety-three-year-old married man, with a five-year history of Alzheimer's Disease, socially withdrew and shouted at his wife's visitors. Twenty-five mg orally of trazodone at bedtime was sufficient to overcome his irritable behavior, social isolation, and depression. Author biographical information. Abstract. Case report. 20 references.

3.035. Hatcher, Betty J., Jerry D. Durham and Michelle Richey. "Overcoming Stroke-Related Depression." **Journal of Gerontological Nursing** 11, No. 11 (1985): 34-39.

Every minute 1.2 Americans experience a stroke (cerebrovascular accident). However, between 1968 and 1981, the death rate from stroke declined 46%, partly as a result of lifestyle changes. Strokes kill annually, in the U.S., approximately 275,000 persons. An additional 300,000 persons are left with disabilities. Depression, which frequently accompanies stroke, can be treated by a nurse-psychotherapist (NPT). This was illustrated by the case study of a sixty-six-year-old female stroke victim. Treatment was accomplished with the aid of a health history and biopsychosocial assessment, followed by nursing interventions. Author bioghraphical information. 2 photographs. 13 references.

3.036. Herr, Keela A. and Paula R. Mobily. "Chronic Pain and Depression." **Journal of Psychosocial Nursing** 30 (September 1992): 7-12.

Sixty-nine elderly individuals, with at least a three-month history of chronic back pain, were the subjects. These subjects had a mean age of seventy-three, ranging from sixty-four to ninety years. The Beck Depression Inventory (BDI), West Haven-Yale Multidimensional Pain Inventory (WHYMPI), Pain Disability Index (PDI), and Chronic Pain Experience Instrument (CPEI) were some of the assessment instruments used. Nonsteroidal anti-inflammatory drugs, opiate analgesics, antidepressants, heat, cold, massage, relaxation techniques, and cognitive therapies were options in the management of pain and depression. Author biographical information. 1 table. 20 references.

3.037. Holahan, Charles J., Rudolf H. Moos, Carole K. Holahan and Penny L. Brennan. "Social Support, Coping and Depressive Symptoms in a Late-Middle-Aged Sample of Patients Reporting Cardiac Illness." **Health Psychology** 14 (March 1995): 152-163.

3.038. Hooper, C.R. and R.E. Dunhle. "A Team Approach to the Treatment of the Depressed Elderly Aphasic." Abstract in **Gerontologist** 21, Special Issue (October 1981): 125.

3.039. Jacobs, M.R., M.E. Strauss, M.B. Patterson and J.L. Mack. "Differences between Depressed and Non-Depressed Alzheimer's Disease (AD) Patients on the Cerad Behavior Rating Scale for Dementia." Abstract in **Gerontologist** 35, Special Issue 1 (October 1995): 377.

3.040. King, Deborah A., Eric D. Caine, Yeates Conwell and Christopher Cox. "The Neuropsychology of Depression in the Elderly: A Comparative Study of Normal Aging and Alzheimer's Disease." **Journal of Neuropsychiatry and Clinical Neurosciences** (Spring 1991): 163-168.

3.041. King, S. "Depression and Social Support in Older Patients with Chronic Obstructive Pulmonary Disease." Abstract in **Gerontologist** 29, Special Issue (October 1989): 17A.

After the Beck Depression Inventory and Social Provisions Scale were used to assess eighty ambulatory patients, with chronic obstructive pulmonary disease (COPD), the researchers noted that depression in these patients was alarmingly high.

3.042. Kinzie, J. David, Peter Lewinsohn, Robert Maricle and Linda Teri. "The Relationship of Depression to Medical Illness in an Older Community Population." **Comprehensive Psychiatry** 27 (May-June 1986): 241-246.

3.043. Kirshen, A.J., O. Agbayewa, J. Clark, N. Pillay and M. Morse. "Post-Stroke Depression: Is It Really That Frequent?" Abstract in **Gerontologist** 28, Special Issue (October 1988): 283A-284A.

Seven females and four males, who were the victims of a first stroke, were screened with numerous assessment instruments between two and six weeks after the stroke. There was in these patients only one case of depression.

3.044. Kumar, V., W.W. Barker, R. Duara and J. Ruiz. "Positron Emission Tomography (PET) Findings in Depressed Alzheimer's Disease (AD) Patients."

Abstract in **Gerontologist** 32, Special Issue 2 (October 1992): 65.

Positron emission tomography (PET) was used to study glucose metabolism in depressed and nondepressed Alzheimer's Disease (AD) patients. There was no difference, in either group of patients, in the glucose metabolism in frontal and parietal lobes. Depressed AD patients who had mild dementia, and had been ill less than four years, had significantly lower glucose metabolism in the right temporal lobe.

3.045. Kurlowicz, Lenore H. "Perceived Self-Efficacy, Functional Ability and Depressive Symptoms in Older Elective Hip Surgery Patients." Abstract in **Gerontologist** 36, Special Issue 1 (October 1996): 69-70.

3.046. Logsdon, R.G. and L. Teri. "Depression in Alzheimer's Disease: A Comparison of Measures." Abstract in **Gerontologist** 33, Special Issue 1 (October 1993): 312.

Depressed Alzheimer's Disease (AD) patients and their family caregivers were the subjects. The caregivers rated patient depression on each of five widely used depression measures. Surrogate reports were highly consistent internally. Questionnaire measures were highly correlated as were two interview measures.

3.047. Logsdon, R.G. and L. Teri. "The Pleasant Events Schedule AD: Psychometric Properties and a Comparison of Scores of Depressed and Non-Depressed Alzheimer's Disease Patients." Abstract in **Gerontologist** 34, Special Issue 1 (October 1994): 191.

The Pleasant Events Schedule Alzheimer's Disease (PES-AD) was administered to twenty-three nondepressed AD patients and twenty-seven depressed AD patients. This instrument had good reliability, with alphas ranging from .88 to .91. The scores for depressed and nondepressed subjects were significantly different.

3.048. Lyness, J.M., D.A. King, Y. Conwell, C. Cox and E.D. Caine. "Medical Illness as a Predictor of One-Year Outcome in Late-Life Major Depression." Abstract in **Gerontologist** 35, Special Issue 1 (October 1995): 224-225.

3.049. Magni, Guido and Diego de Leo. "Anxiety and Depression in Geriatric and Adult Medical Inpatients: A Comparison." **Psychological Reports** 55 (October 1984): 607-612.

This study which was carried out in Padova, Italy, compared, regarding anxiety and depression, a geriatric population and an adult population. The geriatric population consisted of 178 male and female inpatients with a mean age of 75.6 years. The adult population was made up of 201 male and female inpatients with a mean age of 43.9 years. The subjects were assessed with the Anxiety Factor Score and the Depression

Factor Score. The geriatric subjects had higher depression scores, the adults higher anxiety scores. Women in both groups had significantly higher depression than did men. Geriatric subjects with, for example, central nervous system (CNS) and blood disorders, had significantly higher depression scores than did subjects with other diseases. Author biographical information. Abstract. 4 tables. 19 references.

3.050. McCarten, J., J. Mach, J. Cleary and M. Kuskowski. "Insight into Memory Loss: Correlations with Alzheimer's Disease and Depression." Abstract in **Gerontologist** 29, Special Issue (October 1989): 139A-140A.

3.051. McPherson, Wendy Elizabeth. "Vision Loss and Depression in the Elderly: Are They Related?" **Masters Abstracts** 28: 520. M.S. D'Youville College, 1989. UMI Order No. AAD13-39404. DIALOG, Dissertation Abstracts Online.

Thirty-two male and female persons over sixty-five, and with normal vision, comprised the first group of subjects. Thirty-two male and female persons over sixty-five, and with vision loss, comprised the second group of subjects. All subjects were administered the Beck Depression Inventory. Vision was tested with a Rosenbaum Pocket Screener. Vision loss and depression in the elderly did not appear to be related.

3.052. Molchan, S., J. Hill, R. Martinez, B. Lawlor, A. Mellow, K. Thompson, D. Rubinow, B. Vitiello and T. Sunderland. "CSF Somatostatin and Depressed Mood in Alzheimer's Disease." Abstract in **Gerontologist** 30, Special Issue (October 1990): 215A.

Decreased CSF somatostatin-like immunoreactivity (SLI) is found in individuals with Alzheimer's Disease (AD) and individuals with depression. CSF SLI correlated with depression in sixty AD patients. When CSF SLI levels were increased in AD patients, emotional and intellectual functioning improved in these individuals.

3.053. Montgomery, P.S., A.W. Gardner, P.A. Abbott and M.C. Hochberg. "Depression and Quality of Life in Older Adults with Intermittent Claudication." Abstract in **Gerontologist** 36, Special Issue 1 (October 1996): 275.

3.054. Morro, Beverly C. "Post-Hospital Depression and the Elderly Cardiac Patient." **Social Work in Health Care** 14, No. 2 (1989): 59-66.

3.055. Mossey, J.M. "Depressive Symptomatology in Older Females Following Hip Fracture." Abstract in **Gerontologist** 28, Special Issue (October 1988): 284A.

3.056. Mossey, J.M. "Does the Relationship between Depression and Poor Physical Function Reflect Reality or Reporting Biases?" Abstract in **Gerontologist** 36, Special Issue 1 (October 1996): 207.

3.057. Mossey, Jana M., Kathryn Knott and Rebecka Craik. "The Effects of Persistent Depressive Symptoms on Hip Fracture Recovery." **Journals of Gerontology** 45 (September 1990): M163-M168.

A sample of 196 white females, with a mean age of 78.5 years, and who were recovering from hip fracture surgery, was studied regarding depression. Depression was measured by the Center for Epidemiological Studies Depression (CES-D) scale, at an initial postsurgery interview and two, six, and twelve months later. Depressive symptoms were categorized into four primary groups: (1) persistently low, (2) persistently high, (3) initially high, then low, and (4) initially low, then high. Affective state influenced rather than reflected the recovery process. Author biographical information. Abstract. 4 tables. Acknowledgments. 19 references.

3.058. Nebes, Robert D., Christopher B. Brady and Charles F. Reynolds, III. "Cognitive Slowing in Alzheimer's Disease and Geriatric Depression." **Journals of Gerontology** 47 (September 1992): P331-P336.

Four groups of subjects were tested: (1) Alzheimer patients (twenty-one persons), (2) depressed elderly patients (twenty-four persons), (3) normal young persons (twenty-three), and (4) normal elderly persons (twenty-four). The Hamilton Rating Scale for Depression, Mini-Mental State Exam, Dementia Rating Scale, and Geriatric Depression Scale were administered. These subjects had to determine the number of dots in an array. The larger the array size, the longer the response time for all the subjects. Only in the Alzheimer patients was there a significantly greater reflecting rate of enumeration. This suggested cognitive slowing in only the Alzheimer patients. Author biographical information. Abstract. 3 tables. 1 figure. Acknowledgments. 32 references.

3.059. Neshkes, R. and J. Cummings. "Delusions, Hallucinations and Depression in DAT and MID." Abstract in **Gerontologist** 26, Special Issue (October 1986): 112A.

Thirty patients with Alzheimer Disease (DAT) and fifteen patients with multi-infarct dementia (MID) were studied regarding delusions, hallucinations, and depression. One finding: hallucinations appeared more frequently in the MID patients. A second finding: depression was more common in the MID patients.

3.060. Ogrocki, P.K., M.M. Lee and M.E. Strauss. "Family History of Depression as a Liability for Depressive Syndromes in Alzheimer's Disease." Abstract in **Gerontologist**, 36 Special Issue 1 (October 1996): 249.

Alzheimer's Disease patients with no prior episode of major depression were classified into three groups: (1) major depression (twenty-eight patients), (2) minor depression (twenty-five patients), and (3) no depression (eighty-three patients). Family history regarding dementia and depression were studied. Groups differed regarding family history of depression, but not regarding dementia. Depression in these patients was neurobiological not simply reactive.

3.061. Ouslander, Joseph G. "Physical Illness and Depression in the Elderly." **Journal of the American Geriatrics Society** 30 (September 1982): 593-599.

Numerous physical illnesses are associated with depression in the elderly. Examples include: (1) hypoxia, (2) Addison's Disease, (3) pneumonia, (4) meningitis, (5) tuberculosis, (6) hepatitis, (7) Paget's Disease, (8) stroke, and (9) Parkinson's Disease. Drugs used to treat physical illness can also cause depression in this age group. Examples include: (1) reserpine, (2) meperidene, (3) isoniazid, (4) lidocaine, and (5) cimetidine. Diagnostic studies can be helpful in the evaluation of somatic symptoms in elderly persons who appear to be depressed. A few examples of these tests: (1) electrocardiogram, (2) CAT scan, and (3) electroencephalogram. Author biographical information. 5 tables. 50 references.

3.062. Oxman, Thomas E., Daniel H. Freeman, Eric D. Manheimer and Therese Stukel. "Social Support and Depression After Cardiac Surgery in Elderly Patients." **American Journal of Geriatric Psychiatry** 2 (Fall 1994): 309-323.

3.063. Parmar, H., M.A. Plant, P. Katz and J. Karuza. "Depression, Affect and Attributions: Consequence of Stroke Patients and Caregiver Perspectives." Abstract in **Gerontologist** 31, Special Issue 2 (October 1991): 45.

3.064. Popovich, J., L. Fogg, M. Young, M. Lopez and K. Potempa. "Generalizability of the Beck Depression Inventory to Elderly Stroke Patients and Two Comparison Populations." Abstract in **Gerontologist** 36, Special Issue 1 (October 1996): 113-114.

3.065. Pressman, Peter, John S. Lyons, David B. Larson and James J. Strain. "Religious Belief, Depression and Ambulation Status in Elderly Women with Broken Hips." **American Journal of Psychiatry** 147 (June 1990): 758-760.

Thirty female patients, sixty-five years or older, were the subjects. These patients did not have a psychiatric history nor were they cognitively impaired. All had had hip fractures which had been surgically corrected. These subjects were assessed twice while in hospital. The patients' physical therapist assessed ambulation status. The Geriatric Depression Scale and Index of Religiousness were administered. There was less depression and better ambulation in the more religious patients. Author biographical information. Abstract. 14 references.

3.066. Rabins, Peter V., Karen Harvis and Suzanne Koven. "High Fatality Rates of Late-Life Depression Associated with Cardiovascular Disease." **Journal of Affective Disorders** 9 (September 1985): 165-167.

3.067. Roberts, V.J., F.C. Goldstein, K.P. Girardot, D.C. Strasser and M. Rusin.

"Depressive Symptomatology, Functional Disability and Rehabilitation Outcome in Hospitalized Elderly Patients Following Hip Fracture." Abstract in **Gerontologist** 34, Special Issue 1 (October 1994): 209.

Thirty-eight percent of fifty-eight elderly hospitalized patients, with hip fractures, had elevated Geriatric Depression Scale (GDS) scores, supporting a 1989 study that such patients are at risk for depression.

3.068. Robinson, Robert G. and Sergio E. Starkstein. "Mood Disorders Following Stroke: New Findings and Future Directions." **Journal of Geriatric Psychiatry** 22, No. 1 (1989): 1-15.

3.069. Rovner, B.W., M. Ganguli and S. Bell. "Depression and Disability Associated with Low Vision: The MoVIES Project." Abstract in **Gerontologist** 36, Special Issue 1 (October 1996): 276.

3.070. Roy, Ranjan. "A Psychosocial Perspective on Chronic Pain and Depression in the Elderly." **Social Work in Health Care** 12, No. 2 (1986): 27-36.

3.071. Ruiz, Bertha Alicia Aguirre. "Hip Fracture Recovery in Older Women: The Influence of Self-Efficacy, Depressive Symptoms and State Anxiety." **Dissertation Abstracts International** 54: 1337B. D.N.S. University of California, San Francisco, 1992. UMI Order No. AAD93-19012. DIALOG, Dissertation Abstracts Online.

3.072. Rybarczyk, B. and M. Martelli. "Zung Depression Scores for Stroke Patients Enrolled in a Rehabilitation Program." Abstract in **Gerontologist** 27, Special Issue (October 1987): 191A-192A.

3.073. Salzman, Carl and Richard I. Shader. "Depression in the Elderly. I. Relationship between Depression, Psychologic Defense Mechanisms and Physical Illness." **Journal of the American Geriatrics Society** 26 (June 1978): 253-260.

3.074. Schein, R.L. and C.F. Emery. "Psychosocial and Physiological Predictors of Depression in Older Adults with Chronic Obstructive Pulmonary Disease (COPD)." Abstract in **Gerontologist** 35, Special Issue 1 (October 1995): 224.

3.075. Shmuely-Dulitzki, Yocheved. "The Relationship between Low Vision, Depression and Functional Disability in the Elderly." **Dissertation Abstracts International** 55: 1697A. D.S.W. University of Pennsylvania, 1994. UMI Order No. AAD94-27410. DIALOG, Dissertation Abstracts Online.

Seventy elderly patients at a vision clinic were the subjects. The Geriatric Depression Scale and a visual impairment examination by an ophthalmologist were part of the assessment procedure used. One finding: severity of visual impairment correlated highly with depression. A second finding: severity of depression was the strongest variable associated with functional impairment.

3.076. Sinha, Asha. "Neuropsychological Functioning of the Elderly with Degenerative Brain Disease and Depressive Disorder." **Dissertation Abstracts International** 48: 3145B. Ph.D. University of Alberta, 1987. DIALOG, Dissertation Abstracts Online.

Two groups of elderly persons were the subjects: (1) young elderly, ranging in age from fifty-five to seventy-four years and (2) old elderly, seventy-five years and older. Five assessment measures were used: (1) Luria-Nebraska Neuropsychological Battery, (2) Halstead-Wepman Aphasia Screening Test, (3) Trail Making Test, (4) Wechsler Memory Scale, and (5) Wisconsin Card Sorting Battery. Alzheimer's Disease (AD) and Multi-Infarct Dementia (MID) groups, when compared to normal controls and depressives, performed significantly worse on all neuropsychological measures. None of the scores of the depression group fell in the organic range. Depressed patients, when compared to normal control groups, performed poorly on most neuropsychological measures. The AD and the MID groups did not perform significantly differently. Although the neuropsychological tests differentiated the dementia groups from the depressive group, these tests did not differentiate the two dementia groups.

3.077. Smith, H.D., S.I. Zimmerman, J.R. Hebel, K. Fox and J. Magaziner. "The Importance of Depressive Symptoms through Two Months Following Hip Fracture." Abstract in **Gerontologist** 34, Special Issue 1 (October 1994): 297.

3.078. Smith, L.A., P.A. Parmelee, T.L. Harralson, M. Olderman and J. Hollender. "Depression, Pain and Disability among Persons with Osteoarthritis of the Knee." Abstract in **Gerontologist** 36, Special Issue 1 (October 1996): 71.

In a study of 225 persons with osteoarthritis, 63% of whom were female, one-third of the sample (mean age of 69.7 years) had significant depressive symptomatology. Functional disability, pain, and neuroticism were three variables with which depression was significantly associated.

3.079. Speck, C.E., W.A. Kukull, D.E. Brenner, G. Van Belle, J.D. Bowen, W.C. McCormick, L. Teri, M. Pfanschmidt, J. Thompson and E.B. Larson. "Depression as a Risk Factor for Alzheimer's Disease." Abstract in **Gerontologist** 32, Special Issue (October 1992): 95.

The researchers, controlling for gender and age in this study of 398 individuals, concluded that reported history of depression is not a risk factor for Alzheimer's Disease.

3.080. Terran, Eileen Myrtle. "Story Narratives of Elderly Adults with Alzheimer's Disease or Major Depression." **Dissertation Abstracts International** 53: 4614B. Ph.D. University of California, Los Angeles, 1992. UMI Order No. AAD9302446. DIALOG, Dissertation Abstracts Online.

The subjects in this study consisted of: (1) ten with mild to moderate Alzheimer's Disease (AD), (2) ten with major depression (MD), and (3) ten normal elderly controls. Each subject was asked to look at pictures in a wordless picture book and to tell the story. Each subject's narration was recorded on audio tape, transcribed then analyzed. The AD subjects were not able to: (1) state the main idea of the story, (2) tell a complete story, and (3) state the direct consequences of the theme. All the normal controls and eight of the subjects with MD performed the tasks correctly.

3.081. Thomas, P.A. and M.E. Ochs. "Antidepressant Usage in Stroke Rehabilitation." Abstract in **Gerontologist** 26, Special Issue (October 1986): 257A.

3.082. Thomas, P.A. and M.E. Ochs. "Assessment of Depression and Cognitive Loss During Stroke Rehabilitation." Abstract in **Gerontologist** 25, Special Issue (October 1985): 5.

3.083. Tresch, Donald D., Marshal F. Folstein, Peter V. Rabins and William R. Hazzard. "Prevalence and Significance of Cardiovascular Disease and Hypertension in Elderly Patients with Dementia and Depression." **Journal of the American Geriatrics Society** 33 (August 1985): 530-537.

3.084. Von Dras, D. and W. Lichty. "Diabetes Control and Depression." Abstract in **Gerontologist** 28, Special Issue (October 1988): 201A.

Eighty-two male and female Type I and Type II diabetics, ranging in age from eighteen to seventy years, were the subjects. Glycosylated hemoglobin concentration was used to determine level of diabetes control. The Zung Self-Report Depression Scale was used to measure symptoms of depression. Glycosylated hemoglobin concentration and depression were significantly related. One-third of the sample was depressed. Age was not related to glycosylated hemoglobin concentration or depression scores.

3.085. Waxman, H.M., R. Weinrit, G. McCreary and E.A. Carner. "Somatic Complaints, Chronic Medical Illness and Depression among Community Elderly." Abstract in **Gerontologist** 25, Special Issue (October 1985): 164.

3.086. Wetherell, J.L., M. Gatz and N.L. Pedersen. "Depression as a Risk Factor for Alzheimer's Disease in a Twin Sample." Abstract in **Gerontologist** 36, Special Issue 1 (October 1996): 247.

3.087. Wilkie, F., P. Prinz, M. Vitiello and H. Potter. "Memory Impairments Related to Clinical Depression, Alzheimer's Disease and Age." Abstract in **Gerontologist** 26, Special Issue (October 1986): 144A.

3.088. Williams, Ann K. and Richard Schulz. "Association of Pain and Physical Dependency with Depression in Physically Ill Middle-Aged and Elderly Persons." **Physical Therapy** 68 (August 1988): 1226-1230.

One hundred fourteen middle-aged and elderly persons, afflicted with various physical illnesses, took part in two interviews conducted approximately three months apart. These persons were assessed for depression with the Center for Epidemiological Studies Depression (CES-D) scale. Pain and depression were determined to be highly interactive. A depressed person was quite likely to report higher levels of pain; a person with severe pain was quite likely to become depressed. Depression decreased as social support and age increased. Author biographical information. Abstract. 3 tables. 27 references.

3.089. Williamson, Gail M. and Richard Schulz. "Pain, Activity Restriction and Symptoms of Depression among Community-Residing Elderly Adults." **Journals of Gerontology** 47 (November 1992): P367-P372.

The subjects were 228 outpatients from geriatric clinics at the University of Pittsburgh. These subjects were fifty-five years of age or older and lived in the community. Their mean age was seventy-two years. The Center for Epidemiological Studies Depression (CES-D) scale and Cumulative Illness Rating Scale (CIRS) were used for assessment purposes. This study revealed, in part, that pain and illness contributed significantly to functional disability, and that pain and activity restriction should, for treatment purposes, be targeted simultaneously. Author biographical information. Abstract. 3 tables. Acknowledgments. 30 references.

3.090. Wragg, Robin E. and Dilip V. Jeste. "Overview of Depression and Psychosis in Alzheimer's Disease." **American Journal of Psychiatry** 146 (May 1989): 577-587.

3.091. Zuccala, G., A. Cocchi, R. Bernabei, C. Cattel and P.U. Carbonin. "Perceived Health Status and Functional Ability in Heart Failure: The Impact of Depression." Abstract in **Gerontologist** 33, Special Issue 1 (October 1993): 8.

♦ *Chapter 4* ♦

Institutional and Home Environments

4.001. Abraham, Ivo L., Lillian J. Currie and Marcia M. Neundorfer. "Effects of Cognitive Group Interventions on Depression and Cognition among Elderly Women in Long-Term Care." **Journal of Women and Aging** 4, No. 1 (1992): 5-24.

Fifty-six elderly women, residing in nursing homes, were the sample. These women participated in cognitive-behavioral therapy, focused visual imagery, or educational discussion group sessions. Each treatment group lasted twenty-four weeks. Cognition and depression were assessed four times, ranging from four weeks prior to treatment initiation to four weeks after treatment termination. Cognitive-behavioral and focused visual imagery group therapy produced significant improvement in the cognitive functioning of these subjects. Women in the educational discussion groups, unlike women in the other two groups, did not have statistically significant improvements in their cognition scores. Author biographical information. Abstract. 4 tables. 40 references.

4.002. Ames, David. "Depression among Elderly Residents of Local-Authority Residential Homes: Its Nature and the Efficacy of Intervention." **British Journal of Psychiatry** 156 (May 1990): 667-675.

Assessment of 390 residents of local-authority homes for the elderly revealed that ninety-three residents had depression. These residents, furthermore, had a high rate of physical illness, participated in little social activity, and had infrequent visitors. It was difficult to implement social interventions for these individuals. Twenty-five percent of these residents died within one year. Author biographical information. Abstract. 3 tables. Acknowledgments. 40 references.

4.003. Ames, David. "Depressive Disorders among Elderly People in Long-Term Institutional Care." **Australian and New Zealand Journal of Psychiatry** 27 (September 1993): 379-391.

4.004. Bergeron, Jerilyn Ann. "Outcomes of Short-Term Individual Therapy for Elderly Clients Experiencing Reactive Depression in a Skilled Nursing Facility." **Masters Abstracts** 29: 48. M.S.W. Southern Connecticut State University, 1990.

UMI Order No. AAD13-40218. DIALOG, Dissertation Abstracts Online.

Three elderly clients, temporarily residing in a skilled nursing facility because of short-term rehabilitation, experienced reactive depression. A thirty-day social work intervention was used with these clients. The Beck Depression Inventory, observer checklist, and client perception questionnaire were the assessment instruments administered. At the end of thirty days, a sense of autonomy and enhanced coping skills was restored in all three clients. There was also, in all these individuals, a significant decrease in reactive depression.

4.005. Beuker, B. and G.F. Meunier. "Factors Involved in Depressed Nursing Home Residents: Age, Prescribed Medications, Years Spent in Nursing Home and Depression Scale Scores." Abstract in **Gerontologist** 26, Special Issue (October 1986): 198A.

4.006. Blumstein, T., Ziva Shapira, A. Walter-Ginzburg, Z. Fuchs, P. Ruskin, A. Lusky, Y. Gindin and B. Modan. "The Effect of a Kibbutz Lifestyle on Depressive Symptoms in the Oldest-Old." Abstract in **Gerontologist** 35, Special Issue 1 (October 1995): 30.

4.007. Bohlinger, Evelyn Fitzwater. "The Effects of the Frequency of Pet Therapy Sessions on the Depressive Symptoms of Elderly Nursing Home Residents." **Masters Abstracts** 24: 244. M.S.N. University of Cincinnati, 1985. UMI Order No. AAD13-26395. DIALOG, Dissertation Abstracts Online.

4.008. Buschmann, M.B. and L. Hollinger. "The Relationship between Depression and Touch in Elderly Nursing Home Residents." Abstract in **Gerontologist** 31, Special Issue 2 (October 1991): 45.

After eighty elderly nursing home residents were assessed with a variety of instruments, including the Rosenberg Self-Esteem Scale and the Life Satisfaction Index, it was determined depression was inversely related to self-esteem, life satisfaction, and touch.

4.009. Cataldo, Janine K. "Hardiness and Death Attitudes: Predictors of Depression in the Institutionalized Elderly." **Archives of Psychiatric Nursing** 8 (October 1994): 326-332.

4.010. Chalifoux, Z., M. Boyd, S. Reel and I. Abraham. "The Relationship of Geriatric Depression to Hopelessness, Life Dissatisfaction, Cognition and Medical Status in Nursing Home Residents." Abstract in **Gerontologist** 31, Special Issue 2 (October 1991): 46.

4.011. Christopher, Frima. "The Effects of Group Psychotherapy on Mental Status, Social Adaptation and Depression in Elderly Persons in Long-Term Care with Age-

Onset Organic Brain Syndrome." **Dissertation Abstracts International** 47: 4289A. Ph.D. New York University, 1986. UMI Order No. AAD87-06305. DIALOG, Dissertation Abstracts Online.

4.012. Conn, D.K. and Z. Goldman. "Pattern of Use of Antidepressants in Long-Term Care Facilities for the Elderly." Abstract in **Gerontologist** 32, Special Issue 2 (October 1992): 8.

All patients receiving antidepressants in a geriatric hospital and a home for the aged were the subjects. Approximately 11% of the patients in the hospital and approximately 13% in the home received an antidepressant. Doxepin was the most commonly prescribed antidepressant. Pain, agitation, and insomnia were reasons other than depression for the use of an antidepressant. Thirty-two months was the mean duration for patients receiving antidepressants. Sixty percent of patients had been depressed prior to being institutionalized. Approximately 34% of patients receiving antidepressants were likely to have a history of stroke.

4.013. Davidson, H.S., P.H. Feldman and E.A. Latimer. "Impact of Home Care Reform on Satisfaction with Care and Depressive Symptoms among Frail Elderly Home Care Recipients." Paper presented at the **122nd Annual Meeting and Exhibition of the American Public Health Association, Washington, DC, October 30-November 3, 1994.** DIALOG, Conference Papers Index.

4.014. Dean, Alfred, Bohdan Kolody, Patricia Wood and Georg E. Matt. "The Influence of Living Alone on Depression in Elderly Persons." **Journal of Aging and Health** 4 (February 1992): 3-18.

Structured interviews were used regarding noninstitutionalized men and women, fifty years of age or older, residing in New York State. These subjects were assessed concerning depression, disability, undesirable life events, financial strain, social support from friends, and interaction frequency. Depression was higher in elderly persons who lived alone. Living alone appeared to have a more pronounced effect on men than on women. Marital status by itself was not a risk factor for depression. Author biographical information. Abstract. 2 tables. 1 figure. 34 references.

4.015. Dhooper, Surjit S., Sharon M. Green, Marlene B. Huff and Judy Austin-Murphy. "Efficacy of a Group Approach to Reducing Depression in Nursing Home Elderly Residents." **Journal of Gerontological Social Work** 20, No.3-4 (1993): 87-100.

Sixteen nursing home residents, who were mildly to moderately depressed, were the sample. The mean age of these subjects was 77.6 years; 75% were females. Cardiovascular problems were the primary reason for admission. These subjects, assigned to either a treatment or a control group, were assessed with the Zung Self-

Rating Depression Scale. The treatment group participated in nine hour-long weekly sessions. Reminiscing about childhood memories was one of the session topics. The treatment group also studied problem-solving. At the end of nine weeks, 75% of the treatment group were not depressed. There was less depression in the control group. Author biographical information. Abstract. 3 tables. 26 references. Appendix.

4.016. Dunkle, Ruth E. "The Effect of Elders' Household Contributions on Their Depression." **Journal of Gerontology** 38 (November 1983): 732-737.

Six hundred forty-seven families from twenty-seven counties in Ohio, Pennsylvania, and New York comprised the sample in this study. The elder in these families lived with the caregiver. Spouse, child, or grandchild were caregivers to 410 care recipients. The elder's depression was significantly affected by the elder's contribution to the household. Providing advice, entertainment in the home, giving gifts, and remembering birthdays were examples of contributions by the elder. Depression tended to decrease when the elder's contributions to the household increased. Author biographical information. Abstract. 3 tables. 22 references.

4.017. Elder-Jucker, Patricia Louisa. "Effects of Group Therapy on Self-Esteem, Social Interaction and Depression of Female Residents in a Home for the Aged." **Dissertation Abstracts International** 39: 5514B. Ph.D. Temple University, 1979. UMI Order No. AAD79-10046. DIALOG, Dissertation Abstracts Online.

4.018. Fishman, Martin Scott. "An Investigation of the Relationship between Depression, Choice and Control, and Learned Helplessness among Aged Persons Living in Two Types of Care Facilities." **Dissertation Abstracts International** 45: 3055B. Ph.D. California School of Professional Psychology, Los Angeles, 1984. UMI Order No. AAD84-28837. DIALOG, Dissertation Abstracts Online.

This research, involving 135 elderly persons, ranging in age from sixty-five to ninety-six years, and residing in - low and high - care facilities, revealed that perceived choice and control was significantly related to depression, supporting an extension of the learned helplessness model of depression.

4.019. Foster, Jeffrey, J. Cataldo and M. Solovay. "Prediction of Depression in Nursing Home Patients During the First Year of Hospital Stay." Abstract in **Gerontologist** 29, Special Issue (October 1989): 167A.

A one-year study of depression was conducted regarding 104 newly-admitted patients to a long-term care facility. There were predictor variables associated with depression at the time of admission. Lower life satisfaction was one example. Worsened overall health status was a predictor variable during succeeding months.

4.020. Garfein, Adam. "Computerized Depression Inventory for Older Adults Living in Long-Term Care Facilities." Abstract in **Gerontologist** 25, Special Issue

(October 1985): 1.

The Computerized Depression Inventory for Older Adults Living in Long-Term Care Facilities (CDI-LTC) is a program used to diagnose depression. This program is an application of Lotus 1-2-3 and runs on the IBM PC. CDI-LTC is part of a research project at Cornwall Manor, a retirement community in Pennsylvania. This program is not intended to replace professional clinicians.

4.021. Gentili, A., D.K. Weiner and M. Kuchibhatla. "The Impact of Depression on Self-Rated Health in Nursing Home Residents." Abstract in **Gerontologist** 35, Special Issue 1 (October 1995): 76.

Forty-eight nursing home residents with a mean age of seventy-seven years were the subjects. Interviews with these subjects revealed that depressive symptoms were present in 42% of these individuals. Although self-rated health (SRH) correlated with depressive symptoms, it did not correlate with age or gender.

4.022. Gerety, M.B., C.D. Mulrow, J.W. Williams, Jr., D.R. Royall, D.N. Kanten, C.A. Aguilar and J.E. Cornell. "Identifying Depression in the Nursing Home: Performance of Diagnostic Tools." Abstract in **Gerontologist** 32, Special Issue 2 (October 1992): 36.

Sixty-eight nursing home residents were administered depression scales: (1) the Center for Epidemiological Studies for Depression (CES-D) scale, (2) Geriatric Depression Scale (GDS), (3) Brief Carrol Depression Rating Scale (BCDRS), and (4) Hamilton Depression Rating Scale (HAM-D). The HAM-D was the most specific scale. The CES-D exhibited relatively low sensitivity.

4.023. Giambanco, V., M. Lantz and E. Buchalter. "Side Effects of Antidepressants among Very Old Nursing Home Residents." Abstract in **Gerontologist** 35, Special Issue 1 (October 1995): 135-136.

One hundred twenty residents of a nursing home were surveyed, concerning their treatment with antidepressants during a two-year period. Retrospective chart review was used to assess side effects and adverse drug reactions. Side effects were more common among residents with dementia. Behavioral side effects - aggression, for example - occurred more frequently among residents treated with SSRIs (selective serotonin reuptake inhibitors).

4.024. Giambanco, V., M. Lantz, K. Sridharan, S. Lerner, J. Morgan and D. Epstein. "Antidepressant Therapy and Weight Change in Very Old Nursing Home Residents." Abstract in **Gerontologist** 34, Special Issue 1 (October 1994): 322.

One hundred forty-three residents of two nursing homes received antidepressant therapy for longer than three months. Eighty-four years was the mean age and six months was the mean length of therapy. Female gender and trazodone were two characteristics associated with weight gain. Male gender and fluoxetine were two characteristics associated with weight loss. The mean change for the residents overall was +1.9 pounds.

4.025. Goddard, Perilou and Laura L. Carstensen. "Behavioral Treatment of Chronic Depression in an Elderly Nursing Home Resident." **Clinical Gerontologist** 4 (April 1986): 13-20.

An eighty-six-year-old female nursing home resident was the subject in this research. She was most depressed, especially during mornings and early evenings, when she was inactive and unattended. Her environment was modified to provide her with self-initiated pleasant activities, when she was relatively inactive. She noted a significant positive increase in her mood. Short-term behavioral intervention involved minimal staff time and little financial expenditure. Author biographical information. Abstract. 1 table. 10 references.

4.026. Haight, B. "Depression in the Elderly: Incidence and Correlates in High-Rise Apartments and Nursing Homes." Abstract in **Gerontologist** 32, Special Issue 2 (October 1992): 222.

Registered nurses interviewed, during one-hour interviews, 188 elderly persons relocated to nursing homes and high-rise apartments. These relocated persons were also assessed for depression. None of these subjects were clinically depressed. A significant other and an unsafe environment were two variables which made a significant difference regarding the presence of depression. Subjects with cancer, for example, were more depressed than subjects with arthritis.

4.027. Heston, Leonard L., Judith Garrard, Lukas Makris, Robert L. Kane, Susan Cooper, Trudy Dunham and Daniel Zelterman. "Inadequate Treatment of Depressed Nursing Home Elderly." **Journal of the American Geriatrics Society** 40 (November 1992): 1117-1122.

4.028. Hibel, Doris Ethel. "The Relationship between Reminiscence and Depression among Thirty Selected Institutionalized Aged Males." **Dissertation Abstracts International** 32: 2253B. D.N.SC. Boston University School of Nursing, 1971. UMI Order No. AAD71-26667. DIALOG, Dissertation Abstracts Online.

4.029. Hindle, Janet Suzanne. "The Effects of Loss of Meaningful Relationships and Loss of Control over Decision-Making on Depression and Transient Confusion in the Institutionalized Elderly." **Dissertation Abstracts International** 50: 1853B. Ph.D. New York University, 1988. UMI Order No. AAD89-10634. DIALOG, Dissertation Abstracts Online.

One hundred elderly patients, 76% of them women, residing in nursing homes in

Tennessee, were the subjects. These subjects, ranging in age from sixty-five to ninety-five years, resided from one month to one year in the nursing homes. The effect of depression on confusion was statistically significant. The effect of loss of meaningful relationships and loss of control over decision-making on depression was also statistically significant.

4.030. Holcomb, Ralph John. "Mitigating the Effects of Depression in Elderly Males through Environmental Manipulation: A Field Experiment." **Dissertation Abstracts International** 53: 2985A. Ph.D. University of Minnesota, 1992. 100 UMI Order No. AAD92-33993. DIALOG, Dissertation Abstracts Online.

Elderly male subjects - mean age, seventy-six years - who observed an aviary, in an adult day care setting, had a positive change in depression scores.

4.031. Hollinger-Samson, Nancy. "The Relationship between Staff Empathy and Depression in the Institutionalized Aged." **Dissertation Abstracts International** 56: 2328B. Ph.D. George Washington University, 1995. UMI Order No. AADAA-I9530260. DIALOG, Dissertation Abstracts Online.

Sixty-two residents of six metropolitan Washington, D.C., nursing homes were assessed with the Geriatric Depression Scale and the Barrett-Lennard Relationship Inventory. A significant relationship between perceived - but not resonated or expressed staff empathy - and geriatric depression was confirmed by bivariate and regression analyses.

4.032. Hyer, Lee and Dan G. Blazer. "Depressive Symptoms: Impact and Problems in Long-Term Care Facilities." **International Journal of Behavioral Geriatrics** 1 (Fall 1982): 33-44.

4.033. Hyer, Lee A. and Eileen Hyer. "Clinical Depression in Long-Term Care Facilities: Practical Issues." **Activities, Adaptation and Aging** 6 (Fall 1984): 33-44.

4.034. Igou, J.F. and O.K. Caracci. "Relationship between Locus of Control and Depression in Institutionalized Elderly." Poster paper presented at the **113th Annual Meeting of the American Public Health Association, Washington, DC, November 17-21, 1985.** DIALOG, Conference Papers Index.

4.035. Katz, I.R., M.P. Lawton and P. Parmelee. "Incidence and Stability of Depression and Cognitive Impairment among Institutional Aged." Abstract in **Gerontologist** 28, Special Issue (October 1988): 10A.

4.036. Katz, Ira R., Patricia A. Parmelee and Joel E. Streim. "Depression in Older Patients in Residential Care: Significance of Dysphoria and Dimensional Assessment." **American Journal of Geriatric Psychiatry** 3 (Spring 1995): 161-169.

4.037. Krach, Peg. "Nursing Assessment of Elderly Alcoholics in the Home." **Journal of Gerontological Nursing** 16, No. 11 (1990): 32-38.

It may be more difficult to detect alcohol abuse in the elderly than in younger individuals. Self-neglect or repeated falls, rather than being viewed as indicators of alcohol abuse, may be accepted as signs of aging. It is common for elderly alcoholics to drink in reaction to losses and to be late-onset abusers. Older drinkers are likely to drink daily. The aged lack information concerning what constitutes alcohol abuse. In a study of fifteen individuals, fifty-five years of age or older, and who had been for at least five years diagnosed as alcoholics, 90% of these individuals reported taking psychotropic medications. Fifty percent reported being depressed. Author biographical information. 7 tables. 1 figure. 25 references.

4.038. Lantz, M., V. Giambanco, E. Buchalter, S. Lerner and J. Meyer. "Characteristics of Antidepressant Use in Long-Term Care Facilities." Abstract in **Gerontologist** 36, Special Issue 1 (October 1996): 136.

A survey was conducted of 784 residents of two nursing homes, regarding use, over thirty-six months, of antidepressants. Sixty-five percent of the antidepressants were prescribed for depression. Therapy ranged from three to thirty-six months, with SSRIs (selective serotonin reuptake inhibitors) being the antidepressant most frequently prescribed. The average daily dose utilized of trazodone was 84 mg.

4.039. Lardaro, Theresa Ann. "Progress of Depression in Hospitalized Elderly Relocating to Their Own Home or Institution." **Dissertation Abstracts International** 45: 2619A. ED.D. Columbia University Teachers College, 1984. UMI Order No. AAD84-24237. DIALOG, Dissertation Abstracts On-line.

Fifty elderly persons with cardiovascular disease were patients at an acute care hospital. These patients were awaiting relocation to a nursing home or to their own home. They were assessed for depression within days of admission and within days of being told where they would be relocating. There was no major direct impact on depression scores regardless of where the patients were to be relocated.

4.040. Lesher, Emerson L. "Validation of the Geriatric Depression Scale among Nursing Home Residents." **Clinical Gerontologist** 4 (April 1986): 21-28.

Thirty-nine women and twelve men with a mean age of 82.73 years, and residing at the Philadelphia Geriatric Center, were the subjects. These subjects were assigned to one of three groups: (1) nondepressed, (2) depressive features, and (3) major depression. The Schedule for Affective Disorders and Schizophrenia and the Geriatric Depression Scale were administered orally to these subjects. The Geriatric Depression Scale was a valid measure for depression. This scale correctly identified all the subjects who had major depression. Author biographical information Abstract. 1 table. 17 references.

4.041. Marten, Marie Lucille Cherry. "The Relationship of Level of Depression to Perceived Decision-Making Capabilities of Institutionalized Elderly Women." **Dissertation Abstracts International** 43: 2855B. D.N.SC. Catholic University of America, 1982. UMI Order No. AAD83-02478. DIALOG, Dissertation Abstracts Online.

Forty-eight women between sixty-five and ninety-two years of age, residing in one of four types of institutions, were administered several assessment instruments, including: (1) the Beck Depression Inventory and (2) the Twenty-Four-Item Fact Sheet for Sociodemographic Data. Budgeting money was the most relevant area of decision-making.

4.042. Masand, Prakash S. "Depression in Long-Term Care Facilities." **Geriatrics** 50, Supplement 1 (October 1995): S16-S24.

There are in nursing homes approximately 1.5 million elderly residents. This figure is expected to be 3 million within thirty years. Up to 85% of elderly residents of long-term care settings are depressed. Loss of autonomy, physical illness, and awareness of one's mortality may account for depression in these individuals. The risks of tricyclic antidepressants (TCAs) significantly outweigh their benefits in the treatment of depression in the elderly. Anxiety, dry mouth, and orthostasis are some of the side effects of TCAs. The selective serotonin reuptake inhibitors (SSRIs) are preferable to the TCAs because they are better tolerated and have greater overdose safety. Author biographical information. 4 tables. 1 photograph. 43 references.

4.043. Matteson, Mary Ann. "Group Reminiscing for the Depressed Institutionalized Elderly." Chapter in **Working with the Elderly: Group Process and Techniques**, Second Edition, by Irene Burnside, 287-297. Monterey, CA: Wadsworth Health Sciences Division, 1984.

4.044. Meeks, S., K.P. Walker and L.L. Gibson. "'Negative Symptoms,' Health, Depression and Level of Functioning among Nursing Home Residents." Abstract in **Gerontologist** 30, Special Issue (October 1990): 22A.

4.045. Meyers, B., J. Toner, M. Leung and B. Gurland. "Geriatric Depression in a Long-Term State Psychiatric Hospital." Abstract in **Gerontologist** 28, Special Issue (October 1988): 284A.

4.046. Morrill, Belinda. "Malnutrition in Institutionalized Elderly Male Veterans: The Significance of Learned Helplessness Theory for Understanding the Relationships among Depression, Hopelessness and Reduced Dietary Intake." **Dissertation Abstracts International** 55: 5080B. Ph.D. State University of New York at Albany, 1994. UMI Order No. AADAA-I9504101. DIALOG, Dissertation Abstracts Online.

Individual coping styles of twenty-six institutionalized elderly males significantly predicted eating behaviors and nutritional status in these persons. The coping styles were based on depression, hopelessness, and helplessness. Institutionalization alone did not have much effect on nutritional status.

4.047. Mullins, Larry C. and Elizabeth Dugan. "The Influence of Depression, and Family and Friendship Relations, on Residents' Loneliness in Congregate Housing." **Gerontologist** 30 (June 1990): 377-384.

The subjects studied were 208 elderly persons, residing in ten senior housing apartments in a city in Florida. The degree of loneliness experienced by these persons was related to frequency of and satisfaction with neighbor contact. Reported loneliness was not significantly affected by the existence or nonexistence of, for example, children or neighbors, grandchildren, or siblings. Abstract. Author biographical information. 2 tables. 54 references.

4.048. Nelson, Patricia Beatty. "Social Support, Self-Esteem and Depression in the Institutionalized Elderly." **Issues in Mental Health Nursing** 10 (Winter 1989): 55-68.

Twenty-six men and women, with a mean age of eighty-one years, and residing in a nursing home and a retirement home, were the subjects. The Norbeck Social Support Questionnaire, Rosenberg Self-Esteem Scale, and Geriatric Depression Scale were the assessment instruments. For each subject, the mean number of persons in his or her social network was 9.12, networks ranging in size from one to twenty-four members. Health care providers constituted 8% of the network members. Seventy-one percent of the sample were not depressed. High self-esteem was noted in 56.2% of the sample. Author biographical information. Abstract. 4 tables. 38 references.

4.049. Novaky, Denise. "The Quality of Depression among Nursing Home Elderly." **Dissertation Abstracts International**. 48: 884B. Ph.D. Fairleigh Dickinson University, 1987. UMI Order No. AAD87-12646. DIALOG, Dissertation Abstracts Online.

4.050. Parmelee, P.A., I.R. Katz and M.P. Lawton. "Incidence of Depression in Long-Term Care Settings." Abstract in **Gerontologist** 31, Special Issue 2 (October 1991): 45.

4.051. Parmelee, Patricia A., Ira R. Katz and M. Powell Lawton. "Anxiety and Its Association with Depression among Institutionalized Elderly." **American Journal of Geriatric Psychiatry** 1 (Winter 1993): 46-58.

4.052. Parmelee, Patricia A., Ira R. Katz and M. Powell Lawton. "Depression and Mortality among Institutionalized Aged." **Journals of Gerontology** 47 (January 1992): P3-P10.

4.053. Parmelee, Patricia A., Ira R. Katz and M. Powell Lawton. "The Relation of Pain to Depression among Institutionalized Aged." **Journals of Gerontology** 46 (January 1991): P15-P21.

The sample consisted of 598 residents of a multilevel care facility. This sample, which was 70% female, ranged in age from sixty-one to ninety-nine years. The following were some of the assessment instruments used: (1) McGill Pain Questionnaire, (2) Geriatric Depression Scale, (3) Profile of Mood States, (4) Physical Self-Maintenance Scale, and (5) Cumulative Illness Rating Scale. Subjects classified as major depressives reported more intense pain than subjects classified as minor depressives. More depressed individuals were more likely to report pain. Author biographical information. Abstract. 5 tables. Acknowledgments. 37 references.

4.054. Parmelee, Patricia A., Morton H. Kleban, M. Powell Lawton and Ira R. Katz. "Depression and Cognitive Change among Institutionalized Aged." **Psychology and Aging** 6 (December 1991): 504-511.

4.055. Parmelee, Patricia A., M. Powell Lawton and Ira R. Katz. "Psychometric Properties of the Geriatric Depression Scale among the Institutionalized Aged." **Psychological Assessment** 1 (December 1989): 331-338.

4.056. Phillips, Charles, Catherine Hawes, John Morris, Vince Mor and Brant Fries. "Validating a Mood Scale Based on the Minimum Data Set (MDS) for Nursing Home Residents." Abstract in **Gerontologist** 32, Special Issue 2 (October 1992): 254.

4.057. Power, Cynthia A. and Lawrence T. McCarron. "Treatment of Depression in Persons Residing in Homes for the Aged." **Gerontologist** 15 (April 1975): 132-135.

Fifteen depressed residents, from two homes for the aged in Terre Haute, Indiana, comprised a treatment group, which received fifteen weeks of interactive-contact treatment. The fifteen residents in the control group did not receive this treatment. The Brief Psychiatric Rating Scale and the Zung Self-Report Depression Scale were used to assess each participant in this study. Attentional response getting, verbalization, and resident participation comprised the interactive-contact treatment. The treatment group improved; the control group deteriorated in mental health. Author biographical information. Abstract. 2 figures. 13 references.

4.058. Rein, Ronald R. "The Predictive and Causal Relationship between Social Support and Depression among the Elderly During Their First Month of Admission to Nursing Facilities and the Relationship between These Variables and the Demographic Characteristics of This Population." **Dissertation Abstracts International** 54: 1680B. Ph.D. New School for Social Research, 1992. UMI Order No. AAD93-03515. DIALOG, Dissertation Abstracts Online.

Sixty individuals, fifty-five years or older, who were residents at six facilities in New York, and who were admitted for the first time without discharge plans to nursing facilities, were the subjects. A few of the findings: (1) Catholic and Jewish individuals tended to report greater depression one month after admission; (2) white individuals tended to perceive greater availability of support one month after admission; and (3) older individuals tended to report greater satisfaction upon admission and one month after admission.

4.059. Reker, G.T. "Predictors of Late-Life Depression in Community and Institutional Elderly." Abstract in **Gerontologist** 35, Special Issue 1 (October 1995): 458.

Eighty-seven institutionalized and ninety-nine community-residing adults, with an average age of 77.8 years, were the subjects. Hierarchical multiple regression revealed that personal meaning accounted for most of the variance in depression. Personal meaning and meaningful social contacts offered ways of transcending depression in old age.

4.060. Robison, J.T., S.V. Kasl, C. Mendes de Leon and T.A. Glass. "Housing Type and Social Networks: Effects on Disability and Depression." Abstract in **Gerontologist** 36, Special Issue 1 (October 1996): 381.

Residents of public elderly housing, private elderly housing, and older residents in the community were studied, regarding social, physical, and emotional functioning. A total of 2,812 individuals participated in this study. Community dwellers had stronger social networks than the other two groups of participants. Housing type was related to changes in disability and depression.

4.061. Rovner, Barry W., Pearl S. German, Larry J. Brant, Rebecca Clark, Lynda Burton and Marshal F. Folstein. "Depression and Mortality in Nursing Homes." **Journal of the American Medical Association** 265 (February 27, 1991): 993-996.

A total of 454 elderly men and women, admitted to nursing homes in the Baltimore, Maryland, area, were the subjects in this investigation. These subjects were examined upon admission by a psychiatrist. The Modified Present State Examination and Mini-Mental State Examination were two instruments used to assess these subjects. The **Diagnostic and Statistical Manual of Mental Disorders**, Revised Third Edition, was used to measure depressive symptoms. The Psychogeriatric Dependency Rating Scale was used in interviews of nursing staff and families. There were depressive symptoms in 18.1% of the nursing home residents, major depressive disorder in 12.6%. Nursing home physicians did not recognize the majority of cases. Major depressive disorder increased the likelihood of death by 59%. Author biographical information. Abstract. 3 tables. 37 references.

4.062. Ryden, M., M. Snyder, K. Krichbaum, C. Heine, C. Gross, K. Savik, M. Kaas,

V. Pearson, J. Hanscom, E. Hagens, H. Lee and W. Liao. "Trajectory of Depression in Newly-Admitted Nursing Home Residents." Abstract in **Gerontologist** 36, Special Issue 1 (October 1996): 207.

4.063. Selth, Catherine. "Development of the Behavioral Observation of Depression in the Elderly Scales (The BODES) and Validation of a Visual Analogue Scale of Depression with Elderly Nursing Home Residents." **Dissertation Abstracts International** 52: 2313B. Ph.D. Pennsylvania State University, 1990. UMI Order No. AAD91-17741. DIALOG, Dissertation Abstracts Online.

Nursing aides used the Behavioral Observation of Depression in the Elderly Scales (BODES) for seven days to assess the depressive symptoms of elderly nursing home residents. BODES was compared to the Geriatric Depression Scale (GDS) and the Montgomery-Asberg Depression Rating Scale (MADRS). Results of a Visual Analogue Scale of Depression (VASD) were compared to markers of convergent and known-groups validity. The BODES demonstrated variable test-retest reliability across days and shifts, and consistently poor known-groups validity. The BODES, however, seemed to be worthy of further development.

4.064. Shives, Louise J. "Relocation and the Hospitalized Elderly: Depression as an Adaptive Response to Long-Term Care." **Masters Abstracts** 28: 583. M.S.N. University of Florida College of Nursing, 1989. UMI Order No. AAD13-39589. DIALOG, Dissertation Abstracts Online.

Elderly subjects who were relocated from a hospital to a long-term care facility were the subjects. The first group of subjects were thirty individuals who anticipated a limited stay. The second group of subjects were thirty individuals who anticipated an extended stay. The Geriatric Depression Scale revealed some degree of depression in 83% of all the subjects. Depression increased in both groups, after they were relocated. Levels of depression remained higher for subjects anticipating an extended stay than for subjects anticipating a limited stay.

4.065. Simon, Donald Alan. "Social Support Networks and Depression in Elderly Residents of Nursing Homes." **Dissertation Abstracts International** 53: 1407A. Ph.D. Temple University, 1992. UMI Order No. AAD92-27525. DIALOG, Dissertation Abstracts Online.

Social support questionnaires and a self-rating depression scale were used in a study of fifty elderly nursing home residents. A majority of these residents reported significant levels of depression. Lower levels of depression were related to social integration and a sense of self-worth. Religious participation was related to higher levels of social support.

4.066. Simpson, Sara, Robert Woods and Peter Britton. "Depression and Engagement in a Residential Home for the Elderly." **Behavior Research and Therapy**

19, No. 5 (1981): 435-438.

4.067. Snowdon, John. "Dementia, Depression and Life Satisfaction in Nursing Homes." **International Journal of Geriatric Psychiatry** 1 (July-September 1986): 85-91.

It was possible to test, with the Mental Status Questionnaire (MSQ), 84% of 320 elderly persons admitted, over a two-year period, to nursing homes in Sydney, Australia. Of these persons, 73.5% were cognitively impaired. Most demented patients responded satisfactorily to the depression questionnaire used by C.J. Gilleard and others. Author biographical information. Abstract. 1 table. Acknowledgments. 32 references. 1 appendix.

4.068. Snowdon, John and Neil Donnelly. "A Study of Depression in Nursing Homes." **Journal of Psychiatric Research** 20, No. 4 (1986): 327-333.

4.069. Snyder, Mariah, Muriel Ryden, Kathleen Krichbaum, Christine Heine, Cynthia Gross, Kay Savik, Valinda Pearson, Nora Hagans and Heeyoung Lee. "Impact of Transition to Nursing Home on Cognition, Depression and Morale." Abstract in **Gerontologist** 35, Special Issue 1 (October 1995): 57.

Allowing new residents to nursing homes to have familiar possessions, providing these residents with consistent staff, and spending extra time with new residents may ease the transition to nursing homes. These conclusions were based on a study of thirty-eight elderly individuals - average age of eighty-four years - at three nursing homes.

4.070. Spaid, Wanda M. "Correlates of Depression in Institutionalized and Noninstitutionalized Elderly." Abstract in **Gerontologist** 32, Special Issue 2 (October 1992): 209.

One hundred eight elderly persons residing in four types of residences - nursing homes, group homes, retirement communities, own homes - were interviewed, regarding the relationships between key factors in quality of life. More satisfaction with friends and residence, better health, and fewer aversive social contacts were associated with significantly less depression, regardless of type of residence. Frequency of visits by family and extent of leisure activities were variables not found significant.

4.071. Steely, Mildred Ruby. "Effect of Reminiscence on Self-Esteem and Depression of Institutionalized Elderly." **Masters Abstracts** 30: 100. M.S.N. University of Florida College of Nursing, 1991. UMI Order No. AAD13-45582. DIALOG, Dissertation Abstracts Online.

Thirty-one elderly individuals, residing in long-term care facilities, were the subjects.

These subjects attended for eight weeks either a reminiscence or activity group. Depression and self-esteem were assessed during three test periods. Depression and self-esteem improved during these test periods. Depression and self-esteem in the reminiscence and activity groups was not significantly different.

4.072. Stein, Steven Alan. "Sociometry and Life Review: Improving Affect and Social Support among Elderly Residents of an Assisted-Living Community." **Dissertation Abstracts International** 54: 1246A. Ph.D. Kent State University, 1993. UMI Order No. AAD93-20733. DIALOG, Dissertation Abstracts Online.

The elderly residents of an assisted-living community were the subjects in this study. These subjects took part in a sociometric and life review intervention. Friendliness, sociability, support, and depression were measured. Interviews, photographs, and life review groups were used. Photographs helped the subjects reinforce positive social networking. Beck Depression Inventory mean post-test scores were significantly lower than the pretest scores. This research emphasized the importance among the elderly of shared relationships for reducing depressive symptoms.

4.073. Weiss, Benjamin Z. and Michael J. Salomon. "Combined Intervention: An Eclectic Approach to the Treatment of Social Phobias and Depression in Elderly Long-Term Care Patients." **Clinical Gerontologist** 7 (Fall 1987): 51-62.

Steve G., a sixty-four-year-old male afflicted with chronic schizophrenia; Larry S., a fifty-seven-year-old male with a seizure disorder and chronic alcohol abuse condition; and Bertha T., an eighty-three-year-old woman, widowed for six years, were treated for social phobias and depression, with an eclectic treatment approach. Aspects of psychodynamic, behavior, and cognitive therapy were utilized. Author biographical information. Abstract. 13 References.

4.074. Wofford, A., I. Abraham, S. Holroyd and P. Lichtenberg. "Differentiating between Dimensions of Geriatric Depression in Nursing Home Residents: A Factor Analysis of the Geriatric Depression Scale." Abstract in **Gerontologist** 33, Special Issue 1 (October 1993): 175.

4.075. Wyckoff, Shelley Ann Rice. "The Effects of Housing and Race Upon Depression and Life Satisfaction of Elderly Females." **Dissertation Abstracts International** 45: 1890A. ED.D. George Peabody College for Teachers of Vanderbilt University, 1983. UMI Order No. AAD84-12751. DIALOG, Dissertation Abstracts Online.

Black and white females, sixty-five years of age and older, and residing in Huntsville, Alabama, were the subjects. There were four samples: (1) thirty-one elderly black females residing in planned housing, (2) thirty-one elderly black females residing in unplanned housing, (3) forty-one elderly white females residing in planned housing, and (4) forty-one elderly white females residing in unplanned housing. White females in planned housing experienced more life satisfaction than black females in this type of housing. Black females in unplanned housing experienced less depression than white females in this type of housing.

4.076. Yu, L.C., K.L. Johnson, D.L. Kaltreider, W.E. Craighead and T. Hu. "Relationship between Depression, Functional Status and Cognitive Status among Institutionalized Elderly Women." Paper presented at the **122nd Annual Meeting and Exhibition of the American Public Health Association, Washington, D.C., October 30-November 3, 1994.** DIALOG, Conference Papers Index.

◆ Chapter 5 ◆

Nationality, Race, Ethnicity

5.001. Baker, Barbara Elaine. "A study of the Effects of a Six-Week Counseling Group on Well-Being and Depression Scores and Ratings of Self-Perceived Health of Elderly African-American Participants." **Dissertation Abstracts International** 51: 2125A. Ed.D. Peabody College for Teachers of Vanderbilt University, 1990. UMI order No. AAD90-27441. Dialog, Dissertation Abstracts Online.

5.002. Baker, F.M., David V. Espino, Beverly H. Robinson and Bess Stewart. "Assessing Depressive Symptoms in African-Americans and Mexican-American Elders." **Clinical Gerontologist** 14, No. 1 (1993): 15-29.

5.003. Barargan, M. and A.R. Barbre. "The Effects of Depression, Health Status and Stressful Life Events on Self-Reported Memory Problems Among Aged Blacks." Abstract in **Gerontologist** 33, Special Issue 1 (October 1993): 288.

A total of 1,250 Black elderly subjects were assessed, concerning self-reported memory problems. More than 48.3% reported poor memory and forgetfulness. Hearing problems and a higher level of depression were two significant predictors of self-reported memory problems.

5.004. Bazargan, Mohsen and Verneda P. Hamm-Baugh. "The Relationship Between Chronic Illness and Depression in a Community of Urban Black Elderly Persons." **Journals of Gerontology** 50 (March 1995): S119-S127.

5.005. Bazargan, Mohsen and Baqar A. Husaini. "Depression and Other Correlates of Self-Reported Difficulty in Initiating and Maintaining Sleep among African-American Elderly." Abstract in **Gerontologist** 34, Special Issue 1 (October 1994): 22-23.

Of 998 African-American elderly, 68.3% did not have any difficulty falling asleep. Fewer than 13% reported receiving less than four hours of sleep nightly. African-American elderly women, and those who did not exercise, had significantly more self-reported sleep problems.

5.006. Bekaroglu, Mehmet, N. Uluutku, S. Tanriover and I. Kirpinar. "Depression in an Elderly Population in Turkey." **Acta Psychiatrica Scandinavica** 84 (August 1991): 174-178.

5.007. Bennett, J. and J. Liang. "Income and Depression in the Japanese Elderly." Abstract in **Gerontologist** 34, Special Issue 1 (October 1994): 191-192.

Although lower income was directly associated with greater financial difficulty and poorer health, it was not directly associated with depression in a survey of 2,200 Japanese adults, sixty years of age and older.

5.008. Black, Sandra A., Kyriakos S. Markides and Todd Q. Miller. "Symptom Differences in Depression in Older Mexican-Americans." Abstract in **Gerontologist** 35, Special Issue 1 (October 1995): 41.

The Center for Epidemiological Studies Depression (CES-D) scale was used to determine in 2,734 elderly Mexican-Americans, residing in the community, prevalence rates and symptoms of depression. Prevalence rates for older males were 16% and for older females 31%. Depression was as common in these individuals as in older European-Americans.

5.009. Blanchard, Annette. "The Mexican-American Elderly: Generational Status, Social Supports and Depression." **Dissertation Abstracts International** 54: 3844A. Ph.D. California School of Professional Psychology, Fresno, 1993. UMI Order No. AAD94-08185. DIALOG, Dissertation Abstracts Online.

The Geriatric Depression Scale (GDS) and Center for Epidemiological Studies Depression (CES-D) scale were used to measure depression in 162 Mexican-Americans sixty years of age and over, living in Fresno, California. This research revealed that first-generation Mexican-Americans were more depressed than other generations of Mexican-Americans. No relationship was found between depression and frequency of social support.

5.010. Brown, Diane R., Norweeta G. Milburn and Lawrence E. Gary. "Symptoms of Depression among Older African-Americans: An Analysis of Gender Differences." **Gerontologist** 32 (December 1992): 789-795.

Noninstitutionalized African-American community residents, in a large U.S. eastern city, were studied. There were 148 respondents sixty-five years of age and older. Trained interviewers collected data during face-to-face interviews. The Center for Epidemiological Studies Depression (CES-D) scale was used to measure depression. The Recent Life Change Questionnaire (RLCQ) was used to assess stress. No gender differences, in terms of depressive symptomatology, were found in this sample. Social roles associated with childrearing were suggested as one reason for no gender differences in depressive symptomatology. Abstract. Author biographical information. 2 tables. 33 references.

5.011. Dean, L.L. and B.J. Gurland. "Comparison of Rates of Depression and Dementia among White Ethnic Groups in New York City." Abstract in **Gerontologist** 24, Special Issue (October 1984): 290.

Elderly Italians, Jews, and Anglo-Saxon Protestants, residing in New York, were compared regarding rates of depression and dementia. The rates were not significant for dementia. The rates for depression were: (1) Jews, 19% depressed, (2) Italians, 8% depressed, and (3) Anglo-Saxons, 13% depressed.

5.012. Dubanoski, J., E. Heiby, V. Kameoka, E. Wong and S. Wong. "Prediction of Life Satisfaction and Depression among Asian, Caucasian and Hawaiian Community-Dwelling Elders." Abstract in **Gerontologist** 34, Special Issue (October 1994): 112.

5.013. Elliott, Susan Diane. "Social Support, Depression and the Elderly: A Bicultural Study of African-American and Mexican-American Groups." **Masters Abstracts** 30: 55. M.S.W. California State University, Long Beach, 1991. UMI Order No. AAD13-45858. DIALOG, Dissertation Abstracts Online.

Twenty-five African-American churchgoers and eighteen Mexican-Americans, over the age of fifty-five, were the subjects. All these subjects were interviewed face-to-face. The Lubben Social Network Scale (LSNS) and Geriatric Depression Scale (GDS) were administered. There was in both groups a high level of social support in the majority of subjects. Depression scores in the majority of subjects were within the normal range.

5.014. Gardner, Margaret Ann. "Prevalence and Correlates of Depressive Symptoms in Aged Black Females: Some Preliminary Findings." **Dissertation Abstracts International** 50: 5879B. Ph.D. University of Kentucky, 1989. UMI Order No. AAD89-18927. DIALOG, Dissertation Abstracts Online.

5.015. Hamm, V.P., M. Bazargan, A.R. Barbre and L. Harris. "The Relationship between Chronic Illness and Depression in a Community of Black Elderly." Abstract in **Gerontologist** 32, Special Issue 2 (October 1992): 255.

Depression in 1,022 Black elderly, residing in New Orleans, Louisiana, was highest in those persons who reported kidney, vision, and/or circulation problems.

5.016. Hamm, V.P., L.A. Culpepper, M. Bazargan and A.R. Barbre. "Heart Disease, Lifestyle and Depression in Black Elderly." Abstract in **Gerontologist** 31, Special Issue 2 (October 1991): 146.

5.017. Husaini, B.A., V.A. Cain and R.S. Castor. "Predictors of Depression over Time among the Black Elderly: Gender Differences." Abstract in **Gerontologist** 33, Special Issue 1 (October 1993): 312.

5.018. Husaini, Baqar A. and Stephen T. Moore. "Arthritis Disability, Depression and Life Satisfaction among Black Elderly People." **Health and Social Work** 15 (November 1990): 253-260.

This research took place in Nashville, Tennessee, where 600 Black elderly individuals were the sample. These individuals resided in the community, ranged in age from fifty-five to eighty-five years, and had a median age of seventy. Approximately 61% of the sample had arthritis. The individuals most likely to have arthritis were female, single, and lived alone. These individuals were also more depressed than those who did not have arthritis. Furthermore, lower levels of life satisfaction were associated with arthritis. Author biographical information. Abstract. 1 table. 2 figures. 25 references.

5.019. Husaini, Baqar A., Richard Whitten-Stovall, Robert Castor, Van A. Cain and Jane Worley. "Changes in Depression, Socio-Medical Factors and Coping Behaviors among the Black Elderly." Abstract in **Gerontologist** 30, Special Issue (October 1990): 276A.

5.020. Katterjohn, Aurora Limon. "The Effect That Biculturalism, Religious Orientation, Family Support and Friends' Support Have on the Psychological Well-Being (More Life Satisfaction and Less Depression) in Mexican-American Elderly Women." **Dissertation Abstracts International** 53: 3777B. Ph.D. University of Maryland, 1991. UMI Order No. AAD92-22706. DIALOG, Dissertation Abstracts Online.

Sixty-seven Mexican-American elderly women, from senior citizens centers in Los Angeles, California, were the subjects. These subjects were administered several questionnaires. Family support was the most important resource available. The greater the family support, the higher the psychological well-being and support from friends. Only family support was related to depression. Bicultural women had less depression.

5.021. Kemp, Bryan J., Frederick Staples and Walde Lopez-Aqueres. "Epidemiology of Depression and Dysphoria in an Elderly Hispanic Population: Prevalence and Correlates." **Journal of the American Geriatrics Society** 35 (October 1987): 920-926.

5.022. Kennedy, G.J., H.R. Kelman, C. Thomas, J. Chen, N. Katsnelson and I. Efremova. "The Prevalence of Depressive Symptoms among Older Jewish Community Residents." Abstract in **Gerontologist** 36, Special Issue 1 (October 1996): 251.

When 680 Jews were studied regarding depression, 31% of Jews born in Eastern Europe were depressed compared to 18% of Jews born in the U.S., or elsewhere. Disadvantages in health, disability, education, and income may account for the higher prevalence of depression in the Eastern-European-born Jews.

5.023. Kua, Ee-Heok. "Depressive Disorder in Elderly Chinese People." **Acta Psychiatrica Scandinavica** 81 (April 1990): 386-388.

5.024. Lalive d'Epinay, Christian J. "Depressed Elderly Women in Switzerland: An Example of Testing and of Generating Theories." **Gerontologist** 25 (December 1985): 597- 604.

Elderly people in an urban area, Geneva, and rural area, Central Valais, were the subjects of study for this research in Switzerland. The subjects in Geneva were categorized as: (1) small owners and self-employers; (2) blue-collar workers; (3) white-collar employees; and (4) upper-middle and upper class. The subjects in Central Valais were categorized as: (1) farmers; (2) small owners and craftsmen; (3) blue-collar workers; and (4) middle and upper class. The purpose of this study was to learn about the relationship between sociocultural conditions and patterns of coping. An analysis of life histories was included in the methodology. Depression was more than twice as prevalent in farm women as in farm men. Conflict between traditional and contemporary values accounted for the depression. A theory of culture shock was discussed. Abstract. Author biographical information. 2 tables. 2 figures. 28 references.

5.025. Lam, R.E., J.T. Pacala and S.L. Smith. "Factors Related to Depressive Symptoms in an Elderly Chinese-American Sample." Abstract in **Gerontologist** 36, Special Issue 1 (October 1996): 96.

A high prevalence (12.9%) of clinically significant depressive symptoms were found in elderly Chinese-Americans, who were administered a questionnaire and a Chinese version of the Geriatric Depression Scale. Life satisfaction, social support, and command of the English language were inversely correlated to depressive symptoms.

5.026. Lamm, R.S. "A Transcultural Study of the Association between Depression, Chronic Illness and Health Culture among the Elderly in Three Communities." Abstract in **Gerontologist** 35, Special Issue 1 (October 1995): 42.

5.027. Lawrence, R.H. and R.E. Roberts. "Gender Differences in the Structure of Depressive Symptoms among Elderly Mexican-Americans." Abstract in **Gerontologist** 29, Special Issue (October 1989): 296A.

5.028. Lee, D.J. and O. Gomez. "Depression and Hearing Loss in Hispanic Adults." Abstract in **Gerontologist** 35, Special Issue 1 (October 1995): 376.

The relationship between depression and hearing loss was studied in three groups of Hispanic adults, ranging in age from twenty to seventy-four years: (1) Cuban-Americans, (2) Mexican-Americans, and (3) Puerto Ricans. No association between depression and hearing loss was found in any of these groups.

5.029. Lee, D.J., O. Gomez-Marin and B.L. Lam. "Depressive Symptoms and Visual Acuity in Hispanics." Abstract in **Gerontologist** 36, Special Issue 1 (October 1996): 248.

5.030. Lee, Hing chu B., F.K. Helen and Patrick P.K. Kwong. "Cross-Validation of the Geriatric Depression Scale Short Form in the Hong Kong Elderly." **Bulletin of the Hong Kong Psychological Society** No. 32-33 (January-July 1994): 72-77.

5.031. Lomranz, Jacob, Bernard Lubin, Nitza Eyal and Alik Joffe. "Measuring Depressive Mood in Elderly Israeli: Reliability and Validity of the Depression Adjective Check Lists." **Psychological Reports** 68 (June 1991): 1311-1316.

5.032. Lyu, Shu-Yu. "Predictors and Correlates of Depressive Symptoms and Help-Seeking Behavior among Elder Individuals in Taiwan." **Dissertation Abstracts International** 57: 1447B. Ph.D. University of California, Los Angeles, 1996. UMI Order No. AADAA-I9620712. DIALOG, Dissertation Abstracts Online.

5.033. Madianos, M.G., G. Gournas and C.N. Stefanis. "Depressive Symptoms and Depression among Elderly People in Athens." **Acta Psychiatrica Scandinavica** 86 (October 1992): 320-326.

5.034. Mahard, R. "The CES-D as a Measure of Depressed Mood in the Elderly Puerto Rican Population." Abstract in **Gerontologist** 25, Special Issue (October 1985): 165.

5.035. Mahard, Rita E. "The CES-D as a Measure of Depressive Mood in the Elderly Puerto Rican Population." **Journals of Gerontology** 43 (January 1988): P24-P25.

The Center for Epidemiological Studies Depression (CES-D) scale was administered to sixty elderly Puerto Ricans, 80% of whom were females and resided in New York. Half these subjects were clinically depressed and received treatment at a community mental health center. The other half of these subjects resided in the community and did not receive treatment. The CES-D discriminated strongly between patients and nonpatients. There was no evidence CES-D scores differed by interviewer. Author biographical information. Abstract. 1 table. Acknowledgments. 10 references.

5.036. Mui, A.C. "Geriatric Depression Scale as a Community Screening Instrument for Elderly Chinese Immigrants." Abstract in **Gerontologist** 36, Special Issue 1

(October 1996): 348-349.

Fifty elderly Chinese immigrants to the U.S. - twenty-five men and twenty-five women - participated in the development of a Chinese language version of the Geriatric Depression Scale Long Form (GDS-LF) and Short Form (GDS-SF). Cronbach's alpha for the GDS-LF was .90 and for the GDS-SF .72. Internal consistency was high for the GDS-LF, but not for the GDS-SF.

5.037. Mui, Ada C. "Self-Reported Depressive Symptoms among Black and Hispanic Frail Elders: A Sociocultural Perspective." **Journal of Applied Gerontology** 12 (June 1993): 170-187.

The subjects in this study were 1,272 Black, frail elderly persons and 211 Hispanic, frail elderly persons. Both Black and Hispanic women expressed more depressive symptoms than did men in these two groups. Hispanic elders reported more depressive symptoms than did Black elders. A predictor of depressive symptoms for both groups was less sense of control in life. Fewer formal care providers for Black elders was associated with more depressive symptoms. Author biographical information. Abstract. 5 tables. 44 references.

5.038. Niino, N. "Depressive Symptoms among the Elderly in Japan: Prevalence and Effects of Social Network Support." Abstract in **Gerontologist** 32, Special Issue 2 (October 1992): 138.

The relationship between depressive symptoms and social network support was assessed for eighty-seven institutionalized elderly in Japan. No close friends and dissatisfaction with family relationships significantly correlated with depressive symptoms.

5.039. Niino, N., B.E. Fries and N. Ikegami. "Crossnational Comparison of the Relationship between Depression and Physical Function among Institutionalized Elderly in the U.S.A. and Japan." Abstract in **Gerontologist** 35, Special Issue 1 (October 1995): 218-219.

5.040. Pang, Keum-Young. "A Cross-Cultural Understanding of Depression among Elderly Korean Immigrants: Prevalence, Symptoms and Diagnosis." **Clinical Gerontologist** 15, No. 4 (1995): 3-20.

5.041. Park, Seon Woong. "Personal and Social Resources and Their Effects Upon Depression, Self-Esteem and Status in the Family: A Case Study of the Korean Elderly in Gyeongnam Province, Korea." **Dissertation Abstracts International** 55: 1706A. Ph.D. State University of New York at Buffalo, 1994. UMI Order No. AAD94-29837. DIALOG, Dissertation Abstracts Online.

5.042. Phillips, C.J. and A.S. Henderson. "The Prevalence of Depression among

Australian Nursing Home Residents: Results Using Draft ICD-10 and DSM-III-R Criteria." **Psychological Medicine** 21 (August 1991): 739-748.

5.043. Pilgram, Beverly Oretha. "Depression in Elderly Black Women." **Masters Abstracts** 29: 571. M.S. Memphis State University, 1991. UMI Order No. AAD13-44013. DIALOG, Dissertation Abstracts Online.

5.044. Polich, T.M. and D. Gallagher-Thompson. "Effects of Social Support on Level of Hispanic Caregiver's Depression and Burden Relative to Acculturation." Abstract in **Gerontologist** 32, Special Issue 2 (October 1992): 309-310.

5.045. Polo, A.D. and J. Rodriguez. "Puerto Ricans Elderly and the Suicide Phenomena: A Retrospective Epidemiologic Study, 1980-1990." Paper presented at the **122nd Annual Meeting and Exhibition of the American Public Health Association, Washington, D.C., October 30-November 3, 1994**. DIALOG, Conference Papers Index.

5.046. Rodriguez, Israel. "Depression and Support Systems among the Elderly Widowed: A Comparison of Hispanics and Non-Hispanics Utilizing the Geriatric Depression Scale and the Multidimensional Scale of Perceived Social Support." **Dissertation Abstracts International** 54: 507B. PSY.D. Miami Institute of Psychology of the Caribbean Center for Advanced Studies, 1992. UMI Order No. AAD93-04627. DIALOG, Dissertation Abstracts Online.

Thirty Cuban-American widows and thirty non-Hispanic widows, ranging in age from sixty to eighty years, were the subjects. The Geriatric Depression Scale and the Multidimensional Scale of Perceived Social Support were used to assess both groups of widows. One finding: no significant differences on either scale between the two cultural groups. A second finding: higher levels of social support and less depression for the non-Hispanic group. A third finding: age and living alone were two demographic variables which were not significant.

5.047. Rogers, L. Perkowski, C. Stroup and K. Markides. "Multiple Morbidity, Self-Rated Health and Depression in Middle-Aged and Older Mexican-Americans." Abstract in **Gerontologist** 29, Special Issue (October 1989): 295A.

5.048. Santos-Vilella, Fabiola and Jose Rodriguez. "Comparing the Geriatric Depression Scale and the Beck Depression Inventory in a Puerto Rican Elderly Sample: A Pilot Study." Abstract in **Gerontologist** 36, Special Issue 1 (October 1996): 350.

5.049. Schrijnemaekers, Veron J. and Meindert J. Haveman. "Depression in Frail Dutch Elderly: The Reliability of the Zung Scale." **Clinical Gerontologist** 13, No. 3 (1993): 59-66.

5.050. Spagnoli, Alberto, Giovanni Foresti, Alastair MacDonald and Paul Williams. "Dementia and Depression in Italian Geriatric Institutions." **International Journal of Geriatric Psychiatry** 1 (July September 1986): 15-23.

Elderly residents in geriatric institutions in Milan, Italy, were administered the modified Italian version of the Organic Brain Syndrome (OBS) scale and the Depression Scale of the Comprehensive Assessment and Referral Evaluation (CARE). Dementia or depression or both appeared to affect half the elderly residents. One-third of the residents presented a depressive syndrome, requiring professional intervention. Author biographical information. Abstract. 3 tables. Acknowledgments. 29 references. 1 appendix.

5.051. Stroup-Benham, C.A., J.S. Goodwin and K.S. Markides. "Relationship between Low Blood Pressure and Depression among Elderly Mexican-Americans." Abstract in **Gerontologist** 35, Special Issue 1 (October 1995): 455.

The subjects were 3,050 Mexican-Americans, age sixty-five and older. Subjects who used antihypertensive medication and those without complete CES-D data were excluded. Low diastolic blood pressure (BP) was defined as less than 75 mm Hg, low systolic BP as less than 120 mm Hg. Males and females categorized as hypotensive had higher mean CES-D scores than subjects of either sex who were normotensive.

5.052. Weaver, G.D. and L.E. Gary. "Life Stress and Psychosocial Resources as Predictors of Depressive Symptoms among Black Women." Abstract in **Gerontologist** 30, Special Issue (October 1990): 276A.

5.053. Yang, P.S. and A.C. Mui. "Depression among Elderly Chinese Immigrants: An Exploratory Study." Abstract in **Gerontologist** 36, Special Issue 1 (October 1996): 387.

Health status, living situation, and stressful life events were variables studied, regarding fifty elderly Chinese immigrants. Good health and satisfaction with assistance received from family members indicated little likelihood of depression.

5.054. Yaniz, Manuel Jose. "Geriatric Assessment: Risks of Functional Disability, Dementia and Depression among Hispanic Elderly Living at Home with Caregivers Support." **Dissertation Abstracts International** 51: 4612B. Ph.D. Illinois Institute of Technology, 1990. UMI Order No. AAD91-05337. DIALOG, Dissertation Abstracts Online.

Two groups of individuals were studied: (1) fifty-one frail Hispanic elderly living at home and (2) fifty-one primary caregivers. There was high prevalence of functional impairment among the Hispanic elderly. There were physical and emotional disorders among a large proportion of the caregivers. Dementia in the Hispanic elderly was a predictor of increased involvement and increased distress among their caregivers.

5.055. Yatomi, N. and H. Sugisawa. "A Cross-Cultural Comparison of Depressive Symptoms in American and Japanese Elderly: An Analysis Using Item Response Theory (IRT)." Abstract in **Gerontologist** 36, Special Issue 1 (October 1996): 114-115.

5.056. Zamanian, Kaveh. "Acculturation and Depression in Mexican-American Elderly." **Dissertation Abstracts International** 54: 1118B. Ph.D. California School of Professional Psychology, Fresno, 1992. UMI Order No. AAD93-10580. DIALOG, Dissertation Abstracts Online.

One hundred fifty-nine Mexican-Americans, sixty years of age and older, were interviewed via telephone in Fresno, California. Three examples of research instruments used: (1) Acculturation Rating Scale for Mexican-Americans (ARSMA), (2) Geriatric Depression Scale (GDS), and (3) Center for Epidemiological Studies Depression (CES-D) scale. One example of a finding: low-acculturated individuals scored consistently higher regarding depression than did high-acculturated or bicultural individuals. It may be possible to buffer elderly Mexican-Americans from depression by having these individuals incorporate aspects of the dominant culture.

5.057. Zhang, A.Y., S. Foreman and L.C. Yu. "Determinants of Depression among Elderly Chinese." Abstract in **Gerontologist** 35, Special Issue 1 (October 1995): 41.

Household harmony and filial support decreased depression in elderly Chinese.

Chapter 6

Bereavement, Anxiety, Religiosity

6.001. Allgulander, Christer and Philip W. Lavori. "Causes of Death among 936 Elderly Patients with 'Pure' Anxiety Neurosis in Stockholm County, Sweden and in Patients with Depressive Neurosis or Both Diagnoses." **Comprehensive Psychiatry** 34 (September-October 1993): 299-302.

6.002. Ball, Elaine Marie. "The Relationship between Intrinsic-Extrinsic Religiosity and Post-Bereavement Depression in Elderly Widows." **Masters Abstracts** 33: 170. M.S.N. University of Florida College of Nursing, 1993. UMI Order No. AAD13-58068. DIALOG, Dissertation Abstracts Online.

Thirty-three widows, residing in three retirement communities in Florida, were the subjects. Twenty-five of these widows were over seventy years of age and had been widows for two to five years. This study revealed that intrinsic religious orientation may be a factor in preventing depression, the reason being that widows with more extrinsic religiosity were more depressed than widows with intrinsic religiosity.

6.003. Blazer, Dan, Dana C. Hughes and Nancy Fowler. "Anxiety as an Outcome Symptom of Depression in Elderly and Middle-Aged Adults." **International Journal of Geriatric Psychiatry** 4 (September-October 1989): 273-278.

6.004. Bleiker, Eveline M., Henk M. Van der Ploeg, Jaap Mook and Wim C. Kleijn. "Anxiety, Anger and Depression in Elderly Women." **Psychological Reports** 72 (April 1993): 567-574.

6.005. Breckenridge, James N., Dolores Gallagher, Larry W. Thompson and James Peterson. "Characteristic Depressive Symptoms of Bereaved Elders." **Journal of Gerontology** 41 (November 1986): 163-168.

This study had two groups of individuals, a bereaved group and a control group. The bereaved group consisted of 196 individuals, the control group of 145 individuals. Both groups were administered the Beck Depression Inventory (BDI) and responses categorized as mild, moderate, or severe. The bereaved group was later described, for comparison purposes, as those expecting the death of a spouse and those not expecting the death. Severity - mild, moderate, or severe - of distress on BDI items was compared for the "expected" and "not expected" subjects. The likelihood of self-deprecatory cognitions was no greater among the bereaved group than among the control group. Author biographical information. Abstract. 3 tables. 24 references.

6.006. Charlson, Sheila Fern Ostrow. "Depression in the Elderly: A Comparison Study of Recently Bereaved and Nonbereaved Samples." **Masters Abstracts** 21: 65. M.S. University of Utah, College of Nursing, 1982. UMI Order No. AAD13-18360. DIALOG, Dissertation Abstracts Online.

6.007. Clayton, Paula J., James A. Halikas and William L. Maurice. "The Depression of Widowhood." **British Journal of Psychiatry** 120 (January 1972): 71-77.

6.008. Colenda, Christopher C. and Stanley L. Smith. "Multivariate Modeling of Anxiety and Depression in Community-Dwelling Elderly Persons." **American Journal of Geriatric Psychiatry** 1 (Fall 1993): 327-338.

6.009. Conlin, M.M. and E.B. Fennell. "Depression, Anxiety and Health Locus of Control Orientation in an Out-Patient Elderly Population." Abstract in **Gerontologist** 23, Special Issue (October 1983): 180.

6.010. Crook, Thomas. "Diagnosis and Treatment of Mixed Anxiety-Depression in the Elderly." **Journal of Clinical Psychiatry** 43 (September 1982): 35-43.

6.011. Curl, Anita. "Agitation and the Older Adult." **Journal of Psychosocial Nursing** 27 (December 1989): 12-14.

Agitation can be viewed as inappropriate human activity caused by confusion or not explainable by apparent needs. Sleep disturbances, wandering, and aggression have been attributed to agitation. Agitation, rather than being a disease, is a symptom. Delirium, dementia, depression, and parkinsonism may cause agitation. Haloperidol, chlorpromazine hydrochloride, thiothixene, and diazepam are drugs frequently used in the pharmacological management of agitation. Initially, the lowest effective dose should be administered and the patient carefully monitored. Author biographical information. 8 references.

6.012. Deberry, Stephen, Susan Davis and Kenneth E. Reinhard. "A Comparison of Meditation-Relaxation and Cognitive/Behavioral Techniques for Reducing Anxiety and Depression in a Geriatric Population." **Journal of Geriatric Psychiatry** 22, No. 2 (1989): 231-247.

Fourteen males and eighteen females, ranging in age from sixty-five to seventy-five years, volunteered to participate in this research because of various complaints, including, in part, anxiety, tension, insomnia, and sadness. Seventy-eight percent of these subjects had lost a spouse within the past thirty-three months. The Spielberger Self-Evaluation Questionnaire was used to assess state-trait anxiety; the Beck Depression Inventory was used to assess depression. The subjects were then assigned to one of three groups: (1) relaxation-meditation, (2) cognitive restructuring, or (3) pseudo-treatment control. Each group met twice a week for ten weeks, for forty-five minute sessions. The researchers learned that meditation-relaxation was significantly effective for reducing state anxiety in the anxious subjects. The researchers also learned that constant practice of relaxation-meditation was necessary to maintain low-level state anxiety. Meditation-relaxation was not effective in treating depression. Author biographical information. 2 tables. 2 figures 47 references.

6.013. Elkowitz, Edward B. and Arcilio T. Virginia. "Relationship of Depression to Physical and Psychologic Complaints in the Widowed Elderly." **Journal of the American Geriatrics Society** 28 (November 1980): 507-510.

A study of ten widows and eight widowers, ranging in age from sixty-nine to seventy-four years, revealed, after assessment with the Zung Depression Scale, that the widows expressed more physical and psychological complaints than did the widowers. Author biographical information. Abstract. 2 tables. 2 figures. 15 references.

6.014. Eyde, D.R. and J.A. Rich. "A Family-Based Model for Routine Management of Anxiety, Depression and Paranoia in the Aged." Abstract in **Gerontologist** 20, Special Issue (1980): 101.

6.015. Fernandez, F. "Management of Anxiety/Depressive Syndromes in the Elderly." Paper No. 18B presented at the **1994 Annual Meeting of the American Psychiatric Association, Philadelphia, Pennsylvania, May 21-26, 1994.** DIALOG, Conference Papers Index.

6.016. Frances, Allen and Joseph A. Flaherty. "Elderly Widow Develops Panic Attacks, Followed by Depression." **Hospital and Community Psychiatry** 40 (January 1989): 19-20 and 23.

6.017. Futterman, A., B. Rybarcyk, L. Thompson and D. Gallagher. "Judgment of Marital Satisfaction and Depression among Elderly Widows and Widowers." Abstract in **Gerontologist** 28, Special Issue (October 1988): 115A-116A.

The Locke Wallace Index was used to rate the marital satisfaction of 212 bereaved elders. These elders were also administered three times, over a two-year period, the Beck Depression Inventory, following the loss of their spouse. There were 162 nonbereaved individuals in a comparison group. Increased emotional distress was associated with less marital satisfaction in the nonbereaved group. Increased emotional distress was associated with greater marital satisfaction in the elders.

6.018. Gilewski, Michael J., Norman L. Farberow, Dolores E. Gallagher and Larry W. Thompson. "Interaction of Depression and Bereavement on Mental Health in the Elderly." **Psychology and Aging** 6 (March 1991): 67-75.

6.019. Grimby, A. "Bereavement among Elderly People: Grief Reactions, Post-Bereavement Hallucinations and Quality of Life." **Acta Psychiatrica Scandinavica** 87 (January 1993): 72-80.

6.020. Harrington, Virginia Lee. "Mortality During Bereavement in an Elderly Population." **Dissertation Abstracts International** 47: 1383A. Ph.D. University of Utah, 1986. UMI Order No. AAD86-16083. DIALOG, Dissertation Abstracts Online.

The first group of subjects were 192 elderly persons experiencing spouse bereavement; the second group of subjects were 104 nonbereaved elderly persons. These subjects were matched for age, sex, and socioeconomic status. Six nonbereaved and fifteen bereaved persons died during the first two-and-a-half years of bereavement. Anxiety, depression, dissatisfaction, and living arrangements were some of the variables studied. Advanced age was the only significant factor for mortality. Elderly bereaved persons did not experience an increased risk of mortality.

6.021. Jolley, J. "Alienation and Depression in the Small-Town Widow." Abstract in **Gerontologist**, Special Issue (October 1981): 294.

After alienation and depression were studied in relation to social interaction in small-town widows and married women, it was revealed widows were significantly more alienated and depressed than married women.

6.022. Kant, Gail Lynne. "Problem-Solving as a Moderator of Stress-Related Depression and Anxiety in Older and Middle-Aged Adults." **Dissertation Abstracts International** 54: 1100B. Ph.D. State University of New York at Stony Brook, 1992. UMI Order No. AAD93-09980. DIALOG, Dissertation Abstracts Online.

6.023. Kilcourse, J., D. Gallagher, L. Thompson, E. Tanke and J. Sheikh. "Can Rating Scales Differentiate Depression from Anxiety in Older Adults?" Abstract in **Gerontologist** 28, Special Issue (October 1988): 156A.

6.024. Lynch, Michael S. and B. Jan McCulloch. "The Relationship of Religious Motivation to the Dimensions of Depression among Older Rural Adults." Abstract in **Gerontologist** 32, Special Issue 2 (October 1992): 145.

Intrinsic religious motivation and marital status were significant in predicting certain dimensions of depression in one hundred rural adults, sixty-five years of age and older, and residing in rural Kentucky.

6.025. McCoy, Marsha Jane. "Marital Bond, External Confidant Relationship and the Level of Depression During Conjugal Bereavement among the Elderly." **Masters Abstracts** 21: 345. M.S. University of Utah, College of Nursing, 1983. UMI Order No. AAD13-20464. DIALOG, Dissertation Abstracts Online.

6.026. Morgan, D., M. Neal and P. Carder. "Effects of Positive and Negative Relationships on Depression in Widowhood." Abstract in **Gerontologist** 35, Special Issue 1 (October 1995): 427.

Three cohorts of women, ranging in age from sixty to eighty-five years, were studied through their first, second or third year of widowhood. The number of positive and negative exchanges these women experienced in social networks and level of depression were measured at six-month intervals. Change in the number of negative relationships had one of the largest effects on change in depression.

6.027. Mullins, L. and N. McKenzie. "An Examination of the Loneliness and Depressed Mood among Members of a Widowed Persons Support Group." Abstract in **Gerontologist** 36, Special Issue 1 (October 1996): 378.

6.028. Nelson, Patricia Beatty. "Ethnic Differences in Intrinsic/Extrinsic Religious Orientation and Depression in the Elderly." **Archives of Psychiatric Nursing** 3 (August 1989): 199-204.

Sixty-eight elderly persons, residing in the community, participated in this study. Fifty percent of the sample consisted of blacks, 46.9% whites, and 3.1% Mexican-Americans. These subjects ranged in age from fifty-five to seventy-five years or older. Women comprised 78.1% of the sample, men 21.9%. The Mental Status Questionnaire, Age Universal Religious Orientation Scale, and Geriatric Depression Scale were used to assess these subjects. Chi-square analysis indicated more intrinsic religious behaviors among black elderly, and no significant difference between black and white elderly, regarding extrinsic religious orientation. Black elderly were more depressed than white elderly. Author biographical information. Abstract. 2 tables. 22 references.

6.029. Quintiliani, D., L. Angiullo, K. Kiely, M. Egan and A. Futterman. "Personality Traits as Predictors of Depression at 2, 12 and 30 Months Following Spousal Loss." Abstract in **Gerontologist** 32, Special Issue 2 (October 1992): 254.

Personality traits of 212 bereaved elders were assessed. Neuroticism and extroversion were two examples of predictors of depression at two, twelve, and thirty months following spousal loss, neuroticism predicting depression longitudinally.

6.030. Sallis, James Fleming, Jr. "Altering Arousal Level in the Elderly: Effects on

Anxiety and Depression." **Dissertation Abstracts International** 42: 2548B. Ph.D. Memphis State University, 1981. UMI Order No. AAD81-27491. DIALOG, Dissertation Abstracts Online.

Twenty-four depressed and anxious elderly individuals, residing in the community, volunteered to participate in this research. These individuals used learning-based techniques in ten group sessions, concerning depression management, anxiety management, or a placebo condition. There was improvement in all three groups in systolic blood pressure and diastolic blood pressure between pretest and post-test. There was also improvement on the Beck Depression Inventory. There were no improvements by any group on the Pleasant Events Schedule.

6.031. Siegel, Judith M. and David H. Kuy-Kendall. "Loss, Widowhood and Psychological Distress among the Elderly." **Journal of Consulting and Clinical Psychology** 58 (October 1990): 519-524.

Elderly men were more depressed than elderly women, regarding the loss through death of a family member. Men who had a spouse and belonged to a church/temple experienced less severe depression, due to a loss, than did men who did not have a spouse, and did not belong to a church/temple. One hundred percent of widowers who had a recent nonspousal familial loss, and did not belong to a church/temple, were depressed. Author biographical information. Abstract. 3 tables. 25 references.

6.032. Smith, Walter J. "The Etiology of Depression in a Sample of Elderly Widows: A Research Report." **Journal of Geriatric Psychiatry** 11, No. 1 (1978): 81-83.

6.033. Smith, Walter John. "The Desolation of Dido: Patterns of Depression and Death Anxiety in the Adjustment and Adaptation Behaviors of a Sample of Variably-Aged Widows." **Dissertation Abstracts International** 36: 1933B. SC.D. Boston University, Sargent College of Allied Health Professions, 1975. UMI Order No. AAD75-21016. DIALOG, Dissertation Abstracts Online.

6.034. Stevens, John Phillip. "The Effects of Group Rational Behavior Training on Depression, Death Anxiety, Locus of Control and Irrational Beliefs in the Elderly." **Dissertation Abstracts International** 49: 4563B. Ph.D. California School of Professional Psychology, Fresno, 1987. UMI Order No. AAD88-11771. DIALOG, Dissertation Abstracts Online.

A Rational Behavior Training (RBT) group, questionnaire group, and cultural group were compared regarding elderly subjects. Seven, twice-weekly, one-hour sessions were conducted for the RBT and cultural groups. The outcome measures were: (1)Brief Mental Status Questionnaire, (2) Beck Depression Inventory, (3) Templer/McMordie Death Anxiety Scale, (4) Brown's Revised Locus of Control Scale, and (5) Common Beliefs Survey III. Pretest, post-test, and four-week follow-up mean score ranks were compared. One of the eleven hypotheses was supported: the hypothesis favoring the efficacy of the RBT treatment program over control groups.

6.035. Vetter, Norman J. and Diane Ford. "Anxiety and Depression Scores in Elderly Fallers." **International Journal of Geriatric Psychiatry** 4 (May-June 1989): 159-163.

6.036. Vogel, Connie Higgins. "Anxiety and Depression among the Elderly." **Journal of Gerontological Nursing** 8, No. 4 (1982): 213-216.

Moves to remodeled facilities may increase anxiety in the elderly. Changes in facility personnel may also upset the elderly. Staff and residents may find environmental change stressful. For this reason, social networks should be maintained. Depression may increase as self-worth decreases. Life review helps elderly individuals improve self-esteem. Reality orientation through group interaction will help control delusions and hallucinations. Author biographical information. 12 references. Bibliography (4 items). 1 illustration.

6.037. Weiss, Kenneth J. "Management of Anxiety and Depression Syndromes in the Elderly." **Journal of Clinical Psychiatry** 55, Supplement 2 (1994): 5-12.

♦ Chapter 7 ♦

Suicide

7.001. Achte, Kalle. "Suicidal Tendencies in the Elderly." **Suicide and Life-Threatening Behavior** 18 (Spring 1988): 55-65.

Fatigue, agitation, and fretfulness are some of the indicators of depression in old age. The elderly person who is depressed and presuicidal frequently complains about loss of appetite and about aches and pains. This person may make out a will or may overtly express suicidal thoughts. A senior center can help counter the social isolation, loneliness, and rejection experienced by depressed elderly persons. Author biographical information. 14 references.

7.002. Adamek, M.E. and M.S. Kaplan. "Suicide Research and Practice: Neglect of the Elderly?" Paper presented at the **29th Annual Conference of the American Association of Suicidology, St. Louis, Missouri, April 24-27, 1996**. DIALOG, Conference Papers Index.

7.003. Adamek, M.E., M.S. Kaplan and P. Arbore. "Management of Elderly Suicide: A Survey of Facilities in the United States and Canada." Paper presented at the **122nd Annual Meeting and Exhibition of the American Public Health Association, Washington, DC, October 30-November 3, 1994**. DIALOG, Conference Papers Index.

7.004. Agbayewa, B.O., S. Marion and S. Wiggins. "Elderly Suicide in 1981-1991: Regional Differences." Paper presented at the **45th Annual Meeting of the Canadian Psychiatric Association, Victoria, B.C., September 19-22, 1995**. DIALOG, Conference Papers Index.

7.005. Alexopoulos, George S. "Psychological Autopsy of an Elderly Suicide." **International Journal of Geriatric Psychiatry** 6 (January 1991): 45-50.

7.006. Antai-Otong, Deborah. "Suicide Risk?" **Geriatric Nursing** 11 (September-October 1990): 228-230.

James Lewis is a seventy-six-year-old male afflicted with situational depression and grief reaction. He became a widower several months ago, after the death of his wife to whom he was married for fifty years. He and his wife did not have children. Most of their mutual friends are dead. Ethel Sampson is a seventy-year-old retired lawyer, suffering from psychotic depression associated with lifestyle changes and her daughter's recent injury due to an automobile accident. Since her retirement from law practice approximately a year ago, Ethel Sampson has had few social contacts. Elrod Jones is a sixty-seven-year-old male with lung cancer. He is confronted with changing body image and death. These three individuals - Lewis, Sampson, and Jones - were assessed at a hospital emergency department (ED) and treatment recommended. Author biographical information. 1 photograph. Example of a completed psychosocial assessment form. 4 references.

7.007. Baker, F.M. "Suicide among Ethnic Minority Elderly: A Statistical and Psychosocial Perspective." **Journal of Geriatric Psychiatry** 27, No. 2 (1994): 241-264.

7.008. Battin, Margaret P. "Rational Suicide: How Can We Respond to a Request for Help?" **Crisis** 12 (September 1991): 73-80.

7.009. Bauer, Martin Nicholas. "Understanding and Differentiating Late Adulthood Suicide within a Life-Span Developmental Perspective: Protocol Sentence Analysis of Suicide Notes." **Dissertation Abstracts International** 53: 2535B. Ph.D. American University, 1991. UMI Order No. AAD92-25457. DIALOG, Dissertation Abstracts Online.

7.010. Benson, Roger A. and Donald C. Brodie. "Suicide by Overdoses of Medicine among the Aged." **Journal of the American Geriatrics Society** 23 (July 1975): 304-308.

7.011. Bille-Brahe, Unni, Boge Jensen and Gert Jessen. "Suicide among the Danish Elderly: Now and in Years to Come." **Crisis** 15, No. 1 (1994): 37-43.

7.012. Blazer, Dan G., James R. Bachar and Kenneth G. Manton. "Suicide in Late Life: Review and Commentary." **Journal of the American Geriatrics Society** 34 (July 1986): 519-525.

7.013. Brant, Barbara A. and Nancy J. Osgood. "The Suicidal Patient in Long-Term Care Institutions." **Journal of Gerontological Nursing** 16, No. 2 (1990): 15-18.

Three case examples illustrated the suicidal patient in long-term care institutions: (1) a ninety-one-year-old male, (2) a seventy-eight-year-old male, and (3) a seventy-nine-year-old female. The ninety-one-year-old was married, the seventy-eight-year-old was single, and the seventy-nine-year-old was widowed. All three individuals, in addition to having experienced major physical losses, lost, among other things, home, freedom, and privacy. Multiple moves within the institutions, for the old men and old woman, contributed negatively to their overall bad health. Author biographical information. 4 references.

7.014. Buchanan, D.M. "Suicide and Meaning in Life in the Elderly." Paper presented at the **Silver Anniversary Conference of the American Association of Suicidology, Chicago, Illinois, April 1-4, 1992.** DIALOG, Conference Papers Index.

7.015. Burvill, Peter Walter. "Suicide in the Multiethnic Elderly Population of Australia, 1979-1990." **International Psychogeriatrics** 7 (Summer 1995): 319-333.

7.016. Canada. National Task Force on Suicide in Canada. "Elderly." in **Suicide in Canada: Report of the National Task Force on Suicide in Canada,** by Canada. National Task Force on Suicide in Canada, 32-33. Ottawa, ON: National Health and Welfare Canada, 1987.

Deteriorating physical health; increased incidence of depression and dementia; involuntary retirement; social isolation; loneliness; and inadequate income are major determinants of suicide in Canadians over the age of sixty-five.

7.017. Canada. National Task Force on Suicide in Canada. "Elderly." in **Suicide in Canada: Report of the National Task Force on Suicide in Canada,** by Canada. National Task Force on Suicide in Canada, 52-53. Ottawa, ON: National Health and Welfare Canada, 1987.

Examples of suicide prevention and intervention strategies for elderly individuals in Canada: (1) the education of family physicians; (2) public education; (3) telephone crisis centers; and (4) specialized psychogeriatric units in psychiatric and general hospitals.

7.018. Cattell, H.R. "Elderly Suicide in London: An Analysis of Coroners' Inquests." **International Journal of Geriatric Psychiatry** 3 (October-December 1988): 251-261.

7.019. Cattell, Howard and David J. Jolley. "One Hundred Cases of Suicide in Elderly People." **British Journal of Psychiatry** 166 (April 1995): 451-457.

7.020. Clark, D.C. "Narcissistic Crises of Aging and Elderly Suicide." Paper presented at the **Silver Anniversary Conference of the American Association of Suicidology, Chicago, Illinois, April 1-4, 1992.** DIALOG, Conference Papers Index.

7.021. Clark, D.C. and S.H. Clark. "Psychological Autopsy Study of Elderly Suicide." Paper presented at the **Silver Anniversary Conference of the American Association of Suicidology, Chicago, Illinois, April 1-4, 1992.** DIALOG, Conference

Papers Index.

7.022. Cohen, Laurel Beigler. "Suicide and the Elderly: A Growing Problem of Our Time." **Masters Abstracts** 29: 663. M.P.H. New York Medical College, 1991. UMI Order No. AAD13-44581. DIALOG, Dissertation Abstracts Online.

Spousal death, retirement, and physical decline are some of the reasons for suicide by elderly persons. There will be by 2030 approximately 98 million people over sixty-five years of age. The suicide rate presently for persons over sixty-five is four times the rate of the general population.

7.023. Conwell, Yeates, Melanie Rotenberg and Eric D. Caine. "Completed Suicide at Age 50 and Over." **Journal of the American Geriatrics Society** 38 (June 1990): 640-644.

Completed suicides of men and women fifty years of age and over, in Monroe County, New York, were studied. The 246 suicides occurred during the years 1973 to 1976 and 1984 to June 1987. More suicide victims were widowed with increasing age. Significantly fewer suicide victims were single, separated, or divorced. Physical illness and loss became with increasing age the most common precipitants to suicide. Family discord, alcoholism, and isolation were other stressors associated with completed suicide. Author biographical information. Abstract. 2 tables. Acknowledgments. 37 references.

7.024. de Leo, Diego, Giovanni Carollo and Marirosa Dello-BuoNo. "Lower Suicide Rates Associated with a Tele-Help/Tele-Check Service for the Elderly at Home." **American Journal of Psychiatry** 152 (April 1995): 632-634.

7.025. Dennis, Michael S. and James Lindesay. "Suicide in the Elderly: The United Kingdom Perspective." **International Psychogeriatrics** 7 (Summer 1995): 263-274.

7.026. Devons, Cathryn A.J. "Suicide in the Elderly: How to Identify and Treat Patients at Risk." **Geriatrics** 51 (March 1996): 67-68 and 70-72.

In the U.S. between 1980 and 1992, older persons constituted 13% of the population, but committed 19% of all suicides. White men over age eighty-five had the highest suicide rate in any age group. Approximately 80% of suicides in 1988 by men age sixty-five and over were committed with a firearm. Many elderly persons feel lonely, having experienced various losses, including loss of social status, health, independence, and family. The elderly in nursing homes have lost, in part, home, personal freedom, and privacy. Author biographical information. Abstract. 1 photograph. 3 tables. 14 references.

7.027. **Elderly Suicide**. 28 minutes. 1987? Distributed/Produced by Films for the Humanities and Sciences, Princeton, NJ. Videocassette. DIALOG, A-V Online.

Pain, economic stress, and the fear of total dependence are three reasons for suicide by elderly individuals.

7.028.   Elderly   Suicide   Due   to   Depression.   14.5   minutes.   1994. Distributed/Produced by National Public Radio, Washington, DC. Audiocassette.

7.029.   The   Elderly   Suicide   Rate   on   the   Rise.   5   minutes.   1996. Distributed/Produced by National Public Radio, Washington, DC. Audiocassette.

7.030.   Elderly   Suicide: Who   Would   Miss   Me.   30   minutes.   1987. Distributed/Produced by National Public Radio, Washington, DC. Audiocassette. DIALOG, A-V Online.

7.031. Encyclopedia of Aging. s.v. "Suicide."

In addition to depression, loneliness, social isolation, downward mobility, and physical disability are characteristics associated with older white males who commit suicide.

7.032. Encyclopedia of Gerontology. s.v. "Suicide."

7.033. Encyclopedia of Suicide. s.v. "Old Age and Suicide."

7.034. Etzersdorfer, Elmar and Peter Fischer. "Suicide in the Elderly in Austria." **International Journal of Geriatric Psychiatry** 8 (September 1993): 727-730.

7.035. Farberow, Norman L. and Sharon Y. Moriwaki. "Self-Destructive Crises in the Older Person." **Gerontologist** 15 (August 1975): 333-337.

7.036. Finkel, Sanford I. and Marshall Rosman. "Six Elderly Suicides in a 1-Year Period in a Rural Midwestern Community." **International Psychogeriatrics** 7 (Summer 1995): 221-230.

7.037. Gage, Frances Boland. "Suicide in the Aged." **American Journal of Nursing** 71 (November 1971): 2153-2155.

The case of a seventy-one-year-old woman, who survived a fall from a hotel window, and convalesced in hospital, illustrates the dynamics of suicidal behavior in the over-sixty age group. Author biographical information. 1 illustration. 7 references.

7.038. Glass, J. Conrad, Jr. and Susan E. Reed. "To Live or Die: A Look at Elderly Suicide." **Educational Gerontology** 19, No. 7 (1993): 767-778.

According to the National Center for Health Statistics, there were in the U.S. in 1988

6,363 suicides by Americans over the age of sixty-five. One suicide was that of the renowned psychologist, Bruno Bettelheim, who died at the age of eighty-six in a Silver Spring, Maryland retirement home. Bettelheim's wife had recently died and he had had a debilitating stroke which limited his ability to work. There is also the underreporting of elderly suicides by lesser-known individuals. Some physicians may not report a death as a suicide, in order to protect family members from shame or guilt. Nursing homes do not want negative publicity associated with suicides. Elderly individuals are rarely motivated by anger when they attempt suicide. They do not call for help; they want to die. Four types of clues can help predict the likelihood of a suicide: (1) verbal (example: joking about death); (2) behavioral (example: making funeral plans); (3) situational (example: death of a spouse); and (4) syndromatic (example: isolation). Author biographical information. Abstract. 35 references.

7.039. Gold, Roslyn. "Some Variables Associated with Attitudes towards Suicide among the Aged." **Dissertation Abstracts International** 52: 683A. D.S.W. Yeshiva University, 1990. UMI Order No. AAD91-11416. DIALOG, Dissertation Abstracts Online.

One hundred forty white seniors, fifty-eight male and eighty-two female, ranging in age from sixty to eighty-seven years, were the subjects. The Social Readjustment Rating Scale (SRRS) and the Srole Anomie Scale (SAS) were two of the assessment instruments administered to these subjects. Thoughts of suicide were associated with high levels of life stress and high anomie. This data was used to develop a vulnerability scale which was significantly correlated in these subjects.

7.040. Hamilton, John M. "MSW Students' Attitudes toward Suicide among the Elderly." **Masters Abstracts** 33: 1733. M.S.W. California State University, Long Beach, 1995. UMI Order No. AADAA-I1362294. DIALOG, Dissertation Abstracts Online.

When a questionnaire regarding attitudes toward suicide was administered to M.S.W. students, questionnaire results revealed that students with more experience with older adults had a more permissive attitude concerning suicide among the elderly.

7.041. Harris, J.M., M. Martin and J. McFarlane. "Elderly Suicide Prevention Project in Rural County." Paper presented at the **Silver Anniversary Conference of the American Association of Suicidology, Chicago, Illinois, April 1-4, 1992.** DIALOG, Conference Papers Index.

7.042. Heikkinen, Martti E. and Jouko K. Lonnquist. "Recent Life Events in Elderly Suicide: A Nationwide Study in Finland." **International Psychogeriatrics** 7 (Summer 1995): 287-300.

7.043. Hill, Robert D., Dolores Gallagher, Larry W. Thompson and Ted Ishida. "Hopelessness as a Measure of Suicidal Intent in the Depressed Elderly." **Psychology and Aging** 3 (September 1988): 230-232.

7.044. Hoffman, Patricia Kay. "Effects of Contact with Older Adults on Perceptions of Suicide among the Elderly." **Dissertation Abstracts International** 53: 3775B. Ph.D. Saint Louis University, 1992. UMI Order No. AAD92-33800. DIALOG, Dissertation Abstracts Online.

7.045. Horton-Deutsch, Sara L., David C. Clark and Carol J. Farran. "Chronic Dyspnea and Suicide in Elderly Men." **Hospital and Community Psychiatry** 43 (December 1992): 1198-1203.

7.046. Hu, Yow Hwey. "Elderly Suicide Risk in Family Contexts: A Critique of the Asian Family Care Model." **Journal of Cross-Cultural Gerontology** 10 (September 1995): 199-217.

7.047. Kaplan, Mark S., Margaret E. Adamek and Scott Johnson. "Trends in Firearm Suicide among Older American Males: 1979-1988." **Gerontologist** 34 (February 1994): 59-65.

The suicide rate for elderly men in the U.S. steadily increased between 1979 and 1988. Depression, alcoholism, social isolation, and loneliness were a few of the risk factors associated with suicide in this age group. According to National Center for Health Statistics (NCHS) data, firearms were the method of suicide most likely to be used by males sixty-five years of age and older. In 1988 approximately 80% of suicides by men in this age group were committed with firearms. Author biographical information. Abstract. 1 table. 5 figures. 47 references.

7.048. Kettl, P.A. "Suicide in Spinal Cord Injury and the Elderly." Paper No. 46E presented at the **1994 Annual Meeting of the American Psychiatric Association, Philadelphia, Pennsylvania, May 21-26, 1994.** DIALOG, Conference Papers Index.

7.049. Kirsling, Robert A. "Review of Suicide among Elderly Persons." **Psychological Reports** 59 (October 1986): 359-366.

Depressive complaints, bereavement, retirement, and level of unbearability contribute to the decision by elderly persons to commit suicide. Existing suicide prevention programs for the elderly are ineffective. It is necessary to reduce the stigma of mental health services in order for this age group to seek help. The relaxation of mandatory retirement policies would benefit many older persons because they derive from work self-esteem and purpose in life. Author biographical information. Abstract. 20 references.

7.050. Kivela, Sirkka Liisa. "Relationship between Suicide, Homicide and Accidental Deaths among the Aged in Finland in 1951-1979." **Acta Psychiatrica Scandinavica** 72 (August 1985): 155-160.

7.051. Kraaij, V., A.J.F.M. Kerkhof, M. Van Egmond and R.F.W. Diekstra. "Effect of Trauma on Elderly Depression and Suicide." Paper presented at the **29th Annual Conference of the American Association of Suicidology, St. Louis, Missouri, April 24-27, 1996**. DIALOG, Conference Papers Index.

7.052. Kua, Ee-Heok and Soo-Meng Ko. "A Cross-Cultural Study of Suicide among the Elderly in Singapore." **British Journal of Psychiatry** 160 (April 1992): 558-559.

7.053. Kwan, Alex Y. "Suicide among the Elderly: Hong Kong." **Journal of Applied Gerontology** 7 (June 1988): 248-259.

7.054. Lester, D. and F. Moksony. "The Social Correlates of Suicide in Hungary in the Elderly." **European Psychiatry** 9, No. 6 (1994): 273-274.

7.055. Lester, David. "Household Structure and Suicide in Elderly Japanese Women." **Perceptual and Motor Skills** 77 (December 1993): 1282.

7.056. Lester, David and Margot Tallmer. Editors. **Now I Lay Me Down: Suicide in the Elderly**. Philadelphia, PA: Charles Press, 1993. DIALOG, LCMARC-Books.

7.057. Leviton, Dan. "The Significance of Sexuality as a Deterrent to Suicide among the Aged." **Omega** 4 (Summer 1973): 163-174.

7.058. Li, Guohua. "The Interaction Effect of Bereavement and Sex on the Risk of Suicide in the Elderly: An Historical Cohort Study." **Social Science and Medicine** 40 (March 1995): 825-828.

7.059. Long, Jeanne Redmond. "Suicidal Behaviors in Hospitalized Depressed Elderly Persons in Relation to Loss, Chronic Illness and Pre-Existing Mental Illness." **Masters Abstracts** 34: 723. M.S.N. University of Florida College of Nursing, 1994. UMI Order No. AADAA-I1376548. DIALOG, Dissertation Abstracts Online.

7.060. Lyness, Jeffrey M., Yeates Conwell and J. Craig Nelson. "Suicide Attempts in Elderly Psychiatric Inpatients." **Journal of the American Geriatrics Society** 40 (April 1992): 320-324.

Data pertaining to 168 patients, age sixty years and over, who were discharged from Yale-New Haven Hospital from 1979 to 1984, was examined. Fifteen percent of these patients attempted suicide. Overdose of medication accounted for fourteen attempts.

Examples of other methods: (1) ingestion of iodine (one attempt), (2) strangulation (two attempts), (3) hanging (one attempt), and (4) jumping (one attempt). Eighty percent of attempters had a major depressive syndrome. Major depression with psychotic features was associated with severe attempters. Suicide attempt was not significantly correlated with substance abuse. Author biographical information. Abstract. 2 tables. Acknowledgments. 44 references.

7.061. Manton, Kenneth G., Dan G. Blazer and Max Woodbury. "Suicide in Middle Age and Later Life: Sex and Race Specific Life Table and Cohort Analyses." **Journal of Gerontology** 42 (March 1987): 219-227.

7.062. Marshall, James R. "Changes in Aged White Male Suicide: 1948-1972." **Journal of Gerontology** 33 (September 1978): 763-768.

7.063. McIntosh, John L. "Official U.S. Elderly Suicide Data Bases: Levels, Availability, Omissions." **Omega** 19, No. 4 (1988-1989): 337-350.

7.064. McIntosh, John L. "Suicide Prevention in the Elderly (Age 65-99)." **Suicide and Life-Threatening Behavior** 25 (Spring 1995): 180-192.

7.065. McIntosh, John L., Richard W. Hubbard and John F. Santos. "Suicide among the Elderly: A Review of Issues with Case Studies." **Journal of Gerontological Social Work** 4 (Fall 1981): 63-74.

Elderly persons who attempt suicide usually succeed because they are usually more serious about their intentions than are young persons who try to kill themselves. Elderly persons who do not succeed in committing suicide do not succeed because of poor planning, accidental discovery, or lack of coordination. Several interacting factors, rather than a single factor, account for suicide among the elderly. Self-starvation, seclusion, and refusal of medical advice are examples of life-shortening behaviors found in this age group. Author biographical information. Abstract. 2 figures. 1 reference note. 54 references.

7.066. McIntosh, John L. and John F. Santos. "Suicide among Minority Elderly: A Preliminary Investigation." **Suicide and Life-Threatening Behavior** 11 (Fall 1981): 151-166.

Cause-of-death data from the National Center for Health Statistics, and 1976 population estimates, were used to study suicide by age, sex, and race in Chinese-Americans, Japanese-Americans, Filipino-Americans, and Native-Americans. Suicide rates were highest for elderly Chinese-Americans, Japanese-Americans, and Filipino-Americans. Suicide rates were extremely low for elderly Blacks and Native-Americans. Acculturation was a major factor in explaining the differences in suicide rates. Author biographical information. Abstract. 1 table. 2 figures. 50 references. 4 reference notes.

7.067. McManaman, Kathleen Marie. "Acceptability of Suicide in Severely-Ill Elderly and General Favourability toward Elderly." **Masters Abstracts** 31: 439. M.A. California State University, Long Beach, 1992. UMI Order No. AAD13-49907. DIALOG, Dissertation Abstracts Online.

7.068. Mehta, Dinesh, Poyanil Mathew and Shobhana Mehta. "Suicide Pact in a Depressed Elderly Couple: Case Report." **Journal of the American Geriatrics Society** 26 (March 1978): 136-138.

A seventy-one-year-old man and his wife, age sixty-seven, both afflicted with multiple physical problems, and depression, made a suicide pact. After the wife decided she could not adhere to the suicide pact, she and her husband entered a psychiatric hospital. They received, during their three-week hospital stay, pharmacological and nonpharmacological treatment. They were monitored closely for two years after their discharge from hospital. Author biographical information. Abstract. 5 references.

7.069. Mellick, Ellen, Kathleen C. Buckwalter and Jacqueline M. Stolley. "Suicide among Elderly White Men: Development of a Profile." **Journal of Psychosocial Nursing** 30 (February 1992): 29-34.

Twenty-six variables were compared regarding two groups of elderly white men who committed suicide. The first group were men who died in Maricopa County, Arizona, between January 1, 1971 and June 30, 1975. The second group were men who died in Scott County, Iowa, between January 1, 1983 and December 31, 1987. Mean age, marital status, hobbies, time of death, sleep, and drugs were some of the variables studied. In Arizona, 85.38% of the men used a gun to kill themselves; in Iowa, the figure was 63.87%. This was in both states the most common method of suicide. In Arizona, December, January, February, May, and August were the most common months of death; in Iowa, March, April, September, and October were the most common months of death. Author biographical information. 2 tables. 14 references.

7.070. Miller, Marv. "Geriatric Suicide: The Arizona Study." **Gerontologist** 18 (May 1978): 488-495.

By age eighty-five, male suicides outnumber female suicides by approximately 12 to 1. Men tend to use guns, knives, and ropes to commit suicide; women tend to use drugs, gas, and poisons. These latter methods allow time for an intervention before death. Self-inflicted gunshot wounds accounted for more than 85% of the suicides, by white males age sixty and older, in Arizona, during the years 1970 through 1975. Approximately three times as many suicides as controls did not have a confidant at the time of death. Furthermore, suicides had significantly fewer visits with friends and relatives than did controls. Author biographical information. Abstract. 4 tables. 46 references.

7.071. Miller, Marv. "A Review of the Research on Geriatric Suicide." **Death Education** 3 (Fall 1979): 283-296.

Severe physical illness, mental illness, loss of a spouse, retirement, and alcoholism were associated with the suicides of older white males. Author biographical information. Abstract. 1 table. 29 references.

7.072. Muir, G., K. LeClair and D.W. Molloy. "Suicide." Chapter in **Common Sense Geriatrics**, edited by D.W. Molloy, 148-153. Boston, MA: Blackwell Scientific Publications, 1991.

7.073. Osgood, N.J. "Elderly Suicide: Ethical Issues." Paper presented at the **Silver Anniversary Conference of the American Association of Suicidology, Chicago, Illinois, April 1-4, 1992.** DIALOG, Conference Papers Index.

7.074. Osgood, Nancy J. **Suicide in the Elderly: A Practitioner's Guide to Diagnosis and Mental Health Intervention**. Rockville, MD: Aspen Systems, 1985. DIALOG, LCMARC-Books.

7.075. Osgood, Nancy J., Barbara A. Brant and Aaron A. Lipman. "Patterns of Suicidal Behavior in Long-Term Care Facilities: A Preliminary Report on an Ongoing Study." **Omega** 19, No. 1 (1988-1989): 69-78.

The administrators of 463 long-term care facilities responded to questionnaires, regarding suicidal behavior in their facilities. Overt methods of suicidal behavior - from most common to least common - were: (1) wrist-slashing, (2) shooting, (3) asphyxiation, (4) jumping, and (5) hanging. Intentional life-threatening behavior (ILTB) - from most common to least common - consisted of: (1) refusing to eat or drink, (2) refusing medication, (3) injecting foreign objects/substances, (4) serious accidents, and (5) self-mutilations. Author biographical information. Abstract. 4 tables. Acknowledgments. 9 references.

7.076. Osgood, Nancy J. and John L. McIntosh. **Suicide and the Elderly: An Annotated Bibliography and Review**. New York, NY: Greenwood Press, 1986. DIALOG, LCMARC-Books.

7.077. Pollinger-Haas, Ann and Herbert Hendin. "Suicide among Older People: Projections for the Future." **Suicide and Life-Threatening Behavior** 13 (Fall 1983): 147-154.

7.078. Portnoi, V. "Self-Destructive Behavior as Phenomenon of Depression in the Very Old." Abstract in **Gerontologist** 23, Special Issue (October 1983): 114.

Ten depressed geriatric patients, each one over ninety years of age, exhibited sudden changes in behavior. These patients rejected communication with others and demonstrated a desire to die by starvation. None of these patients had a prior history of depression and no indications of organic brain syndromes. Seven patients recovered after treatment with MOAIs.

7.079. Pratt, Clara C., Vicki L. Schmall, Willetta Wilson and Alida Benthin. "A Model Community Education Program on Depression and Suicide in Later Life." **Gerontologist** 31 (October 1991): 692-695.

A community education workshop, concerning depression and suicide in later life, was developed and evaluated in Oregon. This three-hour multimedia program was created for families, older adults, and service providers. The major goal of this program was recognition and intervention regarding depression and suicidal risk in older persons. "The Final Course," an eighteen-minute slide show was part of the workshop. This slide show was about a woman in her seventies, who decided to commit suicide because of the negative impact on her life of a stroke. The community education program was highly praised by most of the participants. Abstract. Author biographical information. 2 tables. 11 references.

7.080. Rachlis, David. "Suicide and Loss Adjustment in the Aging." **Bulletin of Suicidology** No. 7 (Fall 1970): 23-26.

7.081. Richman, Joseph. "The Lifesaving Function of Humor with the Depressed and Suicidal Elderly." **Gerontologist** 35 (April 1995): 271-273.

Case examples illustrate how laughter or humor provide symptom relief, during therapy with depressed and suicidal elderly patients. Five aspects of therapeutic humor: (1) a positive client-counselor relationship, (2) life affirmation, (3) increase in social cohesion, (4) interactivity, and (5) stress reduction. Laughter by individuals in therapy helps increase a sense of community. Author biographical information. Abstract. 13 references.

7.082. Richman, Joseph. **Preventing Elderly Suicide: Overcoming Personal Despair, Professional Neglect and Social Bias**. New York, NY: Springer, 1993. DIALOG, LCMARC-Books.

7.083. Rifai, A. Hind, Charles F. Reynolds and J.J. Mann. "Biology of Elderly Suicide." **Suicide and Life-Threatening Behavior** 22 (Spring 1992): 48-61.

7.084. Rockett, Ian R. and Gordon S. Smith. "Covert Suicide among Elderly Japanese Females: Questioning Unintentional Drownings." **Social Science and Medicine** 36 (June 1993): 1467-1472.

7.085. Saul, Sidney R. and Shura Saul. "Old People Talk about Suicide: A Discussion about Suicide in a Long-Term Care Facility for Frail and Elderly People." **Omega** 19, No. 3 (1988-1989): 237-251.

7.086. Schaller, S. "Anomie and Self-Efficacy in Elderly People with Suicide Ideation." Paper presented at the **29th Annual Conference of the American Association of Suicidology, St. Louis, Missouri, April 24-27, 1996**. DIALOG, Conference Papers Index.

7.087. Secouler, Lori M. "Physicians' Attitudes toward Elder Suicide." **Dissertation Abstracts International** 53: 4384B. Ph.D. Union Institute, 1992. UMI Order No. AAD92-37723. DIALOG, Dissertation Abstracts Online.

Twenty male physicians were divided into two groups - those with less than 16.5 years in practice and those with more than 16.5 years in practice - and were then interviewed. Both groups were likely to treat elderly and younger patients the same way regarding, for example, hospitalization and counseling. However, physicians with less than 16.5 years in practice tended to be more positive regarding elder suicide.

7.088. Seidel, Geoffrey. "Suicide in the Elderly in Antiquity." **International Journal of Geriatric Psychiatry** 10 (December 1995): 1077-1084.

7.089. Sherman, Karen Grove. **Suicide and the Elderly**. Denton, TX: North Texas State University. Center for Studies in Aging, 1980. DIALOG, NTIS.

7.090. Shimizu, Makoto. "Suicide and Depression in Late Life." Chapter in **Aging and Mental Disorders: International Perspectives**, edited by Manfred Bergener, Kazuo Hasegawa, Sanford I. Finkel and Tsuyoshi Nishimura, 91-101. New York, NY: Springer, 1992.

7.091. Stack, Steven. "Audience Receptiveness, the Media and Aged Suicide, 1968-1980." **Journal of Aging Studies** 4 (Summer 1990): 195-209.

7.092. **Suicide and Abuse: The Vulnerable Elderly**. 120 minutes. 1987. Distributed/Produced by Terra Nova Films, Chicago, IL. Videocassette. DIALOG, A-V Online.

7.093. Tennessee. State Center for Health Statistics. **Suicides among the Young and the Elderly in Tennessee, 1950-1986**. Nashville, TN: Tennessee Department of Health and Environment, 1988. DIALOG, LCMARC-Books.

7.094. Tsai, Neng and Zhi-xu Gao. "Epidemiology of Suicidal Death of the Elderly in Shanghai." **Crisis** 11 (November 1990): 114-119.

7.095. Uncapher, Heather and Patricia Arean. "Use of Medical Services and Suicidal Ideation in Older Medical Patients." Abstract in **Gerontologist** 36, Special Issue 1 (October 1996): 254.

Two hundred sixty-five medical outpatients over fifty-five years of age were interviewed and administered the Beck Depression Inventory (BDI). Billing records regarding their medical visits during a year were studied. When these persons were hopeless and suicidal, they more frequently visited their doctor.

7.096. Vannice, Jeff L. "Cognitive-Existential Characteristics and Their Relationship to Suicide Ideation in College Students and the Elderly." **Dissertation Abstracts International** 52: 536B. Ph.D. Texas Tech University, 1990. UMI Order No. AAD91-15359. DIALOG, Dissertation Abstracts Online.

Two groups at high risk for suicide - 340 college students and forty-two elderly persons - were the subjects. They were administered: (1) the Purpose-in-Life Test, (2) the Reasons for Living Inventory, (3) the Rational Behavior Inventory, (4) the Revised UCLA Loneliness Scale, and (5) the Edwards Social Desirability Scale. The college students, compared to the elderly persons, were more accepting of suicide, had less purpose in life, and were lonely.

7.097. Venkoba-Rao, A. "Suicide in the Elderly: A Report from India." **Crisis** 12 (September 1991): 33-39.

7.098. Witzel, Patricia Ann. "Psychological Characteristics Associated with Risk for Suicidal Ideation among Elderly Women." **Dissertation Abstracts International** 56: 6448B. Ph.D. University of Saskatchewan, 1994. UMI Order No. AADAA-INN00210. DIALOG, Dissertation Abstracts Online.

Seventy-six women, sixty-five years of age and older, were assessed with a number of research instruments, including the Center for Epidemiological Studies Depression Scale and the Rosenberg Self-Esteem Scale. None of these women were clinically depressed. A composite score, based on screening measures scores, was derived for each woman. Thirteen women comprised a high-risk group, thirteen a low-risk group. These twenty-six women participated in an open-ended interview. Content and Chi-square analyses were performed. Suicidal ideation was more common among the high-risk group. The approach to physical health, facing death, and the life-review process were some of the psychological factors which differentiated the two risk groups.

7.099. Zweig, R.A. and G.A. Hinrichsen. "Factors Associated with Suicide Attempts in Depressed Older Adults: A Prospective Study." Abstract in **Gerontologist** 32, Special Issue 2 (October 1992): 254.

Thirteen percent of 127 depressed elderly individuals, who were examined demographically and clinically, attempted suicide over a one-year period. Suicide attempts at follow-up were associated with, in part, patient-reported symptoms of self-reproach and seriousness of prior attempts.

◆ Chapter 8 ◆

Social Aspects

8.001. Adkins, Sandra Jean. "The Influence of Social Support on Depression among the Elderly: A Correlational Study." **Masters Abstracts** 29: 47. M.S.W. California State University, Long Beach, 1990. UMI Order No. AAD13-40886. DIALOG, Dissertation Abstracts Online.

8.002. Alvarez, M.F. and D. Cohen. "Psychosocial Networks, Perceived Health and Depressive Symptoms in the Community Aged." Abstract in **Gerontologist** 24, Special Issue (October 1984): 133.

8.003. Blazer, Dan G. "Impact of Late-Life Depression on the Social Network." **American Journal of Psychiatry** 140 (February 1983): 162-166.

The author studied 331 individuals sixty-five years of age and older. These individuals were a subsample of community-based, elderly individuals in Durham County, North Carolina. The Duke Older Americans Resources and Services Depression Scale was used to assess symptoms of major depressive episode. The Duke Older Americans Resources and Services Community Survey Questionnaire was used to assess activities of daily living. It was determined from the subsample at follow-up, thirty months later, that major depressive disorder was a significant predictor of improvement in social supports. Author biographical information. Abstract. 2 tables. 24 references.

8.004. Burnside, Beverly and Grace Hodgins. "The Role of Education in a Program to Treat Depression in Older Women." **Educational Gerontology** 18, No. 5 (1992): 483-496.

SHOP, the Social Health Outreach Program, established in 1983, is a project of the Mature Women's Network Society of Vancouver, British Columbia. SHOP is a community-based program which views a deficient social environment as the cause of and locus of intervention for depression. Pathogenic social arrangements are viewed as the cause of depression in women. These women are neither sick nor cognitively impaired. Education, retooling, and recycling are the major components of SHOP's thirty-five sessions. Author biographical information. Abstract. 55 references.

8.005. Cardone, Lidia. "Self-Efficacy and Social Support as Mediators of Marital Satisfaction and Depression in the Elderly." **Dissertation Abstracts International** 52: 4461B. Ph.D. Illinois Institute of Technology, 1991. UMI Order No. AAD91-36137. DIALOG, Dissertation Abstracts Online.

8.006. Dean, Alfred, Bohdan Kolody and Patricia Wood. "Effects of Social Support from Various Sources on Depression in Elderly Persons." **Journal of Health and Social Behavior** 31 (June 1990): 148-161.

8.007. Dean, Alfred, Bohdan Kolody, Patricia Wood and Walter M. Ensel. "The Effects of Types of Social Support from Adult Children on Depression in Elderly Persons." **Journal of Community Psychology** 17 (October 1989): 341-355.

8.008. Ensel, Walter M. "'Important' Life Events and Depression among Older Adults: The Role of Psychological and Social Resources." **Journal of Aging and Health** 3 (November 1991): 546-566.

A total of 1,199 individuals, 50% males and 50% females, with an average age of seventy-four, were the sample for this investigation. These individuals resided in upstate New York and participated in in-depth personal interviews. The Center for Epidemiological Studies Depression (CES-D) scale was used to measure depression, the ultimate dependent variable. Health-related events exacerbated depression, resulting from an undesirable life event. There was a significant relationship between non-health related events and depression, when health-related events were disregarded. Psychological resources, rather than social resources, were more effective in predicting subsequent level of depression for individuals experiencing health-related events. Author biographical information. Abstract. Author's Note. 1 figure. 2 tables. Appendix. 7 notes. 45 references.

8.009. Estelle, Michelle Marie Hernandez. "Evaluation of Community-Based Services: Effect of Global Intervention on Reduction of Depression in the Elderly." **Dissertation Abstracts International** 53: 6546B. Ph.D. Fuller Theological Seminary, School of Psychology, 1993. UMI Order No. AAD93-11779. DIALOG, Dissertation Abstracts Online.

The Psychological Distress Scale and the Geriatric Depression Scale were used to assess, in new Elderly Services clients, psychological disturbance at entry into the program, and at a two-month follow-up. Significant improvement was noted during the initial two months of intervention. Subjects without home care assistance, during the test period, improved more than subjects with home care help.

8.010. Fielden, Margaret A. "Depression in Older Adults: Psychological and Psychosocial Approaches." **British Journal of Social Work** 22 (June 1992): 291-307.

Reoccurrence of depression in the elderly is less likely if past and present physical and social experiences are understood. Psychological treatments are then more likely to be successful. Re-establishing close relationships - a confiding relationship in particular - may offer a degree of protection from stress associated with, for example, physical illness. A preventative and multidisciplinary approach is necessary. Author biographical information. Abstract. 55 references.

8.011. Frazier, Cynthia Lee. "Depression, Self-Esteem and Physical Health as a Function of Social Support in the Elderly." **Dissertation Abstracts International** 44: 306B. Ph.D. New School for Social Research, 1982. UMI Order No. AAD83-11282. DIALOG, Dissertation Abstracts Online.

One hundred twenty-six elderly subjects, residing in the community, and ranging in age between sixty and ninety-five years, were studied concerning social support, depression, self-esteem, and physical health. Examples of findings: (1) subjects who overestimated their level of support were less depressed, (2) subjects who underestimated their level of support had lower esteem, (3) actual social support did not significantly influence physical health, (4) married persons had more actual support, and (5) females perceived more social support from significant others.

8.012. Garand, F.A., III, J.G. Haugh, D.L. Mozzicato, B.A. Coogan and A.M. Futterman. "Religiosity, Social Support and Depression over Twelve Months in a Community Sample of Older Adults." Abstract in **Gerontologist** 36, Special Issue 1 (October 1996): 246.

8.013. Goldberg, Evelyn L., Pearl Van Natta and George W. Comstock. "Depressive Symptoms, Social Networks and Social Support of Elderly Women." **American Journal of Epidemiology** 121 (March 1985): 448-456.

A total of 1,144 married women, ranging in age from sixty-five to seventy-five years, and residing in Maryland, were interviewed. The interviews were conducted between February and August 1979. The low end of the socioeconomic scale, small social networks, and heterogeneous social networks were associated with a high level of depressive symptoms. Author biographical information. Abstract. 4 tables. 36 references.

8.014. Gorey, Kevin M. and Arthur G. Cryns. "Group Work as Interventive Modality with the Older Depressed Client: A Meta-Analytic Review." **Journal of Gerontological Social Work** 16, No. 1-2 (1991): 137-157.

Nineteen empirical studies, concerning group work intervention and depressed adults sixty-five years of age and older, were analyzed. Due to group work there was 42% positive change in the affective states of the elderly adults, most of the change apparently due to factors outside the control of the group worker. Group work was most effective for depressed elderly who lived alone. Small client groups and brief interventions constituted the most effective format. Author biographical information. Abstract. 3 tables. 35 references.

8.015. Grant, Igor, Thomas L. Patterson and Joel Yager. "Social Supports in Relation to Physical Health and Symptoms of Depression in the Elderly." **American Journal of Psychiatry** 145 (October 1988): 1254-1258.

Eighty-three women and thirty-five men, living independently in the San Diego, California area, and ranging in age from sixty-five to ninety-two years, were the subjects. These individuals were interviewed in their homes every four months for two years. The Social Support Questionnaire was administered three times during this study. Subjects who had more symptoms of depression had fewer emotionally satisfying supports from relatives. Subjects who had physical illnesses had more supports from relatives. Fewer key supports may contribute to dysphoria. Physical illnesses may mobilize meaningful support. Author biographical information. Abstract. 3 tables. 33 references.

8.016. Greenspan, Monte Lance. "The Relationship between the Level of Social Support and Depression among the Frail Elderly." **Masters Abstracts** 27: 42. M.S.W. California State University, Long Beach, 1988. UMI Order No. AAD13-33828. DIALOG, Dissertation Abstracts Online.

Client records, face-to-face interviews, and the Beck Depression Inventory were used to assess twenty-three frail elderly clients, participants in the Multipurpose Senior Services Program. No relationship was found between level of social support and depression.

8.017. Hays, J.C., L.R. Landerman, L.K. George, E.P. Flint, H.G. Koenig and D.G. Blazer. "Through a Glass Darkly: Nuance in the Relationship of Social Support and Depression." Abstract in **Gerontologist** 36, Special Issue 1 (October 1996): 380.

8.018. Konnert, C. and B. Crowhurst. "A Longitudinal Study of Perceived Control, Social Support and Depression in Relocating Elderly." Abstract in **Gerontologist** 36, Special Issue 1 (October 1996): 383.

Sixty individuals with a mean age of eighty-four years were interviewed prior to being relocated. Approximately half of these individuals were available for interviews six and nineteen weeks after being relocated. Perceptions of control and support contributed to well-being at the time of relocation. These influences, however, diminished with time.

8.019. Krames, Lester, Rebecca England and Gordon L. Flett. "The Role of Masculinity and Femininity in Depression and Social Satisfaction in Elderly Females." **Sex Roles** 19 (December 1988): 713-721.

8.020. Looman, W.J., D.M. Bass and L.S. Noelker. "Depression and the Support Networks of the Elderly." Abstract in **Gerontologist** 35, Special Issue 1 (October 1995): 184-185.

8.021. Milanesi, L.C., B.N. Colby and S.I. Mishra. "Within-Person and Situational Factors Contributing to Social Conflict, Social Support and Depression." Abstract in **Gerontologist** 30, Special Issue (October 1990): 311A.

8.022. Milanesi, L.C., R.O. Schmidt, J.K. Johnson, J.L. Kerntop and B.N. Colby. "A Multi-Dimensional Assessment of Social Isolation and Depression among Elderly Women." Abstract in **Gerontologist** 33, Special Issue 1 (October 1993): 289.

8.023. Murphy, Elaine. "The Impact of Depression in Old Age on Close Relationships." **American Journal of Psychiatry** 142 (March 1985): 323-327.

This study took place in London, England, the subjects being elderly patients who had, because of depression, been referred to the London Hospital and the Goodmayes Hospital. There were 124 subjects with a mean age of seventy-four years. These subjects were administered: (1) the Present State Examination, (2) Survey Psychiatric Assessment Schedule, and (3) Bedford College Life Events and Difficulties Schedule. Recovered, relapsed, and continuously ill were how these subjects were categorized. All of them were interviewed one year after an initial interview. Subjects who had recovered one year later also had significantly improved personal relationships. Author biographical information. Abstract. 11 references.

8.024. Niederehe, G. "Psychosocial Network Correlates of Depression in Later Life." Abstract in **Gerontologist** 18, Special Issue (1978): 107.

8.025. Ong, Yong-Lock, Frances Martineau, Christa Lloyd and Ian Robbins. "A Support Group for the Depressed Elderly." **International Journal of Geriatric Psychiatry** 2 (January-March 1987): 119-123.

The rereferral and readmission rate for depressed elderly patients who were discharged from hospital, and who participated in a support group, was lower than for a control group which did not participate in such a group. Author biographical information. Abstract. 2 tables. Acknowledgments. 12 references.

8.026. Oxman, T.E., D.H. Freeman, Jr. and E. Manheimer. "Social Support and Depression in the Elderly." Paper No. 69 presented at the **1994 Annual Meeting of the American Psychiatric Association, Philadelphia, Pennsylvania, May 21-26, 1994**. DIALOG, Conference Papers Index.

8.027. Packard, K.D. and B.A. Edelstein. "Buffering Effects of Coping on Depression

Associated with Negative Social Interactions in Older Adults." Abstract in **Gerontologist** 36, Special Issue 1 (October 1996): 249.

8.028. Palinkas, Lawrence A., Deborah L. Wingard and Elizabeth Barrett-Connor. "The Biocultural Context of Social Networks and Depression among the Elderly." **Social Science and Medicine** 30, No. 4 (1990): 441-447.

8.029. Revicki, D. and J. Mitchell. "Chronic Strain, Social Support, Religious Participation and Depression in Rural Elderly Persons." Abstract in **Gerontologist** 33, Special Issue 1 (October 1993): 151-152.

A total of 2,178 individuals, sixty years of age and older, and residing in eastern North Carolina, were interviewed. Sixty-five percent were women. Forty-three percent were married. Chronic illness was associated with depression. Social contacts were associated with better mental health. Religion was not related to depression.

8.030. Rotenberg, Ken J. and Jocelyn Hamel. "Social Interaction and Depression in Elderly Individuals." **International Journal of Aging and Human Development** 27, No. 4 (1988): 305-318.

8.031. Russell, Daniel W. and Carolyn E. Cutrona. "Social Support, Stress and Depressive Symptoms among the Elderly: Test of a Process Model." **Psychology and Aging** 6 (June 1991): 190-201.

8.032. Saunders, William Bishop. "Functional Disability, Social Support and Depressive Symptoms in the Elderly." **Dissertation Abstracts International** 55: 2679B. Ph.D. University of North Carolina at Chapel Hill, 1994. UMI Order No. AAD94-30855. DIALOG, Dissertation Abstracts Online.

8.033. Scott-Lennox, Jane A. "Gender and Race Differences in Social Support and Its Effects on Depressive Symptom Levels among Chronically Strained Rural Elders." Abstract in **Gerontologist** 32, Special Issue 2 (October 1992): 142.

8.034. Sundberg, N.D. "Boredom, Depression and Social Relations in Young and Old People." Abstract in **Gerontologist** 23, Special Issue (October 1983): 273.

8.035. Wright, Lore K. "Mental Health in Older Spouses: The Dynamic Interplay of Resources, Depression, Quality of the Marital Relationship and Social Participation." **Issues in Mental Health Nursing** 11, No. 1 (1990): 49-70.

◆ Chapter 9 ◆

Caregivers

9.001. Alspaugh, M.L., M.A.P. Stephens, A.L. Townsend and S.H. Zarit. "Patterns of Depressive Symptomatology in Dementia Caregivers: The Relation to Stress and Strain." Abstract in **Gerontologist** 36, Special Issue 1 (October 1996): 218-219.

9.002. Ambinder, A., M. Mittelman, J. Mackell, E. Shulman, G. Steinberg and S. Ferris. "Relationship between Coping Strategies and Depression in AD Caregivers." Abstract in **Gerontologist** 30, Special Issue (October 1990): 369A.

Eighteen spouse caregivers of AD (Alzheimer's Disease) patients became more depressed. These caregivers were less likely to improve their social network satisfaction and had more negative coping strategies. Twenty-six spouse caregivers of AD patients became less depressed. These caregivers recruited additional help and their families were more active in caregiving. Coping measures for both groups of caregivers were evaluated at intake and at four months.

9.003. Bird, R.H. "Depression in Carers of Elderly People Living at Home: Alcohol Misuse Could Be a Factor." **British Medical Journal** 312 (May 11, 1996): 1224.

9.004. Blandford, A. and L. Guse. "Family Caregivers of Cognitively Impaired Institutionalized Persons: Correlates of Depression and Burden." Abstract in **Gerontologist** 34, Special Issue 1 (October 1994): 288.

9.005. Boland, Cynthia L. "The Relationship between Spirituality and Depression in Family Caregivers of the Elderly." **Masters Abstracts** 29: 432. M.S.N. Grand Valley State University, 1990. UMI Order No. AAD13-42881. DIALOG, Dissertation Abstracts Online.

9.006. Brieff, Robert Lewis. "Correlates of Demoralization/Depression and Related Conditions in Primary Support Persons Caring for Dependent Elderly Relatives." **Dissertation Abstracts International** 47: 2273A. ED.D. Columbia University Teachers College, 1986. UMI Order No. AAD86-20339. DIALOG, Dissertation Abstracts Online.

9.007. Chee, Y.K. and J.A. Mancini. "Relationship Quality, Commitment and Depression among Caregivers." Abstract in **Gerontologist** 36, Special Issue 1 (October 1996): 219.

9.008. Collins, C., C.W. Given, B. Given and S. King. "Predicting Depression and Positive Well-Being in Family Caregivers." Abstract in **Gerontologist** 28, Special Issue (October 1988): 82A-83A.

9.009. Cook, J.M., J.L. Pearson and A.H. Ahrens. "Predictors of Change in Depressive Symptoms in Caregivers." Abstract in **Gerontologist** 34, Special Issue 1 (October 1994): 104.

9.010. Coy, B., J.M. Kinney, J.C. Cavanaugh and N.J. Dunn. "Marital Quality, Daily Hassles and Depressive Symptoms among Spousal Caregivers of Alzheimer's Patients." Abstract in **Gerontologist** 32, Special Issue 2 (October 1992): 290.

Thirty-nine caregivers with a mean age of sixty-seven years, and who had been providing care for Alzheimer's Disease (AD) patients for an average of 5.5 years, were the subjects. The care recipients, whose average age was seventy years, were assessed with the Mattis Dementia Rating Scale. The caregivers were assessed with the Dyadic Adjustment Scale, Caregiving Hassles Scale, and the Center for Epidemiological Studies Depression (CES-D) scale. These marriages were not well adjusted relative to noncaregiving couples.

9.011. Drinka, P., T. Drinka, J. Hess and G. Gunter-Hunt. "Correlates of Burden and Depression in Caregivers of Male Geriatric Home Care Patients." Abstract in **Gerontologist** 24, Special Issue (October 1984): 200.

9.012. Drinka, T. and J. Smith. "Depression in Caregivers of Demented Patients." Abstract in **Gerontologist** 23, Special Issue (October 1983): 116.

Seventy-two (80.8%) of eighty-nine caregivers of demented patients were confirmed to be depressed, after interviews and administration of the Carroll Depression Test.

9.013. Dunkin, J.J., J.L. Cummings, S.R. Thompson and S. Wooley. "Relationships between Caregiver Burden and Patient Impairment in Depressed and Non-Depressed Dementia Caregivers." Abstract in **Gerontologist** 36, Special Issue 1 (October 1996): 221-222.

9.014. Eagles, J.M. "Depression in Carers of Elderly People Living at Home: Other Studies Were Misrepresented." **British Medical Journal** 312 (May 11, 1996): 1224.

9.015. Eisdorfer, C., G. Kennedy, W. Wisnieski and D. Cohen. "Depression and

Attributional Style in Families Coping with the Stress of Caring for a Relative with Alzheimer's Disease." Abstract in **Gerontologist** 23, Special Issue (October 1983): 115-116.

Fifty persons looking after a relative with Alzheimer's Disease (AD) were assessed for depression. Assessment revealed that depression was very prevalent. One reason for this was that caregivers felt they had lack of control over the situation. Guilt - its presence or absence - was a significant variable in predicting depression.

9.016. Elkus, Peggy Hulda. "The Impact of Gender, Relationship and Age on Burden and Depressive Symptoms in Family Caregivers of Elderly Dementia Patients." **Dissertation Abstracts International** 50: 2619B. Ph.D. University of Pittsburgh, 1989. UMI Order No. AAD89-21410. DIALOG, Dissertation Abstracts Online.

Spousal or adult child caregivers, who were volunteers from geriatric clinics and Alzheimer's support groups, were the 155 subjects. A good predictor of caregiver burden and depressive symptoms was being female. Gender was the only variable that accounted for significant variance in caregivers' burden or depressive symptoms.

9.017. Fingerman, K.L., D. Gallagher-Thompson, S. Lovett and J. Rose. "Self-Resourcefulness, Coping and Depression amongst Caregivers of the Frail Elderly." Poster Paper No. Q-4 presented at the **102nd Annual Convention of the American Psychological Association, Los Angeles, California, August 12-16, 1994.** DIALOG, Conference Papers Index.

9.018. Fink, Sue V., Loretta Constantino and May L. Wykle. "Depressive Symptoms in Black and White Caregivers." Abstract in **Gerontologist** 35, Special Issue 1 (October 1995): 413.

The subjects in this investigation were 256 white caregivers and 136 black caregivers. Although race helped explain the variance in depressive symptoms, race did not make an independent contribution to this explanation. Black caregivers reported fewer depressive symptoms and less caregiving burden, but more disruptive life events.

9.019. Gallagher, D. and R. Czirr. "Clinical Observations on the Effectiveness of Different Psychotherapeutic Approaches in the Treatment of Depressed Caregivers." Abstract in **Gerontologist** 24, Special Issue (October 1984): 244-245.

Thirteen male and female caregivers, who looked after impaired individuals, including Alzheimer patients, underwent a variety of treatments for depression. These treatment sessions averaged thirty individual sessions. Eleven of the caregivers substantially improved. Mean Beck Depression Inventory and Hamilton scale scores confirmed the improvements.

9.020. Given, B., C.W. Given and K. Ogle. "Depression as an Overriding Variable Explaining Caregivers' Reactions to Caregiving." Abstract in **Gerontologist** 28, Special Issue (October 1988): 246A-247A.

9.021. Hartiens, Jonathan Morse. "The Impact of Day Care Respite on Physical Health, Depression and Marital Satisfaction in Spousal Caregivers of Dementia Victims." **Dissertation Abstracts International** 56: 2941B. Ph.D. Fuller Theological Seminary, School of Psychology, 1995. UMI Order No. AADAA-I9533792. DIALOG, Dissertation Abstracts Online.

9.022. Hernandez, N. and G.A. Hinrichsen. "An Object Relations Perspective on Adult Children Caring for Elderly Depressed Mothers." Abstract in **Gerontologist** 34, Special Issue 1 (October 1994): 191.

9.023. Hinrichsen, G. "Adjustment of Caregivers to Depressed Aged." Abstract in **Gerontologist** 27, Special Issue (October 1987): 187A-188A.

The subjects were spouse or adult child caregivers of depressed aged who were hospitalized because of major depression. The burden of these caregivers was comparable to the burden of caregivers of Alzheimer's Disease (AD) patients.

9.024. Hinrichsen, G. and N. Hernandez. "Problems and Rewards in the Care of Depressed Older Adults." Abstract in **Gerontologist** 31, Special Issue 2 (1991): 121.

Spouses and adult children, the caregivers of depressed frail elderly, identified the problems/rewards associated with their caregiver roles. Psychiatric symptoms and strain in the patient-caregiver relationship were two problems identified.

9.025. Hooker, K., D.J. Monahan, K. Shifren, L. Frazier, N. Greenbaum and D. Sozzi. "Contrasting Parkinson's and Alzheimer's Disease Spouse Caregivers: Relationship of Personality to Anxiety, Stress and Depression." Abstract in **Gerontologist** 32, Special Issue 2 (October 1992): 291-292.

9.026. Keilman, L., B. Given and S. King. "The Relationship between Depression and Spirituality in a Sample of Family Caregivers of Physically Impaired Elderly." Abstract in **Gerontologist** 29, Special Issue (October 1989): 265A.

In-depth telephone and in-home interviews were used to obtain data regarding caregiver spirituality and depression. Self-administered questionnaires were used to obtain information about the latter. The hypothesis tested: spirituality is associated with lower levels of depression.

9.027. Lauzon, Sylvie. "Effects of Caregiving Stressors on Female Spouse Caregivers' Depressive and Physical Symptoms." Abstract in **Gerontologist** 35, Special Issue 1 (October 1995): 122-123.

9.028. Lichtenberg, P. "Further Study of Lewinsohn's Model of Depression in Caregivers." Abstract in **Gerontologist** 29, Special Issue (October 1989): 167A.

9.029. Lichtenberg, P., C. Manning and E. Turkheimer. "Memory Dysfunction in Depressed Spousal Caregivers." Abstract in **Gerontologist** 31, Special Issue 2 (October 1991): 87.

Narrative prose from the Weschler Memory Scale was administered to forty subjects - twenty-one caregivers of demented spouses and nineteen volunteers. The average age of the subjects was in the late sixties. Each subject was assessed with the Geriatric Depression Scale. Depressed caregivers performed significantly worse on immediate prose recall.

9.030. Lichtenberg, Peter A. and Jeffrey T. Barth. "Depression in Elderly Caregivers: A Longitudinal Study to Test Lewinsohn's Model of Depression." **Medical Psychotherapy** 3 (1990): 147-156.

9.031. Liptzin, Benjamin, Mollie C. Grob and Susan V. Eisen. "Family Burden of Demented and Depressed Elderly Psychiatric Inpatients." **Gerontologist** 28 (June 1988): 397-401.

The subjects were thirty-eight hospitalized psychiatric patients. DSM-III criteria were used to diagnose eleven patients with dementia and twenty-seven patients with depression. The Activities of Daily Living, Burden Interview, and Memory and Behavior Problem Checklist were the research instruments used. Hypothesis: the depressed group would, during hospitalization, improve more than would the demented group. This was hypothesized because depression is treatable, dementia usually irreversible. It was also hypothesized that the burden of family caregivers would be reduced. There was no significant difference in burden for family caregivers of either group of patients. Author biographical information. Abstract. 2 tables. 16 references.

9.032. Livingston, Gill, Monica Manela and Cornelius Katona. "Depression and Other Psychiatric Morbidity in Carers of Elderly People Living at Home." **British Medical Journal** 312 (January 20, 1996): 153-156.

In Britain approximately 2 million people provide informal care to elderly and disabled people who live at home. Carers in clinical practice seem psychologically vulnerable. There is in carers of older people with psychiatric disorders an increased risk of depression. This is particularly true of women carers of people with dementia. A confiding relationship may decrease psychiatric morbidity in carers of people with psychiatric disorders. Author biographical information. Abstract. 3 tables. 25 references.

9.033. Marszalek, A.M. and B.J. McDowell. "A Comparison of Depression and Anxiety Levels in Caregivers of Alzheimer's Patients and Non-Demented Patients." Abstract in **Gerontologist** 25, Special Issue (October 1985): 57.

The first group of subjects were seventeen caregivers of Alzheimer's Disease patients; the second group of subjects were fifteen caregivers of nondemented physically dependent persons. Depression and anxiety levels were compared in both groups. The Beck Depression Inventory and the State-Trait Anxiety Inventory were administered to all the subjects. There was a tendency, among all the caregivers, toward mild depression and anxiety.

9.034. Menon, M.P., E.J. Mutran, M.E. Fernandez and J.W. Hatch. "Mental Health of the Helpers: Determinants of Depression among Family Caregivers of the Elderly." Abstract in **Gerontologist** 36, Special Issue 1 (October 1996): 384-385.

Four hundred eighty-one caregivers of an institutionalized family member were interviewed. Females were more depressed than males. Caregiver health and self-loss were most strongly associated with depression. Self-loss had the strongest association with depression among rural caregivers.

9.035. Mittelman, M., E. Shulman, G. Steinberg, S. Ferris, A. Ambinder and J. Mackell. "A Caregiver Intervention Alleviates Depression among Spouses of AD Patients." Abstract in **Gerontologist** 34, Special Issue 1 (October 1994): 68-69.

Individual and family counseling; support group participation; and the availability of a trained counselor for consultation were the components of an intervention in improving the well-being of 206 spouse caregivers of Alzheimer's Disease (AD) patients. The control group - but not the treatment group - became increasingly depressed over time. Treatment ameliorated caregiver reactions to problem patient behaviors, family cohesion, and social network satisfaction.

9.036. Monahan, D.J. and K. Hooker. "Factors Determining Caregiver Type: Social Support, Activities of Daily Living and Depression." Abstract in **Gerontologist** 36, Special Issue 1 (October 1996): 79.

9.037. Monahan, D.J. and K. Hooker. "Social Support and Depression in Spouse Caregivers." Abstract in **Gerontologist** 35, Special Issue 1 (October 1995): 120.

The subjects were spouse caregivers of persons with Parkinson's Disease (PD) and spouse caregivers of persons with Alzheimer's Disease (AD). Spouse caregivers of persons with AD had significantly higher depression scores.

9.038. Neundorfer, M.M., K.A. Smyth, J.C. Stuckey and L.R. Rechlin. "Depression among Spouse Caregivers and the Progression of Alzheimer's Disease." Abstract in **Gerontologist** 35, Special Issue 1 (October 1995): 184.

9.039. Redinbaugh, E.M. and J.K. Kiecolt-Glaser. "Recurrent Syndromal Depression in Caregivers: A Longitudinal Study." Abstract in **Gerontologist** 32, Special Issue 2 (October 1992): 166.

Eighty-two caregivers were interviewed, over a three-year period, at three different intervals. Forty-seven percent were never depressed, 27% were episodically depressed, and 26% were always depressed. Caregiver depression was associated with social support and negative life events. Caregivers who were always depressed reported the greatest number of negative life events.

9.040. Rose, J.M., A.E. O'Reilly, S.A. Lovett and D. Gallagher-Thompson. "Laugh It Off: Mature Ego Defenses May Prevent Depression in Female Caregivers of Frail Elders." Abstract in **Gerontologist** 32, Special Issue 2 (October 1992): 291.

9.041. Schwarz, K.A. "Effects of Informal and Formal Social Support on Strain and Depression of Caregivers." Abstract in **Gerontologist** 35, Special Issue 1 (October 1995): 34-35.

9.042. Silven, D., S. DelMaestro, D. Gallagher, S. Lovett, A. Benedict, J. Rose and K. Kwong. "Changes in Depressed Caregivers' Symptomatology through Psychoeducational Interventions." Abstract in **Gerontologist** 26, Special Issue (October 1986): 179A.

9.043. Son, Yongjin and J. Kim Miller. "Depression Symptoms Reported by Korean Family Caregivers of Alzheimer's and Related Dementias." Abstract in **Gerontologist** 35, Special Issue 1 (October 1995): 87.

Twenty-five Korean caregivers, with a mean age of fifty-two years, were studied concerning depression. The Center for Epidemiological Studies Depression (CES-D) scale indicated these caregivers had a high rate of depressive symptoms. The mean was 22.29. Sleep disturbance was the most frequent somatic complaint. The caregivers also stated they felt lonely.

9.044. Steinberg, G., M. Mittelman, E. Shulman, J. Mackell and A. Ambinder. "AD Caregiver Well-Being: Effect of Treatment on Caregiver Depression." Abstract in **Gerontologist** 32, Special Issue 2 (October 1992): 149.

Depression in caregivers of Alzheimer's Disease (AD) patients increased at different times for different reasons. There should be for these caregivers long-term intervention. Depression decreased in caregivers who received counseling.

9.045. Stommel, M., C. Collins, C.W. Given, S. King and B. Given. "Use of Community Services by Caregivers of Alzheimer's Patients: Does It Influence Caregiver Depression?" Abstract in **Gerontologist** 28, Special Issue (October 1988): 247A.

Family caregivers of Alzheimer's patients, who used family support groups and respite care services, had significantly lower levels of depression.

9.046. Stommel, M., C.W. Given and B. Given. "Caregiver Depression as a Result of Caregiving Processes." Abstract in **Gerontologist** 29, Special Issue (October 1989): 268A.

9.047. Stukenberg, Karl William. "Depression, Stress and Social Support among Middle-Aged and Older Adults." **Dissertation Abstracts International** 52: 2787B. Ph.D. Ohio State University, 1991. UMI Order No. AAD91-20728. DIALOG, Dissertation Abstracts Online.

Fifty-one dementia caregivers over age fifty and fifty-one comparison subjects matched for age, sex, and education were studied. These subjects were assessed at one-year intervals with pencil-and-paper and interview instruments. This research revealed that caregivers, when compared to comparison subjects, were more depressed during the care giving period than prior to this period.

9.048. Teri, Linda, Paula Truax and Jane Pearson. "Caregiver Depression and Burden: What Are the Correlates?" Abstract in **Gerontologist** 28, Special Issue (October 1988): 119A-120A.

An investigation of fifty-five caregivers and their memory-impaired patients revealed that patient behaviors were more closely related to caregiver depression and caregiver burden than to patient cognitive ability or patient behaviors directly related to memory loss.

9.049. Trickett, P., M. Gatz and M. Karel. "A Longitudinal Follow-Up of Depression and Burden in Caregiving and Noncaregiving Relatives of Elderly Family Members." Abstract in **Gerontologist** 31, Special Issue 2 (October 1991): 193.

Data was collected during interviews with members of three generations of twenty-five families. A three-year follow-up included an elderly adult with health problems. Burden was related to generation and caregiver status. Primary caregivers were more burdened than nonprimary caregivers.

9.050. Visintainer, P., R. Schulz, R. Morycz and D. Biegel. "Relationship Orientation as a Predictor of Burden and Depression in Adult Family Caregivers." Abstract in **Gerontologist** 28, Special Issue (October 1988): 246A.

9.051. Whitlatch, C.J., L.S. Noelker, D. Schur, F.K. Ejaz and W.J. Looman. "Depression in Family Caregivers of Institutionalized Demented Elders." Abstract in **Gerontologist** 36, Special Issue 1 (October 1996): 219.

9.052. Williams, Melissa A. "Caregiving and Its Relationship to Depression During Bereavement for Elderly Widows." **Masters Abstracts** 33: 786. M.S.W. California State University, Long Beach, 1994. UMI Order No. AADAA-I1359677. DIALOG, Dissertation Abstracts Online.

After thirty widows over the age of sixty completed a self-administered questionnaire, it was revealed, in part, that: (1) there was no significant relationship between caregiving status and scores on the Beck Depression Inventory and (2) when comparing demographic categories, there was no significant difference in depression scores.

◆ Chapter 10 ◆

Pharmacological Treatments

10.001. Ashford, J. Wesson and Charles V. Ford. "Use of MAO Inhibitors in Elderly Patients." **American Journal of Psychiatry** 136 (November 1979): 1466-1467.

The MAOIs act by breaking down three neurotransmitter monoamines: (1) dopamine, (2) norepinephrine, and (3) serotonin. Depression is related to diminished activity of norepinephrine or serotonin. Antidepressants enhance the activity of these two chemicals. A partial blockage of MAO, which increases with age, may account for the effectiveness of MAOIs in elderly depressed persons. The risk of hypertensive crisis is the reason MAOIs are less safe in the elderly than are tricyclic antidepressants. Author biographical information. 10 references.

10.002. Bennett, Jerry A. and David G. Bienenfeld. "Antidepressant Drug Therapy for Geriatric Patients." **Journal of Practical Nursing** 39 (December 1989): 42-51.

Orthostatic hypotension is the most dangerous MAOI side effect noted in geriatric patients, treated with these drugs, because the elderly tolerate falls poorly. The clinician should, for this reason, watch for orthostatic changes throughout, at least, the first month of treatment. Tyramine-containing foods interact with MAOIs. If excessive amounts of tyramine reach the circulation, hypertension, palpitations, and headache will result. A geriatric patient with fragile atherosclerotic blood vessels could suffer a stroke. Intravenous phentolamine has been an effective treatment for this side effect. Intravenously administered labetalol gradually lowers blood pressure. Author biographical information. 2 tables. 1 figure.

10.003. Blumenthal, Monica D. "Depressive Illness in Old Age: Getting Behind the Mask." **Geriatrics** 35 (April 1980): 34-37, 39 and 43.

The drugs of choice for the treatment of depressive illness in the elderly are, as a rule, the tricyclic antidepressants. These drugs can be ranked in terms of their anticholinergic effects. Four of these drugs ranked from least anticholinergic to most anticholinergic are: (1) imipramine (Tofranil), (2) doxepin (Sinequan), (3) nortriptyline (Aventyl), and (4) amitriptyline (Elavil). Author biographical information.

2 photographs. 3 tables. 10 references.

10.004. Bocksberger, J.P., J.P. Gachoud, J. Richard and P. Dick. "Comparison of the Efficacy of Moclobemide and Fluvoxamine in Elderly Patients with a Severe Depressive Episode." **European Psychiatry** 8, No. 6 (1993): 319-324.

10.005. Bohm, Clause, Donald S. Robinson and Richard E. Gammans. "Buspirone Therapy for Elderly Patients with Anxiety or Depressive Neurosis." **Journal of Clinical Psychiatry** 51 (July 1990): 309.

10.006. Brown, S.L., M.E. Salive, J.M. Guralnik and M. Pahor. "Antidepressant Use in the Elderly: Association with Sociodemographic, Health Status and Access to Health Care." Abstract in **Gerontologist** 33, Special Issue 1 (October 1993): 105.

A total of 13,353 elderly individuals, associated with the four sites of Established Populations for the Epidemiological Studies of the Elderly, were the subjects. There were 423 prescriptions for antidepressants. Three drugs - amitriptyline, doxepin, and imipramine - accounted, at each site, for over 80% of antidepressants prescribed.

10.007. Chacko, R.C., J. Marmion, B. Marsh, R.J. Dworkin and M. Moran. "Lithium Prophylaxis in Elderly Bipolar Outpatients." Abstract in **Gerontologist** 25, Special Issue (October 1985): 191.

The subjects were twenty-one females and four males with a median age of sixty-seven years and diagnosed as having bipolar affective disorder. Twenty of these subjects had a major medical illness. The response to lithium was good in 72% of these subjects. Lithium therapy reduced by 50% the hospitalization rate. Daily dosages ranged from 300 mg to 1200 mg. Five patients did not respond to lithium. Tremor, nausea, and polyuria were the mild side effects in 83% of these subjects.

10.008. Christensen, Daniel D. "Rational Antidepressant Selection in the Elderly." **Geriatrics** 50, Supplement 1 (October 1995): S41-S50.

Atypical depression characterized, in part, by hypersomnia, hyperphagia, and weight gain responds poorly to tricyclics, but quite well to monoamine oxidase inhibitors. A tricyclic antidepressant and electroconvulsive therapy are likely to be effective in the treatment of psychotic depression. Although tricyclics can be fatal in overdose, this is not the case with selective serotonin reuptake inhibitors, if taken alone. Author biographical information. 5 tables. 2 figures. 1 photograph. 41 references.

10.009. Clements, Karen H. "Pharmacological Treatment of Depression in the Elderly." **Canadian Family Physician** 36 (May 1990): 899-904.

The author reviewed forty-one articles published between 1978 and 1988. These articles were about drug side effects and drug effectiveness in depressed elderly persons. Fluvoxamine, fluoxetine, imipramine, amitriptyline, doxepin, nortriptyline, maprotiline, mianserin, and nomifensine were some of the drugs studied. Clinical and research recommendations were made. English abstract. French abstract. Author biographical information. 1 table. Acknowledgments. 24 references.

10.010. Cohen, Lawrence J. "Principles to Optimize Drug Treatment in the Depressed Elderly: Practical Pharmacokinetics and Drug Interactions." **Geriatrics** 50, Supplement 1 (October 1995): S32-S40.

10.011. Cook, Brian L., Paul M. Helms, Robert E. Smith and Merling Tsai. "Unipolar Depression in the Elderly: Reoccurrence on Discontinuation of Tricyclic Antidepressants." **Journal of Affective Disorders** 10 (March-April 1986): 91-94.

10.012. Dunn, C. Gibson and David Gross. "Treatment of Depression in the Medically Ill Geriatric Patient: A Case Report." **American Journal of Psychiatry** 134 (April 1977): 448-450.

The case of Mr. A., a seventy-one-year-old widower, illustrated the treatment of depression in a geriatric patient. Mr. A., prior to treatment, was, in part, tearful, self-critical, and had suicidal ideation. He had retired six years earlier because of chronic obstructive pulmonary disease (COPD). After his wife's sudden death, due to acute myocardial infarction, he experienced a variety of symptoms of depression, two of which were decreased energy and weight loss. Angina pectoris was another of his medical illnesses. He was administered oral amitriptyline, 10 mg initially, later increased to 60 mg. His improved clinical condition was maintained at a three-month outpatient follow-up. Author biographical information. 10 references.

10.013. Dunner, D.L. "An Overview of Paroxetine in the Elderly." **Gerontology** 40, Supplement 1 (1994): 21-27.

10.014. Evans, Mavis E. and Michael Lye. "Depression in the Elderly Physically Ill: An Open Study of Treatment with the 5-HT Reuptake Inhibitor Fluoxetine." **Journal of Clinical and Experimental Gerontology** 14 (September-December 1992): 297-307.

10.015. Ferentz, Kevin. "The Primary Care Setting: Managing Medical Comorbidity in the Elderly Depressed Patient." **Geriatrics** 50, Supplement 1 (October 1995): S25-S31.

Stroke, Parkinson's Disease, Cushing's Disease, diabetes, and rheumatoid arthritis are some of the diseases associated with an increased prevalence of depression. The selective serotonin reuptake inhibitors, compared to the tricyclics, are safer to use in patients with constipation and glaucoma. Tricyclics can, for example, increase intraocular pressure. Fluoxetine is the selective serotonin reuptake inhibitor which should not be administered to patients who have dementia because this drug can more readily produce agitation than can paroxetine or sertraline. Author biographical information. 6 tables. 1 photograph. 38 references.

10.016. Foster, Jeffrey R., William J. Gershell and Alvin I. Goldfarb. "Lithium Treatment in the Elderly. I. Clinical Usage." **Journal of Gerontology** 32 (May 1977): 299-302.

Three case examples illustrated lithium treatment in the elderly at Mount Sinai Hospital in New York. The case examples: (1) an eighty-two-year-old female; (2) a sixty-six year-old married father; and (3) a seventy-six-year-old, recently widowed mother. The research of the authors revealed that lithium was therapeutically effective in elderly and younger patients. Therapeutic and toxic side effects occurred in elderly individuals at much lower dosage than in younger persons. Lithium doses under 900 mg daily were recommended for the elderly and careful clinical monitoring was   also recommended. Author biographical information. Abstract. 10 references.

10.017. Garrard, J., S.J. Rolnick, N. Nitz, L. Luepke, J. Jackson, L.R. Fischer, C. Liebson, P. Bland, R. Heinrich and   L. Waller. "Antidepressant Treatment of Elderly." **Gerontologist** 36, Special Issue (October 1996): 207.

10.018. Georgotas, Anastase, Steven Ferris, Barry Reisberg and Eitan Friedman. "Platelet MAO Inhibition, Clinical Efficacy and Safety of Monoamine Oxidase Inhibitors in Depressed Elderly." Abstract in **Gerontologist** 21, Special Issue (October 1981): 124.

10.019. Goff, Donald C. and Michael A. Jenike. "Treatment Resistant Depression in the Elderly." **Journal of the American Geriatrics Society** 34 (January 1986): 63-70.

Tertiary amines, such as amitriptyline, are more likely than secondary amines, such as nortriptyline, to produce in the elderly orthostatic hypotension. Anticholinergic side effects can be minimized by avoiding the use of amitriptyline. Trazodone, a sedating agent, is recommended when insomnia is present. Desipramine, an activating drug, is recommended during daytime when hypersomnia is present. Blood levels, drawn approximately ten hours after the last dose, may be helpful in patients who do not have an adequate response after approximately four hours. Psychotherapy and pharmacotherapy when used together are more effective in the treatment of depressed elderly individuals than is one treatment method used alone. An undiagnosed medical condition may be present in patients who do not improve when given optimal treatment. Author biographical information. 5 tables. 79 references.

10.020. Gottfries, Carl Gerhard. "Zimeldine in the Treatment of Depression in the Elderly." **Acta Psychiatrica Scandinavica** 68, Supplement 308 (1983): 80-83.

10.021. Gurian, B. and E. Rosowsky. "Successful Treatment of Symptoms of Minor Depression in the Old-Old with Low Dose Methylphenidate (MP)." Abstract in **Gerontologist** 31, Special Issue 2 (October 1991): 88.

Six elderly patients with minor depression, and ranging in age from eighty-five to 105 years, were treated with methylphenidate (MP) 2.5 mg/day to 10 mg/day. There was rapid symptom relief in mood and activity level. There was no evidence of untoward side effects.

10.022. Hill, Connie Dessonville, Alan Stoudemire and Robin D. Morris. "Treatment Outcome of Older Depressives with and without Concurrent Dementia." Abstract in **Gerontologist** 27, Special Issue (October 1987): 193A.

Older depressives with no cognitive impairment, with reversible cognitive impairment, and with a primary degenerative dementia were the three groups of subjects. All these subjects underwent multiple evaluations - medical, laboratory, psychiatric - then were administered tricyclic antidepressants. These subjects were again evaluated at six months, twelve months, and at post-treatment. Depression was reduced in all three groups.

10.023. Katon, Wayne and Murray Raskind. "Treatment of Depression in the Medically Ill Elderly with Methylphenidate." **American Journal of Psychiatry** 137 (August 1980): 963-965.

The case reports of Mr. A., an eighty-two-year-old retired professor; Ms. B., a seventy-three-year-old nursing home resident; and Ms. C., an eighty-five-year-old woman illustrated the effective use of the psychostimulant methylphenidate in the treatment of depression. The therapeutic response began, in each case, during the first few days of treatment. The authors did not observe in these patients adverse effects associated with psychostimulants. Appetite suppression, palpitations, headaches, and insomnia were a few adverse effects attributed to these types of drugs. Author biographical information. Abstract. 16 references.

10.024. Katona, C. "Optimizing Treatment for the Elderly Depressive: New Antidepressants in the Elderly." **Journal of Psychopharmacology** 7, Supplement 1 (1993): 131-134.

10.025. Khan, Arifulla, Hugh Mirolo, Mary Helen Mirolo and Dorcas J. Dobie. "Depression in the Elderly: A Treatable Disorder." **Geriatrics** 48 (June 1993): 14-17.

The selective serotonin reuptake inhibitors (SSRIs) are a new class of antidepressants.

Fluoxetine, one of the SSRIs, may cause nausea. This drug's elimination half-life allows   once-a-day dosing. Sertraline is another SSRI. Neither fluoxetine nor sertraline are of concern regarding overdose. Author   biographical   information. Abstract. 2 tables. 1 figure. 2 references.

10.026. Lafferman, J., P. Ruskin and K. Solomon. "Lithium and Antidepressants in Treatment-Resistant Depression in the Elderly." Abstract in **Gerontologist** 26, Special Issue (October 1986): 225A.

Seven elderly persons, in whom antidepressants were totally ineffective in alleviating depression, were treated with antidepressants and lithium carbonate. Six of these seven persons improved rapidly. It was not clear whether or not lithium carbonate was the sole therapeutic agent responsible for the improvement in depressive symptomatology.

10.027. Lakshmanan, Mark, Lorraine C. Mion and J. Dermot Frengley. "Effective Low Dose Tricyclic Antidepressant Treatment for Depressed Geriatric Rehabilitation Patients: A Double-Blind Study." **Journal of the American Geriatrics Society** 34 (June 1986): 421-426.

Doses of doxepin, ranging from 10 mg to 20 mg daily, were administered for three weeks to depressed geriatric inpatients. Depression was assessed with the Hamilton Depression Scale and the Geriatric Depression Scale. No side effects were found in these patients. Furthermore, these patients were significantly less depressed than those who were given a   placebo. Author biographical information. Abstract. 4 tables. 2 figures. Acknowledgments. 18 references.

10.028. Marcopulos, Bernice Anne. "The Influence of Depression and Antidepressant Medication on Neuropsychological Test Performance in the Elderly." **Dissertation Abstracts International** 48: 296B. Ph.D. University of Victoria, 1986. DIALOG, Dissertation Abstracts Online.

Three groups of individuals participated: (1) twenty-seven community elderly on antidepressants, (2) twenty-seven nonmedicated, depressed controls, and (3) forty-two nondepressed controls. Depressed persons had a tendency to perform more poorly on performance subtests of the WAIS. There was no correlation with any test measures regarding intensity of anticholinergic drug activity and dosage. There was a high correlation between depression and subjects' self-report of: (1) memory problems, (2) functional health, and (3) social activities.

10.029. Miller, M.D., B. Pollock, A.H. Rifai, C.F. Paradis, J.A. Stack and C.F. Reynolds, III. "Comparative Analysis of Nortriptyline Side Effect Profiles of Depressed Geriatric Patients at Various Points in Treatment." Abstract in **Gerontologist** 30, Special Issue (October 1990): 270A.

Fifteen elderly individuals, participating in the Maintenance Therapies of Late Life Depression study, at the University of Pittsburgh, were the subjects. Orthostatic blood pressure, weight, and nortriptyline blood levels were a few of the variables monitored. These variables were compared with Asberg side effect scores at pretreatment, remission, and after four months of continuous remission on nortriptyline. Side effect profiles largely reflected somatic features of depression early in nortriptyline therapy.

10.030. Mittmann, N., U.E. Busto, K.I. Shulman, N. Herrmann, I.L. Silver, D.M. Gardner, E.K. Borden, N.H. Shear and C.A. Naranjo. "Variations in Quality of Life and Depression Levels in Elderly Depressed Outpatients Receiving Pharmacotherapy." Poster Paper No. PII-85 presented at the **95th Annual Meeting of the American Society for Clinical Pharmacology and Therapeutics, New Orleans, Louisiana, March 30, 1972 April 1, 1994.** DIALOG, Conference Papers Index.

10.031. Molloy, D. William, John K. LeClair and E. Anne Braun. "Treating Depression in the Elderly." **Canadian Journal of Geriatrics** 58 (April 1991): 58-63.

The life situation of a seventy-eight-year-old retired businessman was used to illustrate treatment of depression in the elderly. This patient had been a widower for a year and lived alone. He had become more withdrawn. He had become more forgetful and had insomnia. He wondered if life was worth living. Treatment options included: (1) tricyclic antidepressants (examples: nortriptyline and desipramine); (2) tetracyclic antidepressants (examples: trazodone and maprotiline); (3) lithium carbonate; (4) monoamine oxidase inhibitors (examples: tranylcypromine and phenelzine); (5) psychostimulants (example: methylphenidate); (6) ECT (electroconvulsive treatment); and (7) neuroleptics (examples: pimozide and haloperidol). Author biographical information. 16 references.

10.032. Montgomery, S.A. "Depression in the Elderly: Pharmacokinetics of Antidepressants and Death from Overdose." **International Clinical Psychopharmacology** 5, Supplement 3 (July 1990): 67-76.

10.033. Pasternak, R., C. Reynolds, D. Buysse, C. Hoch and D. Kupfer. "Sleep Changes During and After Nortriptyline in Bereavement-Related Depression." Abstract in **Gerontologist** 32, Special Issue 2 (October 1992): 38.

Ten spousally bereaved elders participated in sleep studies. These subjects were administered nortriptyline (NT). Sleep efficiency and sleep quality improved over eight months.

10.034. Payne, Diana L. "Antidepressant Therapies in the Elderly." **Clinical Gerontologist** 7 (Winter 1987): 31-41.

Amitriptyline (Elavil) is a tricyclic with a high sedative quality, desipramine (Norpromine) a tricyclic with a low sedative quality. Dry mouth, blurred vision, tremors, and acute glaucoma are anticholinergic symptoms associated with tricyclic use. Temporary agitation, convulsions, bowel paralysis, and mydriasis can characterize overdosage. Nasal decongestants and bronchodilators contain phenlethylamine and should be avoided by individuals taking MAOIs (monoamine oxidase inhibitors). MAOIs are thought to be less safe than tricyclics because of the danger of hypertensive crisis. Lithium should be used in the elderly to treat recurrent unipolar depression when tricyclic or MAOI therapy is not successful. Alprazolam and bupropion are examples of second generation antidepressants. These drugs do not have any apparent cardiotoxic side effects. Although psychostimulants can rapidly elevate mood, their duration of action is brief. Author biographical information. Abstract. 22 references.

10.035. Pitt, B.M. "Lofepramine in the Elderly." **International Clinical Psychopharmacology** 3, Supplement 2 (November 1988): 49-54.

10.036. Pomara, Nunzio, Miriam Banay-Schwartz, Robert Block, Michael Stanley and Samuel Gershon. "Elevation of RBC Glycine and Choline Levels in Geriatric Patients Treated with Lithium." **American Journal of Psychiatry** 140 (July 1983): 911-913.

10.037. Raffaitin, F. "Efficacy and Acceptability of Tianeptine in the Elderly: A Review of Clinical Trials." **European Psychiatry** 8, Supplement 2 (1993): 117S-124S.

10.038. Reynolds, C.F., J.M. Perel, E. Frank, S.D. Imber, J.E. Thornton, R.K. Morycz, C.L. Cornes and D.J. Kupfer. "Open-Trial Maintenance Pharmacotherapy in Late-Life Depression: Survival Analysis." Abstract in **Gerontologist** 28, Special Issue (October 1988): 236A-237A.

Twenty-seven elderly depressed patients were administered a mean dose of 50 mg/day of nortriptyline, during a median trial period of eighteen months. Hamilton depression ratings were generally below 10. Side effects were minimal and did not increase over time. Depression recurred in four of the patients, who had to be hospitalized. There was at eighteen months a 81.5% survival rate without recurrence of depression.

10.039. Rockwell, Enid, Raymond W. Lam and Sidney Zisook. "Antidepressant Drug Studies in the Elderly." **Psychiatric Clinics of North America** 11 (March 1988): 215-233.

10.040. Roose, Steven P., Stanley Bone, Catherine Haidorfer, David L. Dunner and Ronald R. Fieve. "Lithium Treatment in Older Patients." **American Journal of Psychiatry** 136 (June 1979): 843-844.

Thirty-one patients, ranging in age from sixty to seventy-nine years, were the subjects in this study. Hypertension, followed by arthritis and hypothyroidism, were the three most frequent, chronic medical problems in these subjects. There were four episodes of lithium toxicity, during an eighteen-month period. There were also two cases of lithium toxicity in 164 patients under the age of sixty. Author biographical information. 4 references.

10.041. Salzman, Carl. "Practical Considerations in the Pharmacologic Treatment of Depression and Anxiety in the Elderly." **Journal of Clinical Psychiatry** 51, Supplement (January 1990): 40-43.

10.042. Salzman, Carl, Lon S. Schneider and Barry Lebowitz. "Antidepressant Treatment of Very Old Patients." **American Journal of Geriatric Psychiatry** 1 (Winter 1993): 21-29.

10.043. Strauss, D. and K. Solomon. "Psychopharmacologic Intervention for Depression in the Elderly: A Critical Review." Abstract in **Gerontologist** 20, Special Issue (1980): 208.

As many as 68% of the elderly may be depressed. However, there are relatively few studies concerning the elderly and various drugs used to treat depression in this population. Existing studies indicate major methodological problems.

10.044. Streim, J.E., S. DiFilippo, I.R. Katz, D.W. Oslin, R. Hearn and A. Boyce. "Adverse Events During Antidepressant Treatment: A Re-examination." Abstract in **Gerontologist** 36, Special Issue 1 (October 1996): 273.

10.045. Thienhaus, Ole J. "Depression in the Elderly: Phenomenology and Pharmacotherapy." **Geriatric Medicine Today** 8, No. 1 (1989): 34-37.

10.046. Veith, Richard C. "Depression in the Elderly: Pharmacologic Considerations in Treatment." **Journal of the American Geriatrics Society** 30 (September 1982): 581-586.

10.047. Volz, H.P., H. Muller and H.J. Moller. "Are There Any Differences in the Safety and Efficacy of Brofaromine and Imipramine between Non-Elderly and Elderly Patients with Major Depression?" **Neuropsychobiology** 32, No. 1 (1995): 23-30.

10.048. Wilkins, S., S. Osato, K. Tingus, J. Pickett, M. Mettler, D. McNeilly and R. Kern. "Educational Groups to Increase Medication Adherence in Geriatric Depressed Patients." Abstract in **Gerontologist** 35, Special Issue 1 (October 1995): 74.

Twenty-five depressed geriatric inpatients, with a mean age of sixty-five years, were the subjects. Thirteen subjects participated in a structured educational intervention regarding their medications. Twelve control subjects participated in sessions concerning personal hygiene. Medication adherence was monitored for six months after discharge. The adherence rate for the treatment group was 62% and for the control group 38%.

♦ Chapter 11 ♦

Nonpharmacological Treatments

11.001. Abraham, Ivo L., Sheila A. Niles, Bridget P. Thiel, Karen I. Siarkowski and W. Richard Cowling, III. "Therapeutic Group Work with Depressed Elderly." **Nursing Clinics of North America** 26 (September 1991): 635-650.

Seventeen men and fifty-six women, with a mean age of 84.5 years, from seven nursing homes, were the subjects. Three group approaches were used with these individuals: (1) education, (2) cognitive-behavioral, and (3) focused visual imagery. These interventions benefited depressed elderly individuals even those with mild cognitive impairment who resided in long-term care facilities. Author biographical information. 1 table. 11 references.

11.002. Abrams, Richard. **Electroconvulsive Therapy**. Second Edition. New York, NY: Oxford University Press, 1992.

Many tricyclics often cause in elderly melancholics severe constipation and can precipitate anticholinergic delirium. Some of the most effective results with electroconvulsive therapy (ECT) occur in elderly, debilitated persons, their primary affective disorder masquerading as senile dementia. Risk with ECT does not necessarily increase in elderly patients.

11.003. Alexopoulos, George S., Charles J. Shamoian, John Lucas, Neil Weiser and Henry Berger. "Medical Problems of Geriatric Psychiatric Patients and Younger Controls During Electroconvulsive Therapy." **Journal of the American Geriatrics Society** 32 (September 1984): 651-654.

Two hundred ninety-three psychiatric inpatients - 199 geriatric patients, ninety-four younger controls - were administered electroconvulsive therapy (ECT). Medical treatment or temporary discontinuation of ECT was associated more frequently with the geriatric patients than with the controls. Most medical treatment was cardiovascular in nature; most medical problems were reversible. Author biographical information. Abstract. 1 table. 14 references.

11.004. Arean, Patricia and Jeanne Miranda. "The Prevalence and Treatment of Mood

Disorders in Elderly Primary Care Patients." Abstract in **Gerontologist** 33, Special Issue 1 (October 1993): 312.

Individual and group therapy were used to treat depressed elderly persons. After twelve weeks of cognitive-behavioral therapy, persons in both treatment groups improved. No significant differences were found between the two types of treatment.

11.005. Arland, William Thomas. "A Life Review Intervention with Elderly Subjects Assessing for Impact on Depression and Life Satisfaction." **Dissertation Abstracts International** 51: 2485A. ED.D. University of Maine, 1989. UMI Order No. AAD90-23842. DIALOG, Dissertation Abstracts Online.

Male and female elderly persons, ranging in age from sixty-six to ninety-five years, were the subjects. Subjects who received structured and unstructured life review were compared with control subjects who did not receive any treatment. Self-report measures, pretest and post-test, identified change between group differences. Although interpersonal life review was significantly effective in reducing depression, this treatment was not significantly effective in increasing life satisfaction. No significant difference was discerned between structured and unstructured treatment. Life satisfaction for the subjects decreased as the time they spent in the institution increased. Depression increased as the amount of time they lived in the institution increased.

11.006. Barlow, Jeffrey Paul. "A Group Treatment for Depression in the Elderly." **Dissertation Abstracts International** 46: 4389B. Ph.D. University of Houston, 1986. UMI Order No. AAD86-02302. DIALOG, Dissertation Abstracts Online.

Forty-nine residents of senior citizen apartments participated in group sessions lasting six weeks and designed to increase life satisfaction. The comparison sample was a waiting-list control group. Self-control techniques were used to decrease aversive life influences. Subjects did, at post-test treatment, significantly decrease their depression scores. These subjects, however, did not improve any more than subjects who did not receive treatment. The treatment subjects did not at post-test have higher life satisfaction scores than the control group.

11.007. Benbow, S.M. "Resistant Depression, the Elderly and ECT." Paper presented at the **Spring Quarterly Meeting of the Royal College of Psychiatrists, Dundee, United Kingdom, April 6-7, 1992**. DIALOG, Conference Papers Index.

11.008. Benbow, S.M. "The Role of Electroconvulsive Therapy in the Treatment of Depressive Illness in Old Age." **British Journal of Psychiatry** 155 (August 1989): 147-152.

Temporary memory disorders and confusion may occur in elderly individuals who are treated with electroconvulsive therapy (ECT). These effects are minimized if unilateral electrode placement is used. Some patients, who do not respond to unilateral ECT therapy, will respond to bilateral treatment.

11.009. Blazer, Dan. "Electroconvulsive Therapy for the Severely Depressed Elderly." Abstract in **Gerontologist** 23, Special Issue (October 1983): 292.

11.010. Blazer, Dan. "Major Depression in Later Life." **Hospital Practice** 24 (September 30, 1989): 69-76 and 79.

A seventy-six-year-old married man, residing in the community, typified major depression because of sleep problems, weight loss, lack of appetite, and a desire to die. He was admitted to hospital, after drug therapy, psychotherapy, and electroconvulsive therapy were unsuccessful. A Mini-Mental State Examination, Minnesota Multiphasic Personality Inventory, projective testing, magnetic resonance imaging, dexamethasone suppression test, and polysomnogram were used to assess this individual. He received, over two-and-a-half weeks, eight electroconvulsive treatments. He was subsequently discharged and took twice daily 25 mg of oral desipramine. Occasional problems with sleep were, essentially, his only complaint two years after his second course of electroconvulsive therapy. Author biographical information. 4 figures. 7 references.

11.011. Bostick, Jane E. "The Effects of Group Reminiscence Therapy on Levels of Depression in the Elderly." **Masters Abstracts** 28: 405. M.S. University of Missouri Columbia, 1989. UMI Order No. AAD13-38537. DIALOG, Dissertation Abstracts Online.

Fifteen nursing home residents, ranging in age from sixty-eight to ninety-two years, were the subjects. One group of subjects participated in reminiscence therapy - six weekly sessions. The other group took part in current events sessions. The Geriatric Depression Screening Scale (GDS) was used pretest and post-test. There was no significant decrease in depression when reminiscence therapy was used. There was decreased depression in individuals who participated in the current events sessions.

11.012. Bratter, Bernice, Lew Bank and Judy Gewertz. "Peer Counseling the Depressed Elderly." Abstract in **Gerontologist** 20, Special Issue (1980): 70.

Peer Counseling for Elderly Persons (PEP) was successful in reducing depression, loneliness, and anxiety in depressed older persons. PEP was also successful in increasing in these persons regular exercise and decreasing sleep difficulties.

11.013. Breckenridge, Julia Steinmetz, Antonette M. Zeiss, James N. Breckenridge, Dolores Gallagher and Larry W. Thompson. "Solicitation of Elderly Depressives for Treatment Outcome Research: A Comparison of Referral Sources." **Journal of Consulting and Clinical Psychology** 53, No. 4 (1985): 552-554.

Three types of referrals, concerning elderly depressives to participate in psychotherapy for unipolar depression, were compared. The referrals were: (1) traditional (for example, agency or private practitioner), (2) semitraditional (for example, flyer at church or senior newsletter), and (3) nontraditional (for example, newspaper story or radio talk show). No significant differences were observed concerning type of referral. Author biographical information. Abstract. 1 table. 10 references.

11.014. Burke, William J., Eugene H. Rubin, Charles F. Zorumski and Richard D. Wetzel. "The Safety of ECT in Geriatric Psychiatry." **Journal of the American Geriatrics Society** 35 (June 1987): 516-521.

One hundred thirty-six subjects, forty of them over sixty years of age, were studied regarding electroconvulsive therapy (ECT). There were complications in 35% of the elderly and in 18% of the younger subjects. Severe confusion and falls were among the common complications in the elderly. The more medications subjects took, the more complications there were during ECT. Complications occurred particularly in subjects taking cardiovascular agents. Author biographical information. Abstract. 5 tables. 18 references.

11.015. Burke, William J., James L. Rutherford, Charles F. Zorumski and Theodore Reich. "Electroconvulsive Therapy and the Elderly." **Comprehensive Psychiatry** 26 (September-October 1985): 480-486.

11.016. Burwell, Dorothy. "Psychodrama and the Depressed Elderly." **Canadian Nurse** 73 (April 1977): 54-55.

Psychodrama, long associated with Viennese psychiatrist J.L. Moreno, has been used for thirteen years at the Clarke Institute of Psychiatry in Toronto, Ontario. Case studies illustrate the use of psychodrama in the treatment of depressed elderly men. Abstract. Author biographical information. 1 photograph.

11.017. Campbell, Janis M. "Treating Depression in Well Older Adults: Use of Diaries in Cognitive Therapy." **Issues in Mental Health Nursing** 13, No. 1 (1992): 19-29.

Low-income, well elderly persons, residing in four housing units, were the sample. Eighty women and twenty-three men were diagnosed with depression and three groups established. Cognitive therapy techniques were the basis for nursing intervention in the first group. There was no nursing intervention in the second group, the control group. There was no specific treatment for the third group, although this group received group classes and practice on crafts. The Zung Self-Rating Depression Scale, Mental Status Questionnaire, and Holmes-Rahe Social Readjustment Scale were some of the research instruments used to assess these subjects. Diaries were used for discussion purposes. Depressive symptoms were significantly reduced in the first group. There was no significant change in depression scores in the second (control) group. Depression scores were decreased in the third group. Author biographical information. Abstract. 3 tables. 17 references.

11.018. Cappeliez, P. "Pretherapy Training for Group Cognitive Therapy with Depressed Older Adults." Abstract in **Gerontologist** 33, Special Issue 1 (October 1993): 289.

11.019. Chaisson, Maureen, Larry Beutler, Elizabeth Yost and James Allender. "Treating the Depressed Elderly." **Journal of Psychosocial Nursing** 22 (May 1984): 25-30.

Mental health professionals, representing various disciplines, participated in a ten-week training program in cognitive therapy. Nursing, rehabilitation counseling, and addiction studies are examples of these disciplines. There were only six training sessions - not the usual twenty. Depression levels of elderly subjects declined after eight of twelve trainees, who learned about cognitive therapy, administered this therapy. The Cognitive Therapy Scale (CTS) was used to rate the learning skills of the trainees. The Beck Depression Inventory (BDI) and the Zung Self-Rating Depression Scale (SDS) were used to rate depression in the subjects. 2 photographs. Author biographical information. 1 table. 10 references.

11.020. Czirr, R. and D. Gallagher. "Behavioral Treatment of Depression and Pain in Rheumatoid Arthritis: Rationale and Demonstration." **Gerontologist** 23, Special Issue (October 1983): 232.

A sixty-two-year-old man was afflicted with rheumatoid arthritis (RA) and depression. He learned self-control techniques and progressive relaxation. At the termination of treatment lasting three months, and at six-month follow-up, RA symptoms improved and he was no longer clinically depressed.

11.021. Daniels, Ann A. "Reminiscence Object Relations and Depression in the Elderly." **Dissertation Abstracts International** 54: 3592A. Ph.D. Smith College School for Social Work, 1993. UMI Order No. AAD93-34302. DIALOG, Dissertation Abstracts Online.

Thirty elderly men and women from a housing unit were the nonclinical sample for this investigation. These men and women represented socioeconomic and ethnic diversity. Informative, evaluative, obsessive, and nonreminiscence were the four types of reminiscence identified. A home interview with each respondent was used to gather reminiscence data. The Beck Depression Inventory and Blatt Object Relations Scale were administered. Respondents in the informative group had the lowest level of depression; respondents in the nonreminiscence groups had the highest level of depression.

11.022. Dehope, Eileen Kathryn. "Cognitive Therapy: Intervention with the Depressed Elderly." **Dissertation Abstracts International** 52: 1475A. D.S.W. University of Pennsylvania, 1990. UMI Order No. AAD91-13875. DIALOG, Dissertation Abstracts Online.

Sixty-five elderly persons comprised an experimental group; twenty-three elderly persons comprised a control group. The experimental group underwent in their homes twenty sessions of cognitive therapy. Depression was assessed pretest and post-test with the Beck Depression Inventory. The experimental group experienced a significant decrease in depression; the control group did not exhibit a significant change in depression.

11.023. Dinan, Patricia Lynn. "Effects of Reminiscence Therapy on Self-Esteem and Depression Levels in the Elderly." **Masters Abstracts** 30: 94. M.S.N. San Jose State University, 1991. UMI Order No. AAD13-44256. DIALOG, Dissertation Abstracts Online.

Depression and self-esteem were assessed in thirty-nine subjects before and after six one-hour reminiscence sessions. These subjects were assigned to two experimental groups and two control groups. There was no significant difference between pretest and post-test for depression or self-esteem in any of the four groups.

11.024. Fiorot, Michele Anne. "Personality, Depression and Response to Psychotherapy in Elderly Female Patients." **Dissertation Abstracts International** 49: 236B. Ph.D. University of Miami, 1987. UMI Order No. AAD87-29346. DIALOG, Dissertation Abstracts Online.

Thirty-eight depressed women, ranging in age from fifty-five to eighty-four years, underwent individual psychotherapy. These women were assigned, with the aid of the Millon Clinical Multiaxial Inventory (MCMI), to dependent and compulsive personality groups. Examples of findings: (1) 94% of the women showed dependent traits, compulsive traits, or variations of these traits, (2) precipitants of depression did not differ for the two groups, (3) a small number of women expressed suicidal ideation, (4) dependents at intake reported more anxiety and more depression than did compulsives at intake, and (5) compulsives were significantly more likely to drop out of therapy.

11.025. Fishback, J.B. and S.B. Lovett. "Treatment of Chronic Major Depression and Assessment over Treatment and Follow-Up in an Elderly Female." Abstract in **Gerontologist** 31, Special Issue 2 (October 1991): 64.

A seventy-nine-year-old white female was treated for chronic major depression with cognitive-behavioral treatment - twenty sessions over twenty-nine weeks. Depression scores decreased substantially between beginning and end of treatment. Her diagnosis was changed from major to minor depression. There was no depressive disorder at fifteen and nineteen weeks post-treatment.

11.026. Frances, Allen J., Richard D. Weiner and C. Edward Coffey. "ECT for an Elderly Man with Psychotic Depression and Concurrent Dementia." **Hospital and Community Psychiatry** 40 (March 1989): 237-238 and 242.

11.027. Fraser, R.M. and Ilana B. Glass. "Unilateral and Bilateral ECT in Elderly Patients: A Comparative Study." **Acta Psychiatrica Scandinavica** 62 (July 1980): 13-31.

11.028. Fry, P.S. "Cognitive Training and Cognitive-Behavioral Variables in the Treatment of Depression in the Elderly." **Clinical Gerontologist** 3 (Fall 1984): 25-45.

11.029. Gallagher, Dolores E. and Larry W. Thompson. "Effectiveness of Psychotherapy for Both Endogenous and Nonendogenous Depression in Older Adult Outpatients." **Journal of Gerontology** 38 (November 1983): 707-712.

Thirty outpatients with major depressive disorder were assigned to one of three treatment groups: (1) behavioral, (2) cognitive, or (3) insight-oriented psychotherapy. Age greater than fifty-five, low suicidal risk, and a score greater than 17 on the Beck Depression Inventory (BDI) were three of the criteria for entry into this study. Fifteen patients had endogenous depression; fifteen patients had nonendogenous depression. There were sixteen treatment sessions over a twelve-week period, with evaluation before and after treatment, and four times during a one-year follow-up. Psychotherapy was more effective with the nonendogenous patients. One-third of the endogenous patients were not depressed when treatment was terminated. Author biographical information. Abstract. 2 tables. 25 references.

11.030. Gallagher, Dolores Elizabeth. "Comparative Effectiveness of Group Psychotherapies for Reduction of Depression in Elderly Outpatients." **Dissertation Abstracts International** 39: 5550B. Ph.D. University of Southern California, 1979. DIALOG, Dissertation Abstracts Online.

11.031. Gaspar, D. and L.A. Samarasinghe. "ECT in Psychogeriatric Practice: A Study of Risk Factors, Indications and Outcome." **Comprehensive Psychiatry** 23 (March-April 1982): 170-175.

11.032. Gatz, M. and C. Warren. "Pathways to Electroconvulsive Therapy (ECT): Depressed Elders and Distressed Families." Abstract in **Gerontologist** 29, Special Issue (October 1989): 41A.

Electroconvulsive therapy (ECT) with elderly persons in California increased markedly during 1977-1986. Most of the therapy was done at private psychiatric hospitals. When these persons declined therapy or behaved in a difficult manner, family most often gave informed consent for therapy.

11.033. Genhart, Michael Joseph. "Seasonality, Depression and the Psychological Effects of Phototherapy in an Elderly Sample." **Dissertation Abstracts International** 51: 428B. Ph.D. University of Maryland, 1989. UMI Order No. AAD9012462. DIALOG, Dissertation Abstracts Online.

Seventeen elderly individuals, residing in residential settings for older persons, were studied regarding light, mood, and behavior. Observer ratings and self-ratings of mood were used weekly, for four weeks, to assess the degree of change in mood and behavior in these individuals. There was no reported seasonal variation in the mood of the majority of elderly subjects. There was increased irritability, anxiety, and agitation in subjects exposed to phototherapy.

11.034. Godber, Colin, Henry Rosenvinge, David Wilkinson and Joan Smithies. "Depression in Old Age: Prognosis after ECT." **International Journal of Geriatric Psychiatry** 2 (January-March 1987): 19-24.

One hundred sixty-three persons, who were treated in 1981 with electroconvulsive therapy (ECT), were followed up three years later. One hundred thirteen subjects were alive three years later. Fifty-nine percent were not depressed; 29% had mild symptoms only. Author biographical information. Abstract. 1 figure. 5 tables. 18 references.

11.035. Goldstein, Stanley E. "Depression in the Elderly." **Journal of the American Geriatrics Society** 27 (January 1979): 38-42.

Multiple losses, feelings of helplessness, and reduced self-esteem cause depression in the elderly. The risk of suicide, especially among men, is high in this age group. The elderly rarely make suicidal gestures. Unsuccessful suicide attempts by these persons are relatively rare. When their depression does not respond to medication, electroconvulsive therapy (ECT) should be administered. This treatment, safe and effective, has been used with patients in their eighth decade of life. There have not been in these individuals any fatalities or significant confusional episodes. Author biographical information. Abstract. 15 references.

11.036. Greklek, Barbara J. "A Short-Term Social Work Stress Management Intervention for Elderly Clients Experiencing Reactive Depression." **Masters Abstracts** 30: 45. M.S.W. Southern Connecticut State University, 1991. UMI Order No. AAD13-45271. DIALOG, Dissertation Abstracts Online.

11.037. Hanley-Peterson, P., A. Futterman, L. Thompson, A.M. Zeiss, D. Gallagher and G. Ironson. "Endogenous Depression and Psychotherapy Outcome in an Elderly Population." Abstract in **Gerontologist** 30, Special Issue (October 1990): 51A.

11.038. Hanser, Suzanne B. "A Music Therapy Strategy for Depressed Older Adults in the Community." **Journal of Applied Gerontology** 9 (September 1990): 283-298.

Four clinical case studies illustrated how music therapy strategy helped in the management of depression and/or anxiety in older adults. Case one was a seventy-three-year old widowed female; case two was a sixty-five-year-old female; case three was a seventy-four-year-old male, retired airline pilot; and case four was a sixty-five-year-old male. The Geriatric Depression Scale (GDS), Brief Symptom Inventory (BSI), Self-Esteem Inventory (SEI), and Beck Depression Inventory (BDI) were used pretreatment and post-treatment. The music therapy included imagery and body relaxation. Author biographical information. Abstract. 39 references.

11.039. Holder, Jason Daniels. "The Effects of Low Level Aerobic Activity upon Systolic Blood Pressure, Heart Rate and Depression Levels among the Elderly." **Dissertation Abstracts International** 43: 3817A. ED.D. Boston University School of Education, 1982. UMI Order No. AAD83-09743. DIALOG, Dissertation Abstracts Online.

11.040. Hughes, Colin P. "Community Psychiatric Nursing and the Depressed Elderly: A Case for Using Cognitive Therapy." **Journal of Advanced Nursing** 16 (May 1991): 565-572.

A.T. Beck's cognitive therapy was effective with both depressed young and depressed elderly persons. However, there did not appear to be any substantial evidence this therapy was more effective than other nonpharmacological treatment or that it was more effective than pharmacological treatment. Community psychiatric nurses (CPNs) could use cognitive therapy to treat depression in the elderly. Author biographical information. Abstract. 33 references.

11.041. Jasin, Grace Rizzo. "The Effect of Cognitive-Behavioral Therapy, Therapist Competency and Group Process on Depression among the Elderly." **Dissertation Abstracts International** 47: 3957B. Ph.D. University of Arizona, 1986. UMI Order No. AAD86-23829. DIALOG, Dissertation Abstracts Online.

11.042. Karlinsky, Harry and Kenneth I. Shulman. "The Clinical Use of Electroconvulsive Therapy in Old Age." **Journal of the American Geriatrics Society** 32 (March 1984): 183-186.

The charts of thirty-three elderly inpatients - twenty-two women, eleven men - who received electroconvulsive therapy (ECT) at the University of Toronto, between 1979 and 1981, were studied. The mean age of these patients was 73.2 years. Although this therapy was safe, it was not uniformly effective. There was immediate good outcome for only 42.4% of the patients. Patients who received fewer treatments did better. ECT was safe and age alone should not deter the use of this type of treatment. Author biographical information. Abstract. 2 tables. 1 figure. Acknowledgments. 19 references.

11.043. Kemp, Bryan. "Brief Group Cognitive/Behavioral Therapy for Depressed Older Persons with and without Chronic Illness." Abstract in **Gerontologist** 30, Special Issue (October 1990): 97A.

There were meaningful and significant changes, on most measures, in fifty-four older persons, who underwent twelve weeks of cognitive/behavioral psychotherapy. These persons were followed up for up to one year.

11.044. Kramer, B.A. "ECT Use in Geriatric Depression." Abstract in **Gerontologist** 25, Special Issue (October 1985): 191.

Fifty elderly individuals, ranging in age from sixty-one to eighty-eight years, received, over eighteen months, electroconvulsive treatment (ECT). From two to fourteen treatments were administered. All treatment sessions produced a seizure and were safe and effective. ECT produced substantial improvement in 92% of these individuals. Thirty percent of these individuals received more than eight treatments.

11.045. Landreville, Philippe and Lynda Bissonnette. "Cognitive Bibliotherapy for Geriatric Depression: Predictors of Improvement." Abstract in **Gerontologist** 35, Special Issue 1 (October 1995): 458-459.

There was a significant reduction in depressive symptoms in forty adults, whose mean age was seventy-one years, after these adults participated in a four-week cognitive bibliotherapy program.

11.046. Latour, David and Philippe Cappeliez. "Pretherapy Training for Group Cognitive Therapy with Depressed Older Adults." **Canadian Journal on Aging** 13 (Summer 1994): 221-235.

Subjects sixty-five years of age or older, and without previous psychotherapy experience, were assigned to one of two conditions - pretherapy training or attention-placebo control. These subjects were depressed according to the Beck Depression Inventory and the Geriatric Depression Scale. The pretherapy training promoted a problem-oriented focus in therapy. It did not, however, significantly reduce dropouts. For both conditions, 53.7% of these subjects improved at the end of therapy. Author biographical information. English abstract. French abstract. 2 figures. 1 table. 27 references.

11.047. Leja, Ann M. "Using Guided Imagery to Combat Postsurgical Depression." **Journal of Gerontological Nursing** 15, No. 4 (1989): 6-11.

An experimental group and control group, both consisting of postsurgical hospitalized older adults, comprised the subjects in this research. The experimental group received Guided Imagery Discharge Teaching (GIDT), the control group Routine Discharge Teaching (RDT). The sample consisted of seven white men and three white women, ranging in age from sixty-six to seventy-six years. All these subjects were retired and married and resided with their spouses in single-family homes. These subjects were administered the Beck Depression Inventory (BDI) before discharge and completed another one at home seven days after discharge. There was, following GIDT, a significant decrease in depression. This was attributed, in part, to an increase in perceived self-control on the part of subjects. 1 illustration. Author biographical information. 3 tables. 22 references.

11.048. McNeil, J. Kevin, Esther M. LeBlanc and Marion Joyner. "The Effect of Exercise on Depressive Symptoms in the Moderately Depressed Elderly." **Psychology and Aging** 6 (September 1991): 487-488.

11.049. Milinsky, Tova S. "Stagnation and Depression in the Elderly Group Client." **Social Casework** 68 (March 1987): 173-179.

Treatment for elderly male and female clients, at a Jewish agency, used psychodynamic group therapy. The purpose of this therapy was to neutralize defensive behavior that prevented movement through life. Self-tolerance became the purpose and result of the therapy sessions, this occurring over a five-year period. Author biographical information. 10 footnotes.

11.050. Mintz, Jim, Lois Imber Mintz and Lissy F. Jarvik. "Cognitive-Behavioral Therapy in Geriatric Depression: Reply to Riskind, Beck and Steer." **Journal of Consulting and Clinical Psychology** 53, No. 6 (1985): 946-947.

11.051. Mitchell, Tim. "Family Therapy with Multigenerational Households: Factors Related to Changes in Depression for Dependent and Non-Dependent Elderly." **Dissertation Abstracts International** 54: 683A. Ph.D. Brigham Young University, 1993. UMI Order No. AAD93-16737. DIALOG, Dissertation Abstracts Online.

This study revealed, in part, that elderly persons with a dependent role status and poor health were significantly more depressed than elderly persons with a nondependent role status and good health.

11.052. Moberg, Paul J. and Laurence W. Lazarus. "Psychotherapy of Depression in the Elderly." **Psychiatric Annals** 20 (February 1990): 92-96.

11.053. Mossey, J.M., K.A. Knott and I.R. Katz. "Treatment of Subsyndromal Depressive Symptoms in Hospitalized Ill Elderly." "Abstract in **Gerontologist** 32, Special Issue 2 (October 1992): 275.

Subsyndromal depression is depressed mood which does not meet DSM-III-R criteria for major depression. Six sessions of Interpersonal Counseling (IPC), adapted from Interpersonal Therapy for Depression (IPT), were used to treat depressed hospitalized patients sixty years of age and older. Data pertaining to thirty subjects indicated IPC was feasible and associated with lowered Geriatric Depression Scale (GDS) scores in patients with subsyndromal depression.

11.054. Nadler, D., R. Kalish, R. Weiser and G. Fuller. "Biofeedback and Relaxation Training in the Treatment of Depression in Older Adults." Abstract in **Gerontologist** 18, Special Issue (1978): 105.

11.055. Parent, Carla J. and Ann L. Whall. "Are Physical Activity, Self-Esteem and Depression Related?" **Journal of Gerontological Nursing** 10, No. 9 (1984): 8-11.

Thirty people, age sixty or older, and residing in a senior citizen complex, volunteered to participate in this study. The Functional Life Scale (expanded version), Self-Esteem Scale, and Beck Depression Inventory were used to assess these subjects. Self-esteem scores were higher and depression scores lower, when subjects took part in a regular monthly activity program. Subjects who had hobbies were less depressed than subjects who did not have hobbies. Hobbies such as dancing, walking, and bicycling were positively related to self-esteem. Author biographical information. 3 photographs. 2 tables. 12 references. Bibliography (11 items).

11.056. Parsons, Catherine Lynne. "Group Reminiscence Therapy and Levels of Depression in the Elderly." **Masters Abstracts** 24: 259. M.S.N. University of Florida College of Nursing, 1985. UMI Order No. AAD13-27312. DIALOG, Dissertation Abstracts Online.

11.057. Perrotta, Peter and John A. Meacham. "Can a Reminiscing Intervention Alter Depression and Self-Esteem?" **International Journal of Aging and Human Development** 14, No. 1 (1981-1982): 23-30.

Twenty-one elderly male and female community residents in Buffalo, New York, were the subjects in this investigation. Seven subjects were randomly assigned to each of three groups: (1) a treatment group that received reminiscing intervention, (2) a control group that received current life events intervention, and (3) a no-treatment control group. Neither pretest nor post-test data indicated depression and self-esteem were altered. Author biographical information. Abstract. 21 references.

11.058. Ramsay, Rosaland and Cornelius Katona. "Therapeutic Sleep Deprivation for Depression in the Elderly." **Journal of Clinical and Experimental Gerontology** 12 (September 1990): 191-202.

11.059. Riskind, John H., Aaron T. Beck and Robert A. Steer. "Cognitive-Behavioral

Therapy in Geriatric Depression: Comment on Steuer et al." **Journal of Consulting and Clinical Psychology** 53, No. 6 (1985): 944-945.

11.060. Ronsman, Kaye. "Therapy for Depression." **Journal of Gerontological Nursing** 13, No. 2 (1987): 18-25.

Abraham Maslow's Hierarchy of Needs consists of five types of needs: (1) physiological; (2) safety and security; (3) love, belonging, and affection; (4) esteem and self-respect; and (5) self-actualization. Nurses can integrate these needs into treatment of depression in elderly patients. Physiological; safety and security; and love, belonging, and affection are needs the elderly depressed can meet with the assistance of a nursing care plan. 1 illustration. 2 tables. 18 references. Author biographical information.

11.061. Ruckdeschel, Holly. "Psychotherapy for the Old-Old: Ten Patients Report on Their Treatment for Depression." Abstract in **Gerontologist** 34, Special Issue 1 (October 1994): 275-276.

Individual psychotherapy was more effective in preventing further decline, than in producing cures, in subjects with a mean age of 87.2 years.

11.062. Scogin, Forrest, David Hamblin and Larry Beutler. "Bibliotherapy for Depressed Older Adults: A Self-Help Alternative." **Gerontologist** 27 (June 1987): 383-387.

The Hamilton Rating Scale for Depression was used to assess twenty-nine persons, who were the subjects in this research. These subjects exhibited mild to moderate depression. They were sixty years of age and older; they were recruited through newspaper announcements. These subjects were placed into three treatment groups: (1) cognitive bibliotherapy, (2) delayed cognitive bibliotherapy, and (3) control bibliotherapy. **Feeling Good**, a 1980 book about cognitive therapy by D. Burns, was given to the participants in the cognitive bibliotherapy group and the delayed cognitive bibliotherapy group. **Man's Search for Meaning**, a 1959 book by Viktor Frankl, was given to the control bibliotherapy group. In addition to the Hamilton Rating Scale for Depression, the Beck Depression Inventory (short form), Geriatric Depression Scale, Hopkins Symptom Checklist, and Cognitive Error Questionnaire were used in the outcome measures. This research demonstrated significant treatment effects for older adults. Abstract. Author biographical information. 2 tables. 18 references.

11.063. Scogin, Forrest, Christine Jamison and Kimberly Gochneaur. "Comparative Efficacy of Cognitive and Behavioral Bibliotherapy for Mildly and Moderately Depressed Older Adults." **Journal of Consulting and Clinical Psychology** 57 (June 1989): 403-407.

Participants in this investigation were community-dwelling persons with a mean age of 68.3 years. The Hamilton Rating Scale for Depression and Mental Status Questionnaire were used to assess these individuals. Subjects who participated in the behavioral bibliotherapy condition read the book, **Control Your Depression** (1986); subjects who took part in the cognitive bibliotherapy condition used the book, **Feeling Good** (1980). These two conditions were compared to a control condition and found to be superior to it. Author biographical information. Abstract. 3 tables. 23 references.

11.064. Senesh, D. and P.S. Fry. "Depressotypic Attributions of Control in Later Life Reminiscence." Abstract in **Gerontologist** 28, Special Issue (October 1988): 155A.

11.065. Solomon, Kenneth and Myra R. Zinke. "Group Psychotherapy with the Depressed Elderly." **Journal of Gerontological Social Work** 17, No. 1-2 (1991): 47-57.

Inadequate coping skills are found in three groups of older people. The first group is comprised of most individuals who develop psychopathology. Prior to severe losses, especially the death of a spouse, these individuals adequately coped with stress. However, the overwhelming of their ego defenses and coping skills rendered inadequate their coping skills. The second group are elderly persons who coped adequately when they were younger, but because of brain failure can no longer cope adequately. These individuals have psychopathological symptoms in addition to neurological pathology. The third group are older people afflicted with chronic schizophrenia, mental retardation, unresolved neurotic conflicts, and personality disorders. These individuals never had adequate coping skills. Author biographical information. Abstract. 1 figure. 27 references.

11.066. Soltys, F.G. and M.D. Letson. "Reminiscence as a Clinical Tool in Working with Depressed Older Individuals." Abstract in **Gerontologist** 34, Special Issue 1 (October 1994): 275.

11.067. Steffen, Judith Anne. "Reminiscence, Depression and the Elderly: A Comparative Study." **Dissertation Abstracts International** 55: 1707A. Ph.D. Texas Woman's University, 1994. UMI Order No. AAD94-28325. DIALOG, Dissertation Abstracts Online.

The reminiscences of two groups of elderly persons were compared. These reminiscences pertained to general life cycle issues. A clinical group consisted of persons who had been hospitalized for depression; a nonclinical group consisted of persons who had not been hospitalized for this condition. Themes and patterns, based on responses to eight variables, were used to construct a profile of a clinical subject and a nonclinical subject. The ability of the clinical subject to cope with numerous stressors appeared to have been compromised. This was due to early problems at home and school. This subject seemed to have reached a reconciliation, but not without regrets. The ability of the nonclinical subject to cope with fewer stressors had not been compromised. This was due to positive early home and school experiences. There was no indication this subject had any major regrets and would likely live again the same life.

11.068. Steuer, Joanne L., Jim Mintz, Constance L. Hammen, Mary Ann Hill, Lissy F. Jarvik, Tracey McCarley, Pamela Motoike and Richard Rosen. "Cognitive-Behavioral and Psychodynamic Group Psychotherapy in Treatment of Geriatric Depression." **Journal of Consulting and Clinical Psychology** 52, No. 2 (1984): 180-189.

Geriatric male and female patients, with a mean age of sixty-six years, and residing in the community, were recruited through a variety of ways for this study, including through local newspapers and senior citizen organizations. All these patients, 69% married, 31% divorced, were depressed. Hypertension and arthritis were among the most common medical disorders afflicting these individuals, some of whom had first been depressed in early childhood. The Hamilton Depression Scale (HAMD), Hamilton Anxiety Scale (HAMA), Zung Self-Rating Depression Sale (SDS), and Beck Depression Inventory (BDI) were the assessment instruments used. Twenty patients completed a course of treatment lasting nine months. Cognitive-behavioral and psychodynamic group psychotherapy were both effective in reducing depression and anxiety. Author biographical information. Abstract. 3 tables. 1 figure. 44 references.

11.069. Struckus, Joseph Edward. "The Use of Pet-Facilitated Therapy in the Treatment of Depression in the Elderly: A Behavioral Conceptualization of Treatment Effect." **Dissertation Abstracts International** 51: 1514B. Ph.D. University of Massachusetts, 1989. UMI Order No. AAD90-11804. DIALOG, Dissertation Abstracts Online.

During a twelve-week period, volunteers, accompanied by their dogs, twice weekly visited twenty-five elderly subjects, residing in a nursing facility. The following were some of the assessment instruments used: (1) Social Interaction Rating Scale, (2) Profile of Mood States, and (3) Pet Attitude and Experience Questionnaire. A matched no-treatment group was compared to the experimental group. When treatment was concluded, experimental subjects reported, for example, less depression, anger, and confusion.

11.070. Teri, Linda and Dolores Gallagher-Thompson. "Cognitive-Behavioral Interventions for Treatment of Depression in Alzheimer's Patients." **Gerontologist** 31 (June 1991): 413-416.

Two strategies were used to treat depression in Alzheimer's patients. Cognitive strategies were used for patients with mild cognitive impairment. Behavioral strategies were used for patients with moderate to severe cognitive impairment. Nine symptoms were addressed: (1) dysphoria; (2) psychomotor retardation/withdrawal; (3) psychomotor agitation; (4) complaints; (5) problems concentrating; (6) loss of interest or pleasure; (7) feelings of worthlessness/guilt, thoughts of death/suicide; (8) appetite/weight change; and (9) sleep disturbance. Both strategies, cognitive and behavioral, were used successfully in clinical settings. Author biographical information. Abstract. 1 table. 12 references.

11.071. Thompson, L.W. and D. Gallagher-Thompson. "Cognitive/Behavioral Therapy for Elders' Depression." Paper No. 1E presented at the **1994 Annual Meeting of the American Psychiatric Association, Philadelphia, Pennsylvania, May 21-26, 1994.** DIALOG, Conference Papers Index.

11.072. Thompson, Larry W., Dolores Gallagher and Julia Steinmetz Breckenridge. "Comparative Effectiveness of Psychotherapies for Depressed Elders." **Journal of Consulting and Clinical Psychology** 55 (June 1987): 385-390.

The subjects in this study were at least sixty years of age and were diagnosed with Research Diagnostic Criteria as having major depressive disorder. These subjects were administered: (1) the Mini-Mental State Examination, (2) the Beck Depression Inventory, and (3) the Hamilton Rating Scale for Depression. These subjects were treated for sixteen to twenty sessions with: (1) cognitive therapy, (2) behavioral therapy, or (3) brief psychodynamic therapy. By the end of treatment, depression went into remission in 70% of the cases or the subjects improved substantially. There was treatment failure in 30% of the cases. Delayed treatment patients did not improve. Author biographical information. Abstract. 5 tables. 29 references.

11.073. Thompson, Larry W., Dolores Gallagher, Gloria Nies and Donald Epstein. "Evaluation of the Effectiveness of Professionals and Nonprofessionals as Instructors of 'Coping with Depression' Classes for Elders." **Gerontologist** 23 (August 1983): 390-396.

A course, "Coping with Depression," was taught to depressed elderly individuals by sixteen "professionals" and sixteen "nonprofessional" instructors. The "professionals" had at least one degree and experience as mental health workers. The "nonprofessionals" had at least a high school education. When these individuals had postgraduate training, this training was not in the mental health field. The work experience of "nonprofessionals" was in places such as seniors centers and retirement hotels. The depressed participants had a mean age of 68.4 years. Four assessment measures administered to the participants before and after the course were: (1) Beck Depression Inventory (BDI), (2) Automatic Thoughts Questionnaire (ATQ), (3) Older Persons Pleasant Events (OPPE) schedule, and (4) Older Persons Unpleasant Events (OPUPE) schedule. This research revealed "nonprofessionals" could be as effective as "professionals" in teaching "Coping with Depression." Author biographical information. Abstract. 5 tables. 18 references.

11.074. Tutaj, George Andrew. "The Effectiveness of Group Counseling in Alleviating Depression among the Aged." **Dissertation Abstracts International** 36: 2653A. ED.D. George Washington University, 1975. UMI Order No. AAD75-23417. DIALOG, Dissertation Abstracts Online.

11.075. Waller, Mildred and Mickie Griffin. "Group Therapy for Depressed Elders." **Geriatric Nursing** 5 (September-October 1984): 309-311.

The Special Needs Project for Aurora Seniors was established in Aurora, Colorado, in 1979. This project, cosponsored by four local agencies, had the long-term goal of preventing depression in seniors from increasing to the point where hospitalization was required or the seniors committed suicide. Resocialization and the learning of problem-solving techniques was the focus of group therapy. Stress, frustration, retirement, and loneliness were recurring themes in the group therapy sessions. Attendance increased 77% in 1981. This occurred over the previous eighteen months. There were no suicides and only one hospitalization for myocardial infarction. Author biographical information. 1 table. 1 graph. 11 references.

11.076. Walsh, K., A. Shea, M. Munoz-Ruiz, C. Ouellette, J. Joyce, A. Futterman, L. Carli, A. Zeiss, D. Gallagher and L. Thompson. "Interaction Style in Psychotherapy of Late-Life Depression." Abstract in **Gerontologist** 32, Special Issue 2 (October 1992): 143-144.

11.077. Weiner, Richard D. "The Role of Electroconvulsive Therapy in the Treatment of Depression in the Elderly." **Journal of the American Geriatrics Society** 30 (November 1982): 710-712.

Electroconvulsive therapy (ECT), developed in 1938, induces electrically, in depressed patients, grand mal seizures. The seizure not the electrical stimulus is therapeutic. No therapeutic benefit results if the seizure is prevented. The use of ECT in the treatment of depression in the U.S. declined in the 1950s with the advent of antidepressants. These drugs, unlike ECT, were simpler to use and not as frightening to many patients. Mortality from ECT is approximately 1 per 10,000 patients. Author biographical information. Abstract. 18 references.

11.078. Yang, Janet Anderson and Lynn P. Rehm. "A Study of Autobiographical Memories in Depressed and Non-Depressed Elderly Individuals." **International Journal of Aging and Human Development** 36, No. 1 (1993): 39-55.

11.079. Zerhusen, Jerri D., Kathleen Boyle and Warner Wilson. "Out of the Darkness: Group Cognitive Therapy for Depressed Elderly." **Journal of Psychosocial Nursing** 29 (September 1991): 16-21.

Group cognitive therapy was used successfully to treat depression in male and female nursing home residents. These residents were a sample of sixty men and women, ranging in age from seventy to eighty-two years. Their mean age was seventy-seven years. These subjects resided at Miami Christel Manor, Inc. in Miamisburg, Ohio. A cognitive therapy group had significantly lower Beck Depression Inventory (BDI) scores after treatment than did a music therapy group and a control group after treatment. Author biographical information. 1 photograph. 1 table. 1 figure. 12 references.

◆ Chapter 12 ◆

Treatment Comparisons

12.001. Beutler, Larry E., Forrest Scogin, Patricia Kirkish, David Schretlen, Anne Corbishley, David Hamblin, Keith Meredith, Rebecca Potter, Colin R. Bamford and Alan I. Levenson. "Group Cognitive Therapy and Alprazolam in the Treatment of Depression in Older Adults." **Journal of Consulting and Clinical Psychology** 55 (August 1987): 550-556.

Fifty-six depressed elderly persons were assigned to one of four conditions: (1) alprazolam support, (2) placebo support, (3) cognitive therapy plus placebo support, or (4) cognitive therapy plus alprazolam support. One finding: persons assigned to group cognitive therapy, relative to nongroup therapy subjects, demonstrated consistent improvement in sleep efficiency. A second finding: there were no differences noted between alprazolam and placebo. Author biographical information. Abstract. 2 tables. 2 figures. 23 references.

12.002. Gage, M.J. and J.M. Kinney. "Treatment Approaches for Major Depressive Disorders in the Elderly." Abstract in **Gerontologist** 36, Special Issue 1 (October 1996): 13.

Physician and patient characteristics influenced treatment approaches for major depressive disorder. Older patients were significantly more likely to be prescribed psychotropic medication than were young patients. This treatment approach was used by psychiatrists and nonpscyhiatrists. Psychiatrists viewed psychotherapy as a treatment more appropriate for female patients. These specialists chose pharmacotherapy as the preferred treatment for male patients.

12.003. Jenike, Michael A. "Treatment of Affective Illness in the Elderly with Drugs and Electroconvulsive Therapy." **Journal of Geriatric Psychiatry** 22, No. 1 (1989): 77-112.

Protriptyline, a possibly activating drug, may be administered mornings to a depressed patient who sleeps much more than usual. Trimipramine, a more sedating agent, may be given to a depressed person who is unable to sleep. An adequate trial takes approximately six weeks at therapeutic levels. Many patients who are unresponsive to tricyclics will improve with MAOIs (monoamine oxidase inhibitors). MAOIs have essentially no anticholinergic effects. Lithium can be used to treat mania in the elderly. Lithium, however, can affect both renal and thyroid function. Stimulants such as methylphenidate are used to treat depressed postoperative elderly patients. Psychostimulants, by blocking the reuptake of depleted catecholamines, may be useful in treating stroke-induced depressions. Although persons with heart disease can be administered antidepressants, these persons should be given frequent ECGs, and should be monitored for ankle edema, dyspnea on exertion, and other cardiac symptoms. Electroconvulsive therapy (ECT) may be the preferred treatment for elderly patients because of, for example, the hypotensive effects of antidepressant drugs. Author biographical information. 5 tables. 114 references.

12.004. Liptzin, Benjamin. "Discussion: Treatment of Affective Illness in the Elderly with Drugs and Electroconvulsive Therapy." **Journal of Geriatric Psychiatry** 22, No. 1 (1989): 113-120.

A seventy-eight-year-old woman, who appeared to be depressed, was reacting to a nonsteroidal anti-inflammatory drug. When she stopped taking the drug, her food tasted better, her appetite improved, and she was less "depressed." Another woman - this one in her early sixties - also appeared to be "depressed." CT scan confirmed a brain tumor, which was surgically removed, after which her "depression" disappeared. Electroconvulsive therapy (ECT) is more effective, faster acting than drugs, appears to be safer, and appears to be better tolerated than antidepressants by most older patients. Author biographical information. 10 references.

12.005. McCarron, John Ashley. "The Relative Efficacy of Cognitive Therapy and Chemotherapy for the Treatment of Depression among the Retired Elderly." **Dissertation Abstracts International** 41: 2334B. Ph.D. California School of Professional Psychology, San Diego, 1980. UMI Order No. AAD80-28693. DIALOG, Dissertation Abstracts Online.

12.006. Meyers, Barnett S. "Late-Life Depression and Delusions." **Hospital and Community Psychiatry** 38 (June 1987): 573-574.

A neuroleptic combined with a tricyclic is a more effective method of treating delusional depression than the administration of only a tricyclic. Tertiary amines, however, provide the highest response rates. Electroconvulsive therapy (ECT) is approximately 90% effective in the treatment of delusional depression. Author biographical information. 32 references.

12.007. Pettinati, Helen M. and Kathryn M. Bonner. "Cognitive Functioning in Depressed Geriatric Patients with a History of ECT." **American Journal of Psychiatry** 141 (January 1984): 49-52.

Selected inpatients at the Carrier Foundation in Belle Mead, New Jersey, were the subjects. They met DSM-III criteria for major depressive disorder or schizoaffective disorder. These subjects were scheduled to receive ECT and to participate in a study of drug effects on ECT. Twenty patients were age sixty-five or over; forty-one patients were under age sixty-five. The Trail Making B test was used to assess cognitive functioning. Both groups experienced the same severity of depression. Depressed patients over sixty-five, with a history of ECT, performed more poorly on the Trail Making B Test than older patients with no history of ECT, and younger patients regardless of ECT history. Author biographical information. Abstract. 2 figures. 17 references.

12.008. Phair, Lynne. "George: An Elderly Depressed Patient." **Nursing Times** 86 (February 7, 1990): 64-66.

George was an eighty-two-year-old man, who received inpatient intensive nursing care for depression. Upon admission, he was anxious, preoccupied, and his diet was poor. Nursing staff gained his trust by helping to make his bed and by running small errands for him. Assessment revealed, in part, that his concentration was poor and that he did not sleep well. He scored 99 on an automatic thoughts questionnaire. The mean value for depression is 79.64. Participation in newspaper discussions, music appreciation, and a reminiscence group were part of his treatment program. Thioridazine, 10 mg three times daily, was administered to control his anxiety. He was released after nine weeks. Author biographical information. 1 illustration. 3 references.

12.009. Rodman, J., F. Gantz and J. Schneider. "Short-Term Treatment of Endogenous Depression Using a Combination of Cognitive-Behavioral Psychotherapy and Pharmacotherapy." **Gerontologist** 30, Special Issue (October 1990): 97A.

A seventy-five-year-old female, severely depressed for eighteen months, improved by the fourth week of a sixteen-week treatment program, after she was treated with desipramine and cognitive-behavioral psychotherapy.

12.010. Spar, James E. and Asenath La Rue. "Major Depression in the Elderly: DSM-III Criteria and the Dexamethasone Suppression Test as Predictors of Treatment Response." **American Journal of Psychiatry** 140 (July 1983): 844-847.

Twenty-seven geriatric patients, admitted between May 1980 and July 1981 to the UCLA Neuropsychiatric Institute, were the subjects in this research. These patients met DSM-III criteria for major depression. DSTs were administered to all these patients. Tricyclic antidepressants, MAOIs, and ECT were among the treatment options used. The Inventory of Psychic and Somatic Complaints in the Elderly, Global Assessment Scale, and Profile of Mood States were used for assessment purposes. Patients with a nonsuppressor response to the DST had poorer responses to treatment than patients with a suppressor response. Combined data regarding suppressor and nonsuppressor outcomes indicated over half the entire group improved significantly, this supporting the value of DSM-III criteria for depression in the elderly. Author biographical information. Abstract. 2 tables. 14 references.

12.011. Steuer, J., L.F. Jarvik, R. Gerner, C.L. Hammen, T. McCarley, R. Rosen, S. Cochran and P. Motoike. "Group Psychotherapy vs. Medication in Treatment of Depressed Elderly: A Preliminary Report." Abstract in **Gerontologist** 21, Special Issue (October 1981): 124-125.

One group of depressed geriatric outpatients participated in group psychotherapy; another group took part in tricyclic antidepressant treatment. The Hamilton Depression Scale and the Zung Self-Rating Depression Scale were used to determine the suitability of individuals to participate. The Hamilton Anxiety Scale and the Beck Depression Inventory were also used to assess these subjects. After nine months of treatment, depression and anxiety were significantly reduced in both treatment groups.

12.012. Stoudemire, Alan, Connie D. Hill, Robin Morris, David Martino-Saltzman, Holland Markwalter and Barbara Lewison. "Cognitive Outcome Following Tricyclic and Electroconvulsive Treatment of Major Depression in the Elderly." **American Journal of Psychiatry** 148 (October 1991): 1336-1340.

The Mattis Dementia Rating Scale was used to evaluate patients designated as having major depression, diagnosed with the aid of an interview and the Hamilton Rating Scale for Depression. These patients were then treated with either tricyclic antidepressants or ECT (electroconvulsive treatment). The ECT was followed by tricyclic maintenance therapy. Psychometric testing was repeated six months later. Cognition was generally stable for patients with normal pretreatment cognitive functioning. There was demonstrated improvement in cognition in patients with pretreatment cognitive impairment. The affective and cognitive states of the majority of patients improved. However, chronic depressive symptoms may persist in subgroups of patients. Abstract. Author biographical information. 1 table. 26 references.

◆ *Appendix A* ◆

Information Providers

Back East Productions
77 West Broad Street
BETHLEHEM, PA 18018-5722

Burrelle's Transcripts
Box 7
LIVINGSTON, NJ 07039-0007

DIALOG Information Services, Inc.
3460 Hillview Avenue
PALO ALTO, CA 94304

Films for the Humanities and Sciences
P.O. Box 2053
PRINCETON, NJ 08543

Journal Graphics, Inc.
1535 Grant Street
DENVER, CO 80203

National Public Radio
2025 M Street NW
WASHINGTON, DC 20036

Terra Nova Films
9848 South Winchester Avenue
CHICAGO, IL 60643

University Microfilms International
300 North Zeeb Road
ANN ARBOR, MI 48106

◆ *Appendix B* ◆

Associations

Academy of Psychosomatic Medicine
5824 North Magnolia
CHICAGO, IL 60660

American Association of Suicidology
4201 Connecticut Avenue NW, Suite
310
WASHINGTON, DC 20008

American Geriatrics Society
770 Lexington Avenue, Suite 300
NEW YORK, NY 10021

American Orthopsychiatric
Association
330 7th Avenue, 18th Floor
NEW YORK, NY 10001-3010

American Psychiatric Association
1400 K Street NW
WASHINGTON, DC 20005

American Psychological Association
750 1st Street NE
WASHINGTON, DC 20002-4242

American Public Health Association
1015 15th Street NW
WASHINGTON, DC 20005

American Society for Clinical
Pharmacology and Therapeutics
1718 Gallagher Road
NORRISTOWN, PA 19401-2800

Canadian Association on Gerontology
1306 Wellington Street, Suite 500
OTTAWA, ON K1Y 3B2

Canadian Psychiatric Association
237 Argyle, Suite 200
OTTAWA, ON K2P 1B8

Federation of American Societies for
Experimental Biology
9650 Rockville Pike
BETHESDA, MD 20814-3998

Gerontological Society of America
1275 K Street NW, Suite 350
WASHINGTON, DC 20005

Royal College of Physicians and
Surgeons of Canada
774 Echo Drive
OTTAWA, ON K1S 5N8

Royal College of Psychiatrists
17 Belgrave Square
LONDON, UK SW1X 8PG

Society for Neuroscience
11 Dupont Circle NW, Suite 500
WASHINGTON, DC 20036

Southwestern Psychological
Association
University of Oklahoma
NORMAN, OK 73019

◆ *Appendix C* ◆

Television Programs

"Chronic Depression and Suicide in Older Men Reported On." **Good Morning America** (ABC), July 31, 1996. Journal Graphics.

"Elderly Suicide Rates Climb, But Help Is Available in Both Medication, Sharing with Others." (Newscast). **The 700 Club** (BNO), July 31, 1996. Burrelle's Transcripts.

"Eleanor Purdy, Dr. Charles Reynolds; Late-Life Depression Prevention Program, NIH." (Interview). **NBC Saturday Today** (NBC) January 30, 1993. Burrelle's Transcripts.

"Forever Young, A Guide to Life After 50; Dr. Steven Roose Discusses Defeating Depression." (Profile). **NBC Today** (NBC), October 22, 1996. Burrelle's Transcripts.

"Government Reports That Suicide Rate among the Elderly Rose Nearly 9 Percent in Last 12 Years Reversing Four Decades of Decline." (Newscast). **CBS Evening News** (CBS), January 11, 1996. Burrelle's Transcripts.

"Illinois-Appointed Attorney Fights Electroshock Treatment for Aged Nursing Home Patient." (Newscast). **CBS Evening News** (CBS), December 31, 1993. Burrelle's Transcripts.

"Many Senior Citizens Affected by Depression." **Early Prime** (CNN), September 17, 1996. Journal Graphics.

"Number of Elderly Suicides Alarming, Doctors Agree." **Early** (CNN), January 12, 1996. Journal Graphics.

"Seniors Highest Risk Group for Suicide." (Newscast). **NBC Nightly News** (NBC), May 10, 1996. Burrelle's Transcripts.

"Suicide among the Elderly." (Profile). **60 Minutes** (CBS), June 10, 1990. Burrelle's Transcripts.

Author Index

Note: Some authors use combinations of first name, middle name(s), or initials for their names in different publications.

Groves, L., 2.066
Gruetzner, Howard, 3.030
Grut, Michaela, 2.030
Guerrero, Jose, 3.031
Gugel, Rita Nacken, 3.032
Gunter-Hunt, G., 1.001, 2.009, 9.011
Guralnik, J., 1.075
Guralnik, J.M., 10.006
Gurevich, David, 2.093
Gurian, B., 10.021
Gurland, B., 2.101, 4.045
Gurland, B.J., 2.016, 5.011
Gurland, Barry, 1.014, 1.256
Gurland, Barry J., 1.067, 2.031
Guse, L., 9.004

Hagans, Nora, 4.069
Hagens, E., 4.062
Haggerty, John J., Jr., 2.032
Haidorfer, Catherine, 10.040
Haight, B., 4.026
Hale, W. Daniel, 1.106, 1.107
Halikas, James A., 6.007
Hall, W.D., 1.043
Hall, Wayne D., 1.044
Halpert, S., 1.108
Hamblin, D., 1.243
Hamblin, David, 2.091, 11.062,
    12.001
Hamel, Jocelyn, 8.030
Hamilton, John M., 7.040
Hamm, V.P., 5.015, 5.016
Hamm-Baugh, Verneda P., 5.004
Hammen, C.L., 12.011
Hammen, Constance L., 11.068
Hankin, C., 1.207
Hanley, Ray, 2.084
Hanley-Peterson, P., 1.087, 1.109,
    11.037
Hanna, Vickie, 1.055
Hanscom, J., 4.062
Hanser, S., 1.087
Hanser, Suzanne B., 11.038
Harkins, S.W., 3.033
Harper, R.G., 2.065

Harper, Robert G., 1.110
Harralson, T.L., 3.078
Harrington, Virginia Lee, 6.020
Harris, J.M., 7.041
Harris, L., 5.015
Harris, M. Jackuelyn, 3.034
Harris, Rachel, 1.162
Harrison, Robert, 2.033
Hartiens, Jonathan Morse, 9.021
Harvey, P.D., 2.072
Harvis, Karen, 3.066
Hasegawa, K., 2.035
Hasegawa, Kazuo, 2.035, 2.082, 7.090
Hastrup, Janice L., 1.111
Hatch, J.W., 9.034
Hatcher, Betty J., 3.035
Haug, M.R., 1.195
Haugh, J.G., 8.012
Haveman, Meindert J., 5.049
Hawes, Catherine, 4.056
Hawranik, Pamela, 1.112
Hayes, James P., 1.204
Hayes, Pamela M., 1.113
Hays, J.C., 8.017
Hayslip, Bert, 2.022, 2.043
Hayslip, Bert, Jr., 2.034
Hazzard, William R., 3.083
Hearn, R., 10.044
Hebel, J.R., 3.077
Hedgepeth, Bruce E., 1.107
Heersema, Philip H., 1.037
Heiby, E., 5.012
Heikkinen, Martti E., 7.042
Heine, C., 4.062
Heine, Christine, 4.069
Heinrich, R., 10.017
Helen, F.K., 5.030
Helms, Paul M., 10.011
Henderson, A.S., 2.035, 5.042
Hendin, Herbert, 7.077
Hendrie, Hugh C., 1.114
Hernandez, N., 9.022, 9.024
Heroux, S., 1.212
Herr, Keela A., 3.036
Herrmann, N., 2.098, 10.030

Ruckdeschel, Holly, 11.061
Rudas, N., 1.049
Ruegg, Robert G., 1.233
Ruiz, Bertha Alicia Aguirre, 3.071
Ruiz, J., 3.044
Rusin, M., 3.067
Ruskin, P., 4.006, 10.026
Russell, Daniel W., 8.031
Rutherford, James L., 11.015
Ryan, Ellen Bouchard, 1.252
Rybarczyk, B., 3.072, 6.017
Ryden, M., 4.062
Ryden, Muriel, 4.069

Sacco, William P., 1.065
Sadavoy, J., 1.234
Sagar, R.S., 1.235
Sahakian, Barbara J., 2.089
Salamon, Michael J., 4.073
Salive, M.E., 10.006
Salive, Marcel E., 1.236
Sallis, James Fleming, Jr., 6.030
Salzman, Carl, 1.237, 3.073, 10.041,
    10.042
Samarasinghe, L.A., 11.031
Sands, L., 2.025
Santos, John F., 7.065, 7.066
Santos-Vilella, Fabiola, 5.048
Sathianathan, R., 1.215
Satish, N., 3.013
Sauer, Lori, 2.070
Saul, Shura, 7.085
Saul, Sidney R., 7.085
Saunders, William Bishop, 8.032
Savik, K., 4.062
Savik, Kay, 4.069
Savla, Navin, 2.033
Sayres, L., 3.012
Schaller, S., 7.086
Schechtman, K.B., 1.153
Scheier, L.M., 2.090
Schein, R.L., 3.074
Schein, Rebecca L., 1.238, 1.239
Schifano, Fabrizio, 1.166
Schmall, Vicki, 1.211

Schmall, Vicki L., 7.079
Schmidt, M., 1.118
Schmidt, R.O., 8.022
Schneider, A., 2.066
Schneider, E.L., 1.270
Schneider, J., 12.009
Schneider, L.S., 1.240
Schneider, Lon S., 2.056, 10.042
Schoenberger, James, 1.067
Schretlen, David, 12.001
Schrijnemaekers, Veron J., 5.049
Schuler, P., 1.241
Schulz, R., 1.271, 9.050
Schulz, Richard, 3.019, 3.088, 3.089
Schur, D., 9.051
Schwalm, Virginia Clare, 1.242
Schwarz, K.A., 9.041
Scogin, F., 1.243
Scogin, Forrest, 2.088, 2.091, 11.062,
    11.063, 12.001
Scogin, Forrest Ray, Jr., 2.092
Scott, C.W., 2.068
Scott, R., 1.184
Scott-Lennox, Jane A., 8.033
Seaburg, Eric, 1.089
Secouler, Lori M., 7.087
Seidel, Geoffrey, 7.088
Sells, Sharon, 1.129
Selth, Catherine, 4.063
Sen, P., 1.244
Senesh, D., 11.064
Service, C., 1.024
Service, Connie, 1.032
Shader, Richard I., 1.237, 3.073
Shamoian, C.A., 1.275
Shamoian, Charles A., 1.007, 1.245,
    2.001
Shamoian, Charles J., 11.003
Shapira, Ziva, 4.006
Shea, A., 11.076
Shear, N.H., 10.030
Shelley, Rory, 1.204
Shelly, Carolyn, 2.059
Sherman, Karen Grove, 7.089
Shewchuk, R.M., 1.078

Subject Index

Note: Titles of books are in bold typeface.

Rivermead Behavioral Memory Test,
2.038
Rorschach Depression Index (RDI),
1.103
Rosenberg Self-Esteem Scale, 1.242,
4.008, 4.048, 7.098
Routine Discharge Teaching (RDT),
11.047
rural depressed, 1.049, 1.089, 5.024,
8.029, 8.033

Sandoz Clinical Assessment Geriatric
Scale, 2.066
Schedule for Affective Disorders and
Schizophrenia (SADS), 1.007,
1.099, 1.145, 1.218, 2.001, 2.109,
4.040
Schedule of Recent Events, 1.242
schizophrenia, 2.072, 3.029, 4.073,
11.065
secondary amines, 10.019
Selective Reminding Test, 2.012,
2.027
selective serotonin reuptake inhibitors
(SSRIs), 1.046, 4.023, 4.038,
4.042, 10.008, 10.015, 10.025
self-actualization, 11.060
SELF-CARE (D), 1.020
self-efficacy, 1.058, 3.045, 3.071,
7.086, 8.005
self-esteem, 1.045, 1.085, 1.259,
1.262, 4.008, 4.017, 4.048, 4.071,
5.041, 6.036, 7.049, 8.011, 11.023,
11.035, 11.057
Self-Esteem Inventory (SEI), 11.038
Self-Esteem Scale, 11.055
Self-Evaluation of Life Function
scale, 1.232
self-mutilations, 7.075
self-neglect, 1.277
Self-Rating Depression Scale (SDS),
1.218, 3.005
self-starvation, 7.065
Senile Dementia of the Alzheimer
Type (SDAT), 1.213, 2.019, 2.020,

2.044, 2.045, 2.062, 3.023; battery,
2.013
senior citizen centers, 5.020, 7.001,
11.073
seniors housing, 4.047, 11.006,
11.055
sensory impairment, 1.130, 3.002
serotonin, 1.039, 1.273, 10.001
sertraline, 1.046, 10.015, 10.025
serum cholesterol, 1.231
sexuality, 7.057
shame, 7.038
Shanghai elderly, 7.094
SHORT-CARE, 1.014, 1.067, 1.256,
2.031
Short Zung Interviewer-Assisted
Depression Rating Scale, 1.259
Simultaneous Bilateral Physical
Stimulation Test (SBPST), 2.074
sleep, 1.062, 1.118, 1.134, 1.153,
1.200, 1.227, 2.003, 2.032, 2.037,
3.031, 5.005, 6.011, 7.069, 9.043,
10.033, 11.010, 11.012, 11.058,
11.070, 12.001, 12.003, 12.008
smoking, 1.236
social contacts, 1.112, 4.059, 4.070,
7.006, 8.034
Social Health Outreach Program
(SHOP), 8.004
social interaction, 3.032, 4.017, 6.021,
8.027, 8.030, 8.035
Social Interaction Rating Scale,
11.069
social isolation, 1.041, 1.064, 1.135,
1.224, 3.034, 7.001, 7.016, 7.023,
7.031, 7.038, 7.047, 8.022
social networks, 1.212, 4.048, 4.060,
5.038, 6.026, 6.036, 8.003, 8.013,
8.020, 8.028, 9.002, 9.035
Social Provisions Scale, 3.041
Social Readjustment Rating Scale
(SRRS), 1.250, 7.039
social roles, 1.045, 5.010
social status, 7.026
social support, 1.154, 1.193, 1.267,

7.094; in Singapore, 7.052;
thoughts of, 7.039, 7.086, 7.096,
11.070; and the unemployed,
1.127; in the United Kingdom,
7.025; and the widowed, 1.127
support groups, 3.025, 5.046, 9.035,
9.045
Survey Psychiatric Assessment
Schedule, 8.023
Sweden, Stockholm County, 6.001
Switzerland, Central Valais, 5.024;
Geneva, 5.024
Symptom Checklist-90 (SCL-90),
1.015, 1.107
Symptom Checklist-90-R (SCL-90-R),
1.145
syndromal depression, 9.039

Taiwanese elderly, 5.032
taste, 1.021
telephone crisis centers, 7.017, 7.024
Telephone Interview for Cognitive
Status (TICS), 2.046
temple, 6.031
Templer/McMordie Death Anxiety
Scale, 6.034
Tennessee, 4.029; Nashville, 5.018
terminal drop, 1.038
tertiary amines, 10.019, 12.006
thioridazine, 12.008
thiothixene, 6.011
thyroid, 1.077, 1.261, 12.003
tianeptine, 10.037
Trail Making Test, 3.076, 12.007
tranylcypromine, 10.031
Trapp Depression Inventory (TDI),
1.265
trazodone, 3.034, 4.024, 4.038,
10.019, 10.031
tremors, 10.007, 10.034
tricyclic antidepressants, 10.001,
10.003, 10.008, 10.011, 10.015,
10.022, 10.027, 10.034, 11.002,
12.003, 12.006, 12.010, 12.011,
12.012

trimipramine, 12.003
tuberculosis, 3.061
Turkey, 5.006
Twenty-Four-Item Fact Sheet for
Sociodemographic Data, 4.041
tyramine, 10.002

UCLA Loneliness Scale, 1.242
UCLA Loneliness Scale-Revised,
7.096
UCLA Neuropsychiatric Institute,
12.010
unipolar depression, 1.033, 10.011
University of Pittsburgh, 3.089,
10.029
University of Southern California,
3.016
University of Toronto, 11.042
University of Washington, 2.084,
3.028
uremia, 1.064
urinalysis, 1.077, 1.245

VA Normative Aging Study, 1.207
vegetative factor mean, 3.021
ventricular dilatation, 1.122
verbal fluency, 2.066, 3.009
veterans, 4.046
Veterans Administration (VA)
Hospital, 1.144, 1.218
Veterans Administration (VA)
Medical Center, 1.120, 1.201,
2.018
Veterans Affairs patients, 3.029
videocassettes, 1.060, 1.187, 7.027,
7.092
vignettes, 1.274
vinblastine, 1.077
vision, 1.041, 1.127, 1.256, 3.026,
3.051, 3.069, 3.075, 5.015, 5.029,
10.034
Visual Analogue Scale of Depression
(VASD), 4.063
visual-spatial scanning tasks, 2.056
visuo-motor scanning tasks, 2.056

About the Author

JOHN J. MILETICH is a former Reference Librarian at the University of Alberta. He has published book-length bibliographies in psychology, medical studies, sociology, and gerontology for Greenwood Press.

ISBN 0-313-30113-1

HARDCOVER BAR CODE